MUSIC AND WOMEN

Frontispiece. A *Hekateion* unites the spirits of the
waxing, full, and waning moon: Artemis, Selene,
and Hekate. In this lovely ivory figurine from ancient Greece, dancing maidens invoke the three-fold
goddess to keep them in the flow of all life.

(See page 122.)

MUSIC
AND WOMEN

THE STORY OF WOMEN IN THEIR
RELATION TO MUSIC

BY

SOPHIE DRINKER

COWARD-McCANN, INC.

NEW YORK

28499

CONTENTS

ILLUSTRATIONS

FOREWORD

MY ORIGINAL incentive to write a book about women in their relation to music came from a women's chorus that met for fifteen years in the music room of my home. It was my responsibility to find appropriate music for my friends who gathered here to sing—women like myself, neighbors with husband, children, and home.

From the beginning I was both surprised and shocked at the type of choral literature offered by the music publishers. It was childish, trivial, far too sentimental for these intelligent women who took time out of their busy lives for spiritual exaltation. It was, indeed, listed in many catalogues as music intended for "women's and *children's* voices"! I was amazed that the modern woman, with her high education, her personal liberty, and her active participation in the life of the community, was satisfied to sing, in a group, music manifestly inferior to other works of the same composers for solo voice or mixed chorus.

Almost none of the music we sang was composed by women. Why, I wondered, do my contemporaries, with their aspiration to self-expression, their notable attainments in this direction, neither excel as individual creators of the important music of our civilization nor even use a natural musical ability as a common mode of self-expression? Women musicians are experts in performing vocal and instrumental music, but rarely do they play or sing music that they themselves have composed. Why do they allow themselves to be merely carriers of the creative musical imagination of men? Why do they not use the language of music, as they use gesture and speech, to communicate their own ideas and feelings?

It is not necessary here to emphasize the value of music in relation to spiritual stature. Philosophers of all ages have dwelt upon the importance of music as both an outlet for the spirit and emotions and as discipline for the mind. It is generally recognized that music gives access to regions in the subconscious that can be reached in no other way. By plumbing depths where nature and spirit are in unity, a greater awareness of surrounding conditions may be developed and other inherent native talents may be stimulated into activity. Women's failure to think in terms of their own creative music has the inevitable result of causing a kind of feminine spiritual starvation. Moreover, it thins the quality of musical feeling and expression in general.

My intense interest in the enrichment of women's inner lives led me, therefore, from document to document, from book to book and article to article, from interview to interview with musicologists and specialists in other forms of learning related to this one, in my search for an understanding of women and music.

Among the countless things I wanted and needed to know were these, as illustrative: Had anyone undertaken a methodical analysis of early women's dirges and offered explanations for their composition? Did Victoria create his beautiful women's chorus "Duo Seraphim" for the Empress Maria and the nuns of Descalzas Reales in Madrid? Did ladies in medieval castles merely repeat songs improvised by men for their entertainment or did they evolve songs of their own? In modern times did American women play instruments with men in such musical groups as the Boston Flute Players Club? Where could I get the answers?

Grove's Dictionary of Music and Musicians was more of a puzzle than a source of information for my purposes. General histories of music rarely mention women. Wider histories of a general nature commonly ignore music while dealing with the "people." Fully half of the authors to whom I turned for knowledge, since they took account of women in connection with music, affirmed the passivity of women in this art except as inspirers of masculine musicians. Even in a book on *Woman in Music* carrying chapters headed Bach, Beethoven, Schubert, and Schumann, I discovered that women were depicted only as friends or relatives of these famous men musicians.

Yet I refused to be completely discouraged; I was firmly convinced that the whole story of music had not been told in a single volume, in any compendium of information on music, or in any collected series of works on the subject. I determined to find woman in this larger story of musical creativeness where I believed she belonged.

As I proceeded to read and to make independent inquiries, I did in fact find a great mass of material, both written and pictorial, concerning women and music. There were the rock paintings revealing women musicians. There were myths and legends about the musical activities of hundreds of goddesses and other feminine spirits—symbols and reflections of women in real life. There were the songs and dances of primitive women and of peasants. There were many references in scattered sources to Egyptian, Sumerian, Cretan, Greek, Roman, Chinese, East Indian, Arabian, and Jewish women musicians and also to the famous Saracen singing girls with their descendants at the court of the Great Mogul. There was proof of the participation of Christian women in the music of the early organized groups of Christ's followers. There were descriptions of women musicians from medieval times to the modern age. There were also musical scores demonstrating the character of a considerable amount of women's compositions.

From books in which this factual material appeared I have assembled, classified, and arranged pertinent items in manageable form. With my complete bibliography they may be studied in the Smith College and in the University of Pennsylvania libraries. The material on goddesses has been segregated for an article requested by the *Encyclopaedia Britannica* and will appear there in a forthcoming edition. It is my intention ultimately to make a reference book dealing exclusively with women's symbols and deities. Since pictures are indispensable in a comprehensive history of women and music, illustrations accompany each folio of collected material. Reinforcing the power of the written word, they positively portray musicians and they demonstrate the connection of women musicians with religious rites such as goddess worship and with the personal exuberance of women's spirit.

My distillation of facts for the present volume begins with four chapters on women as musicians in living groups of people called primitives and peasants. Why do I start with women of these types? There are two reasons: one is that the musical activities of such women, as in all modern researches for social origins, suggest the forms that prehistoric musical vitality assumed; the other is the clear evidence that such women are customarily on footings of equality or superiority with men in the realm of musical invention. In conformity with the practices of modern anthropological work, therefore, as well as with the findings that indicate a natural musicianship among women, the background of woman's musicianship in history is first brought to attention.

No doubt it is obvious that this volume is useful as an assortment of information about women's historic musical activities, but its true value would be missed if it were viewed merely in that way. Simply to cull items from it, as one might from a catalogue of musical events or descriptions, would be to tear apart things inseparably related; such as the intimacy between women's musicianship, their emotional reactions to productive labor, and their conceptions of the whole spiritual aspect of life, including their associations with men and children. Great music has always been rooted in religion—when religion is understood as an *attitude* toward superhuman power and the mysteries of the universe. This sensitivity to life, to its aims, its commands, its forms, and to its supporting emotions within men and women is a phase of the feminine being that, if deeply understood, should operate as an incitement to musicians, artists, poets, dancers, and all persons who long for a greater art expression in our modern world.

It is now nearly twenty years since I began to collect facts and to formulate ideas about women in their relation to music. During this long time, certain people have encouraged me beyond the point of polite interest in a neglected subject. Fundamentally, their support consisted in an understanding of my long and hard study in preparation for handling so difficult a matter, coupled with faith that the kind of book I had in mind could illuminate women's aptitude for musical composition, and induce in that light an impulse to more creativeness. From the beginning, the steadfast encouragement of my husband has been my greatest boon. His respect for me as an individual, creative in my own right, gave me the spiritual sustenance required for the expression of any original thinking.

For continuously challenging the validity of my interpretations and helping me to verify them from the authority of their own experience and knowledge, several women have my sincere gratitude. In that respect, Harriet Gratwick, Mabel Carnarius, Lela Vauclain, and my daughters live in these pages. In the early days when my project was in its infancy, Kathi Meyer, at that time librarian of the Paul Hirsch Library at Frankfurt am Main, opened the door to fruitful lines of research. Her wide musicological knowledge, so freely shared, has been a benefaction to me ever since. Katherine Swan, Russian sociologist and philologist, wrote for me an account of the participation of Russian women of all classes in music. Louise Beck, collaborator with Jean Beck in his work on the troubadours of France, gave me details about the musical activities of medieval ladies. Ruth Benedict, in the Department of Anthropology at Columbia University, taught me that woman's musical imagination depends upon the culture pattern of any given group for development as definitely as does any other human characteristic. The first to give me systematic editorial help was Katherine R. Drinker, at one time managing editor of the *Journal of Industrial Hygiene*. From first to last, Ann Chase has been constructively reviewing versions of the manuscript from the point of view of philosophy and psychology, and Catherine Drinker Bowen has as continuously given me the benefit of her great skill in the use of English. Mary R. Beard, who has written on women in long history but exclusive of the woman musician, warmly and generously reassured me that my efforts to introduce this feature of women's capability were socially important.

When I discovered that primitive women often displayed remarkable evidence of creative imagination, Heinrich A. Wieschhoff, curator of the African section of the University of Pennsylvania Museum, patiently answered a myriad of questions about rock paintings and primitive customs. More recently, M. F. Ashley-Montagu, associate professor of anatomy at Hahnemann Hospital in Philadelphia, checked my social anthropological data, and William Schuman, director of the Juilliard School of Music, approved the section on modern developments for the woman musician. The efficiency of Arthur Hamlin, assistant librarian in the service division of the University of Pennsylvania Library, in locating obscure books and articles has been a constant spur to continued research.

To Marjorie Barstow Greenbie I am indebted for final editorial services, which words cannot measure. Her long literary experience, coupled with Sydney Greenbie's wise advice, helped me to keep excessive details within bounds, to explain certain passages that might otherwise have been obscure to the general reader, to highlight several matters that I had perhaps underlighted, to add vivid touches from far-off places, and generally to give me confidence that my history of women in music would find popular appreciation.

I present my message, therefore, in the hope that it will remind every woman—and especially my own little granddaughters, Sophie, Ann, Ernesta, and Caroline—that they have deep, and as yet in our world, untapped reservoirs of imaginative power.

SOPHIE DRINKER

Merion, Pennsylvania
June, 1947

FULL MOON

CHAPTER I

SINGERS OF MAGIC

1.

WHEN the men of New Guinea are away at war, or on a long journey, their women beat upon booming gongs and sing to hasten the coming of the new moon. The first one to see the thin golden crescent in the sky gives a shout and all the women rejoice: "Now we see the moon, and so do our husbands, and now we know that they are well; if we do not sing, they would be sick or some other misfortune would befall them." [1]

No man composed the music. No man stands in the jungle shadows and waves his baton. No audience listens. But as the night silence deepens, and two or three tiny pinpricks of light in the village of thatched huts go out, and the young moon rides high in the sky, the voice of the leader soars as if it would lay hold of the very horns of the moon, and the voices of the others come in, rich and strong, supported by the rolling beat of the drums. The moonlight on their dark eyes and gleaming dark faces lights them into a deadly earnestness. They are not doing this to entertain anybody, even themselves. This is woman's music made by women only, for a woman's purpose. (See Plate 1.)

"If we do not sing our men will die." Theirs is an incantation or singing to invoke the powers that govern the rhythm of life. This moon that appears in the sky like a newborn baby will wax in the following nights like a growing child into a full round being. The women have power to invoke it with singing for the protection of their men, because they are the Daughters of the Moon.

Everywhere in the world simple, unlettered women who live more under the open sky than under roofs, without men's books, without men's churches and universities, feel their being as women peculiarly

3

linked to the celestial being of the moon. For the rhythmic drama of a woman's bodily life, of which childbirth is the great climax, is timed to the cycle of the moon. Her monthly cycle is four weeks or a lunar month. She measures the time it will take her to bring her child to birth by the waxing and waning of the moon. Ten times the thin, gleaming crescent will appear in the sky, ten times it will grow to its full, round, lusty prime, and ten times it will fade and shrink and so grow old and die. Ten times it will be born again. And at the tenth moon the child will be born, and grow like the moon to full splendor, and wane, and die—to be reborn again like the moon, if a woman has faith and makes the proper incantations or singing.

2.

Music in its elemental and primitive form, as still practiced by people of the simpler societies all over the world, is incantation. Incantation from Latin *cantare,* to sing, and *in,* meaning into, is literally a singing into. The primitive musician believes that by directing the force of rhythm and sound upon a thing, a person, or a situation, he can make it conform to his will.

To any honest and simple mind looking out on the wild world of living things, life is identical with rhythm and sound. A dead thing does not make a sound. Its heart does not beat. Therefore life is rhythm and sound. What is more reasonable than the application of rhythm and sound to objects, forcing into them the kind of life one wants them to have?

A Zuñi Indian woman making pottery, for instance, will imitate with her voice the sound of water boiling. This is to make the pot firm and unbreakable when water boils in it. Bavenda women pounding grain imitate the sound made by their pestles—*gu, gu*—in the mortars. Zuñi priestesses sing to the Spirit of Rain: "Fall upon the mountains and on the plains!" [2] As they pronounce the command they drop their voices in a descending scale to imitate the falling rain. Lithuanian women imitate the sounds of words that are themselves suggestive of the rustling of winds, the gurgling of water, and the trilling of birds.

In this primitive world there is rarely poetry without melody. Poems are usually sung. When asked whether words or melody came first into an artist's mind, a Hopi Indian said that song meant words and music conceived simultaneously. Where texts of songs have been written down by some visitor or literate scribe, an accompanying melody can therefore be assumed.

But this music has a practical aim. It is designed to do something. When a girl in Palestine thinking of her distant lover sings:

> "O trees, bend down to shade him,
> O stars, shine brightly for him!" [3]

she is making use of words to control the elements. And when a Greek nurse sings to a wakeful child:

> "The sun is sleeping in the mountains,
> the partridge in the woods—" [4]

her aim is to induce sleep by the power of suggestion inherent in the words. With us such words are merely poetic parlance. But these women believe them to be a practical method of attaining their ends.

As if to make their texts irresistible, women often end their formulas with words like these:

> My words, be strong and sticky, harder than stone,
> Stickier than glue or sulphur, saltier than salt,
> Sharper than a sword, stronger than steel. [5]

Out of the determination to make the words stick grows the musician's artistry. Rhythmical sounds and a variety of imitative tones reinforce the meaning of words and persuade or compel the listener to attend to them. So also do instruments. Women often make rattles by using gourds or by sewing little bags of dried skin and filling them with seeds or pebbles. They make pipes or flutes or stamping tubes by using hollow reeds or bamboo. They make the gourd zithers and probably the musical bow that in Rhodesia has nothing to do with the hunter's bow and is never used by men. Among European peasants women often use harp, dulcimer, and castanets; the tambourine is everywhere their special instrument. In many parts of the primitive world women not only use drums but make the drums themselves.

Except for drums, however, instruments are undeveloped in comparison to ours and exist generally for the purpose of making a noise to frighten away or to attract spirits. The voice is the instrument, and vocal music has attained in many primitive cultures a high state of artistic expression.

Just as it is obvious to the intelligent nature worshiper that life is rhythm and sound, and that if one directs the right rhythm and sound upon something, one puts life into it, so it is equally obvious that women are the proper persons to make incantations. Clearly women are more closely related to the life force than men, because they have the power to make new human beings in their own bodies.

Moreover, in some mysterious way this power in women to make people is related to the waxing and waning of the moon. Here, in the sky, waxing and waning, dying and coming to life again, is the magical prototype of life. And women, who make human beings, are obviously related to the moon in some special way.

So the woman's natural authority is the authority over life and death. By singing, she who understands human birth has the power to bring about birth everywhere. So woman's music is made in the stupendous faith that if it is only made in the right way, it can turn the old into new and bring the dead to life. There is thus concentrated in the single indivisible magic of a woman's incantation the foundation of the modern professions of religion, medicine, and music.

3.

I heard it while traveling—
The woman's song being sung.[6]

From the edge of the frozen tundra in the day-long night of the arctic winter, in Canada and Siberia, to the coral reefs of the Pacific and the green slopes of South Sea islands, which are like mountain peaks half sunk in the sea; from the vast hot spaces of Africa to old villages under the spruce and pine in Finland and Russia; from the foggy Aleutian Islands to Indian pueblos, under the blazing sky of New Mexico; in a thousand villages tucked quietly behind the peaks of the Andes, or forgotten on the slopes of Mount Olympus; in the valleys of the Himalayas and by the springs of the Yangtze and the Yellow rivers, or lost in the folds and crannies of Central Europe— brides, mothers, and old wives are making their own music. Blue-eyed or dark-eyed, pink-cheeked, olive-skinned, deeply brunette; Estonian women with smooth blonde sheets of hair; Indian women with dark braids; African women with tight curls, each oiled and carefully set; dark-skinned Melanesian women with bleached, bushy hair that is like a gold cap atop a vivid dark face—they are singing their incantations, their songs of joy and songs of sorrow. Through their compositions, in which words and music are of one inspiration, there resounds the story of birth, love, work, death, and rebirth, the story of hearth and home, the liturgy of woman's religion.

The primitive woman's authority over life and death, thus expressed in music, is supported by all the circumstances of primitive society.

Bringing life, fostering it with food and warmth, keeping humanity in touch with the spirit world are her normal activities. Her inborn talents all have a high value for the type of society in which she lives. What she does economically brings health and wealth to her people; what she does spiritually gives them contact with the life force. The more she asserts herself and the more she emphasizes her natural ways, the more power she brings to her tribe and the more she develops her own physical, mental, and spiritual stature. Childbearing, far from interfering, actually stimulates the development of creative imagination, especially her musical faculty. For around the physical nourishment and the spiritual aids that the mother must provide for the child, primitive family and social life are organized.

"In olden times, men and women were like two distinct peoples," [7] a Natchez Indian told an eighteenth-century French missionary. The primitive family is a considerable community of women and girls and boys under twelve, to which any number of men are more or less loosely attached. It is closely knit and self-sufficient, sustained by the women's monopoly of basic industry—the production of food and clothing. Women in primitive societies need no by-your-leave from their menfolk. They go about their business, not much caring what the men do, sure that when the time comes men will be drawn back to them by the irresistible double lure of sex and food.

Since primitive industries are centered in the communal household, the women must be well organized. There is the head of the group, usually the old mother or mother-in-law, who lectures the younger ones perpetually. She really doesn't know how she gets anything done with a lot of addlepated girls who are always planning to steal away and meet their lovers under the palm tree or the bamboo tree or the fir tree. She is annoyed with young women who are always mooning over their husbands or worrying about the babies. And she thinks the younger generation has no religion and never will learn to carry a tune or rotate their hips or shake their heels smoothly and rapidly in the community dance. Among the Maoris, where the grand old woman, work boss, priestess, and musician in one, functions at her best, she keeps after the girls from morning till night about their voices and the use of their bodies, while instructing them at intervals in all the other mysteries of life, and boring them to death with the recital of long genealogies. Thus, somehow or other, the new generation of women leaders and musicians is trained.

Subordinate to the old woman leader, but co-operating with her, are other older women, aunts, cousins, and females adopted into the household years before, down to the elder sister who is complete manager of the younger ones and responsible for all their sins.

Often women are organized into religious associations, or secret societies, by which they assert and emphasize their independence and solidarity. In certain African tribes today, women force men to remain in their huts during the performance of the secret rites. Men are convinced that their own vital powers would shrink up forever should they attempt to glance at the women's mysteries. In sex solidarity, women share their normal experiences, work in groups, play games together, help each other in childbirth, and worship their own spirits. Sometimes they speak in different language terms from those of the men. Wherever they dance, they use steps of their own invention, beat drums with their own rhythms, and sing songs of their own creation. (See Plate 2.)

Such institutions tend to develop women leaders whose authority often extends into the larger life of the community. As queen, chieftainess, priestess, prophetess, seeress, oracle, shamaness, magician, musician, and even as old wife who has experienced life, woman exercises a natural control over the members of her society. If and when women celebrate jointly with men at religious ceremonies and games, they perform as an independent unit with their own leaders.

Leadership in the fields where women have natural authority—in music, healing, and ritual—is strengthened by the attitude of the community. Among many simple people woman is highly valued for her natural bond with the life force. She is often regarded as the symbol of life itself. As long as the deep stream of mothers and daughters, bearing husbands and sons in its powerful current, flows on undisturbed, the spirit of the tribe prospers. Mothers symbolically pass the torch of life to their daughters; a girl in the bloom of youth with a moon tattooed on her back, a star on her forehead, and a turtle on her hands must dance to stimulate fertility in field and home. A May queen and a chosen youth must exchange the kiss that awakens life. Without the woman in action, there is no life *and the spirit lies dormant*. Woman's authority rests not only in birth but in the function of nourishing. Mothers are expected to feed their babies at the breast and then to provide other food. So women often identify themselves with the earth, or with grain, or with flowers and fruit. Some of the North American Indians call the corn "old woman who never dies" —the same name they have for the moon. Iroquois women regard the food spirits as their sisters and thank them with song:

> On the planted fields I walked:
> Throughout the fields I went:
> Fair fields of corn I saw there: . . . .
> I have thanked the sustainers of life.[8]

In one of the most beautiful liturgies in existence the Zuñi Indians glorify the nurturing mother. The Maiden-Mothers of the North, West, South, and East carry trays of seeds, each her own kind, as the wonderful truth is chanted:

"Lo, as a mother of her own being and blood gives life and sustenance to her offspring, so have these given unto ye—for ye are their children—the means of life and sustenance. . . . Behold! beautiful and perfect were the maidens, and as this their flesh, derived from them in beauty and by beautiful custom is perfect and beautiful, so shall it confer on those nourished of it, perfection of person and beauty. . . ."[9]

By reason of women's function as the source of food and drink for the newborn child, women are called upon to ensure, by charms and incantations, the water and the food for the community. They have authority over springs and wells, and often are the official rain charmers, passing on their magic powers to a daughter. Some peoples believe that woman's magic touch makes the grain grow. Among European peasants, where the formal ceremonies of the church have not completely superseded women's rites, women clap hands, shout, dance, shake tambourines, play pipes, and sing to celebrate the first day after midwinter and help call the spring and the season of new growth. (See Plate 3.) In Russia when spring is in the air and the birds are expected again, women bake buns in the shape of larks. Their daughters carry the buns out into the fields and call on Láda, goddess of fertility, love, and marriage.

> "Bless, Mother, oi! Mother Láda!
> Bless us to call the spring,
> To see off the winter." [10]

Many expect a priestess rather than a priest, or priestess and priest together, to serve in the religious ceremonies organized for the purpose of praying for prosperity. Great festivals are held at regular intervals and celebrated by men and women together for the purpose of inducing fertility, of renewing the warmth of the sun, of reviving the moon, of giving thanks for harvest, of casting out evil spirits, and of propitiating the nature deities. In some places, women and men beat the drums together and have dances in which both sexes perform. Among the Hootka Indians (U.S.A.) there are mixed choruses in which the men and the women sing in harmony. In other places women have their own dances and their own magic music. The women's choir, with its own leader, brings its own songs. For women to imitate men, or fail to make their own contribution, would be to defeat the purpose of their participation. This purpose is to assert and to emphasize the natural way of women in the scheme of life.

Women's authority over life and death extends to all matters affecting the security or continued life of the tribe. On this account some people even give women authority over the making of war. The Jabo tribe in Africa, for example, has two parliaments—the parliament of the young women and that of the older women. What these parliaments decide often becomes the law of the land. They decide that a stranger who wants to enter their country must not be admitted. And he is not admitted. They tell their men not to go to war and the men do not go.

To every people, war is both a religious undertaking and a practical task. Among primitive people it requires the services of women as the guardians of life. In their role of life givers they are indispensable to military victory. When the Haida Indian men go out to battle, the women sing and dance all night, pointing spears in the direction of the enemy. Women of the Karagive tribe accompany their men to war and beat the war drums. Scouting, fighting, inspiring men with courage, rejoicing at victory, lamenting the fallen, ensuring the continued life of their tribes, and performing different kinds of sympathetic magic with music are all activities regarded as normal for women in wartimes. (See Plate 4.)

Women's songs are valued as a means of transmitting strength to warriors. Among the Omaha Indians there is an old and untranslatable term, *We'Ton waan,* for those verses women sing in front of the empty tent of a man away at war:

> "The timid leader never wins fame,
> Let the tribes hear of you!" [11]

Through women the strength of the warrior may be preserved and transmitted to the tribe even in death. When an African Ibibio man is killed in battle, married women who are his next of kin rescue the corpse. No man may touch it. Weeping and singing sad songs, the scouts bear the dead warrior to a forest glade called *owokafai*— the place of those slain by sudden death. They lay him on a bed made of fresh leaves. Then they cut young branches from a sacred tree and wave the boughs over the genital organs of the warrior to extract his spirit of fertility into the leaves. Knowledge of the rites must be kept from men and from unmarried girls. Only married women, who have felt the virility of men in their bodies, can know the secret of life. To them it was entrusted by their great goddess "in the days when woman, not man, was the dominant sex . . . on the guarding of this secret depended the strength of the tribe. Were the rites once disclosed—few or no babes would be born, barns and herds would yield but scanty increase, while the arms of future generations of fighting men would lose their strength and hearts their courage." [12] This ceremony is conducted to the accompaniment of low, wailing chants, which only these wives of warriors have authority to sing, or even to know.

Even in places close to modern civilization the custom for choirs of women to sing the laments for warriors has persisted. On January 1, 1942, at Honolulu, when a funeral ceremony was held in memory of soldiers and sailors killed at Pearl Harbor, a choir of Polynesian women officiated. According to a newspaper account: "The silence was broken only by sobs and the soft chant for departed warriors sung by six native girls."

The association of women with war, and with music connected in various ways with war, is reflected in the fantastic figure of a terrible giantess. This Forest Demon of the Ibibios, whose women are so important in war and at the same time so musical, carries in her belly all the weapons in the world and also all the music. Bringing life to men engaged in a death struggle with the enemy and making appropriate music is thus impersonated by a woman spirit.

4.

The importance assigned to women in rites vital to the community stimulates women's musical talents. Because a woman is expected to give evidence of this life force flowing through her and because she has invented special powerful ways of using music for the benefit of her group, she is expected to make music. Primitive woman can be a successful musician because she is able both to realize and to idealize her natural capacities for work and for thought. Because her group demands music from her, she can assert and develop her native musical imagination.

Since women are expected to make important use of music, they have all the education in music the tribe can give them. Girls are trained in music and are given many opportunities for dancing, playing instruments, and singing. A girl lives her whole life among people who use music easily as a means of self-expression. She is as familiar with musical techniques as she is with speech and gestures. From the day she is born she hears the language of music and is taught to believe that it is a means of communication to be utilized at will. All children receive their first impressions of rhythm and melody from nurses, older sisters, mothers, and grandmothers. In many places, men initiates of religious cults learn the tribal songs and dances from the priestess in charge. Most primitive people regard women as peculiarly fitted by nature to think in terms of music; they consider music a direct extension of the functions of motherhood.

Talent and training in music are reinforced by adequate institutional support. Women's organization for making music is identical with their organization for the conduct of their worship, work, and play. The hierarchy of musicians consists of leaders, individual artists, and chorus. The chorus is the group of women who are performing their rites, working, or amusing themselves. The leaders and the professionals are the same women who have authority over the group in the ordinary course of daily life. The priestess-musician conducts the religious choir. The work leader conducts the singing of the women workers. In fact, a forewoman is often chosen for her ability to sing well and to have a large repertory of songs and stories. (See Plates 5 and 6.)

Both leaders and choir function under conditions that encourage them to do their best. Individual artists enjoy tremendous prestige and are often called in to perform at funerals, at weddings, and other occasions of community import. In North Russia, where the song leaders (*stihovóditzi*) are particularly musical, the chantress conducts the old rites and observes the old customs with authority often inherited through the mother's line. She knows by heart the ancient portions of the incantations and invocations that must be sung at every ceremony. She improvises new texts and new melodic lines to suit the emergency—a description of the virtues of the deceased, a history of the tribe, a portrayal of national characteristics, or whatever seems to be expected by her followers. The respect accorded her by both men and women is genuine, engendered by an inherited belief in her power to invoke the forces of life and by an admiration for her fertile imagination, which never fails to meet the artistic requirements of her group.

The women's choir functions at childbirth, at all rites of the re-birth, at work, at war, and for entertainment. According to local custom, the chorus sings in unison or in parts. In the Solomon Islands women sing thirds and fifths. In Papago Indian music a drone tone is held by women above the melody. Hottentot women often add a motif that, after an interval, they repeat with variations. An interesting type of part singing is performed by Russian singers. They develop variants to the melody, the effect being a rich harmonic structure quite different from the canonic imitation of western European polyphony. The responsorial form, in which the leader gives the first line of the verse and the chorus responds with additional lines, is universal. Antiphonal singing, which means that one group answers another group, is especially common among the Lithuanians, who, like many peasants, retain early customs. Among primitive women and many European peasant women the woman's chorus is as important a medium for the realization of women's musical ideas as is the solo singer. The solo singer's function is that of leader of the chorus. Though she may sing a portion of the song alone, she is primarily the spokeswoman for the group, who come in, rich and strong, with their own voices. The object of such singing is not the featuring of an individual, but collective expression under leadership.

Where women are recognized as having authority to make music for important ends, where training, organization, and incentives adequate for the kind of music expected of them are provided, primitive and peasant women living today are functioning as authoritative, creative musicians. No man makes their music for them; they make their own. No man leads them; they provide their own leaders. In their societies there is women's music—music conceived by women to fit their own experiences and to accompany their own activities. Women have their own dance steps, their own rhythmic patterns, and their own melodic lines. These are not, in any sense, imitative of men's, but spring wholly from the depths of their own approach to life and from associations lying deep in their inner lives. The explanation women themselves give of the nature of their songs is that some honored heroine or ancestress bequeathed the music to them, or else that they conceived it in a dream.

Though women imitate in their songs the natural sounds of the world around them, a man's voice is one natural sound that they do not imitate. In the entire range of the societies where women are creative musicians, instances of women assuming men's attitudes, taking over men's rites, singing in forced chest tones are rare and inconspicuous. On the other hand, instances of men wearing women's clothes, even castrating themselves, and singing in falsetto like women are, throughout history, frequent in men's religious ceremonies.

A complete collection of women's songs would fill many volumes, since, indeed, half of the folk songs and art songs of primitive and peasant people have been created by women, half of the total number of human beings. But our system of notation is, unfortunately, inadequate to reproduce them. On that account, many melodies to extant texts have been lost, or have become integrated into an ever changing musical idiom.

Wonderful songs and dances do not, of course, spring from every group of primitive people. Some races are not musically minded but develop their talents in other directions. Some merely make a noise with instruments and voice. But when a race is inclined to music, women as well as men, girls as well as boys evince the ability to think in terms of melody and rhythm, and even in harmony. It should be understood without laboring the point that women musicians of primitive and peasant societies are not to be compared to Bach, Beethoven, Brahms, and other musical giants of our civilization. These belong to an entirely different cultural level and cultural ideal. Primitive men are not creating harmony and counterpoint any more than are the women. But the music that women do create is of a quality and type entirely satisfactory to them and to their men, and is the highest that their culture knows. It requires for its composition, moreover, the same germ of emotional and artistic potency—the same capacity for symbolic thinking—that is required for the development of musical imagination at any time.

Most observers and historians of social activities in primitive tribes agree that the great school of primitive music owes its continuance to the woman musician. In both the quantity and the quality of music, women excel. Women dance more and sing more than men do. Women are the chief repositories for racial musical expression. It is they who store the incantations, the dirges, and the epics in their memories and who know the tribal lore. Women are also the chief transmitters of history, which is generally retailed in song and story. In the absence of written records, primitive music is passed on orally and often through the filter of woman's preconceived musical ideas, especially through lullabies and songs at initiation ceremonies.

Examples of primitive tribes in which women's musical activity is conspicuous in tribal life can be chosen from all types of humanity. Beginning in the north, the women of Kamchatka, of other aboriginal Siberian tribes, of the Eskimo peoples, especially those of Greenland, are outstanding musicians as compared to the men of their groups. In the Pacific islands, the Dyak women in Borneo excel in the music of their culture. The Trobriand Islanders, the Fiji Islanders, and many of the Maoris belong in this category. Among the black people of Africa the woman musician is in her element. Bushwomen, Pygmies, the Bavenda, the Ba-Ronga, the Valenge, Dahomeans, Ashantis, Wanyamwezi, the Tuareg, and many others represent woman's musical imagination in action.

Collectors of Oriental songs have commented on the extent of women's musical activity. In Tibet, for instance, and among the Dravidians of India, women musicians are outstanding. Grierson, who collected songs from different sets of people in India, said that he could not have performed his task successfully if he had not had access to the Hindu ladies' private quarters—the place where the old songs were remembered and sung. Women in Siam and Cambodia also excel as musicians. And Jewish women, wherever they live, have a native talent for musical expression. (See Plate 18.)

In the group of European peasants, women musicians stand out with undeniable power. Safarik, a prominent Slav scholar, said: "Wherever there is a Slavonic woman, there also is a song." A good half of the beautiful Russian, Yugoslavian, Bulgarian, Serbian, and Albanian folk songs are the product of women's imagination—their authorship in Russia being established by the use of verbs with feminine endings, such as *hodíla, trepála*. Fauriel, who collected Romaic folk songs, commented upon the fact that many of the most beautiful were women's songs. The folk literature of Greece, Finland, Brittany, Ireland, the Hebrides, and many other places is filled with women's musical poems. Latvian, Estonian, and Lithuanian songs are created almost entirely by women. In the vocal music of these countries men play an altogether secondary role. In Lithuania, especially, the bulk of the musical literature consists of the women's exquisite lyrics—the *daina*.

The manner of many European peasant women's singing is musicianship itself. The singers often have absolute pitch and are able to dispense entirely with instrumental accompaniment. Voices are true, strong, rich, and low. In one Lithuanian folk song a poetess-musician asserts herself with these proud words:

> What a sonorous voice I have!
> It is as if it flowed in gold.
> People from afar are listening.[13]

The group singing of both primitive and peasant women is completely satisfying to performers and listeners. Just as the women are sure of their own worth and confident that their music has a significance for the whole society, so do their rich, warm voices require no support from men or from instruments. The sounds produced by peasant women in chorus are extravagantly admired by both musically untrained listeners and musicologists.

Music created by these peasant musicians is marked by great vigor and richness of imagery, by highly ingenious rhythmic patterns, by a sensitivity to natural surroundings, by conspicuous beauty of melodic content, and by the same refined lyrical quality that graced the art of the ancient Greek poetess-musician.

The greatest heights of primitive and peasant music are reached in connection with those activities in which women have authority. No description, no recording, no evaluation of it can be made, therefore, without a recognition of the woman musician.

5.

It is easy for those who live within our own culture pattern to forget how large a portion of the human race is outside this way of life. It is also easy to take no notice of the fact that, as peoples outside the pattern of western European civilization that was dominant up to World War II bestir and assert themselves, they are not necessarily accepting the patterns that have prevailed in civilization up to this time.

All over the world there are still men and women who hold to the religion in which woman is the natural high priestess and maker of music. Many of these people are not to be regarded as uncivilized remnants of old races who will ultimately be swept into the currents of our present culture. On the contrary, most of them have been in touch with our civilization for centuries, and are now under the administration of some government that offers them all modern benefits —British, French, Dutch, Russian, or American. Most of them are nominally Christian, or are being actively proselytized by missionaries. They have educated leaders trained in the best universities of Europe or America. Withal, in really vital matters they keep to the nature religion and observe more or less the ancient festivals, of which birth is the central mystery and woman the high priestess, able by incantation or music to bend the unseen to her will.

One cannot see this nature religion anywhere in its entirety. One must put it together like the pieces of a picture puzzle—taking a birth rite from Africa, a puberty rite from central Asia—until the whole emerges. On the other hand, secret and unknown to most travelers as these customs are, incomplete, often quite archaic, one cannot underestimate their vitality. In the revolutionary ferment all over the world today, Christians with their roots in the woman's religion but with modern education are lustily reasserting themselves. This is true of the Maoris of New Zealand, whose Princess Te Puea is a genuine political force and earnestly calls for the maintenance of the rites. It is true in the resurgent Indian movement of Latin America, in Mexico and Peru, and it is true in many parts of Russia. In these movements, which are political and social and only incidentally artistic, there is usually a vigorous assertion of the values of that type of communal living in which women's talents as musicians and organizers of rites flowered.

It is true that the woman in these societies is not always a happy creature, that she often lacks freedoms her civilized sisters enjoy, and that she submits to customs discriminatory to her sex. Nevertheless, woman's authority as bearer of life is incorporated into religious dogma. Every individual woman in the tribe has an inestimable spiritual advantage. One of her great advantages is the assumption that the supreme life force may be feminine and manifested by women. She is not limited to one male divinity with no feminine religious officials.

In these lands where women make songs and folk tales set to music, whatever a woman does, what she is, and what she is valued for become projected into some kind of image or symbol. An outstanding woman becomes magnified and glorified into a goddess. When Queen Oya of the Yoruba died about two hundred years ago she was elevated to the rank of a divine power. Today homage is paid to her as the spirit of the giant river Niger.

Hardly a primitive or peasant society exists without its spirits who lead, protect, and represent women. For the Ibibios, the mother of the town is a huge tree. Generation after generation of little brown girls is presented to it. Often the guardian of women is a great rock or water spirit. Often it is the moon. Again it is a supernatural woman. Dzogbemesi—Woman of the Other World—receives the prayers of the African Matse mothers. She punishes all those who would harm her protégées, even their husbands. The Lithuanian Mahra, with loosened hair streaming on her shoulders, holds a woman in labor on her lap. Láda, in Russia, brings the flowers and fruits of summer. "Mother" and "love" are the same word in the language of the Ibibios. Over them there rules a great life giver, whose face is the face of love. This mother-love goddess—Eka Abassi—is such an overwhelming power that no man dares approach her or speak her name above a whisper.

Of all the symbols of womanhood, the moon is the most significant. The mysterious apparent synchronization of woman's monthly cycle and her term of pregnancy with the lunar cycle brings woman and the moon imaginatively together. There is a woman in all moon myths. Even in cultures where the moon is a god, the imagery includes woman either as the mother of the moon, as mate, or as daughter. Over and over again the moon is a god and goddess together—symbol of the growth and change that govern all forms of life on earth. But as goddess alone, the moon has many forms. She may be woman herself who grows and dies and is born again as a maiden, bringing with her the hope for the rebirth. She may be "the old woman who never dies." To the Polynesians she is Hina, the great goddess who has the power to grant immortality. To the Slavs she is Libussa-Baba, who invented birth and death, and who, as Golden Moon, eases birth. Or the moon may be a worker at any of woman's daily tasks and so unite in symbol the worker and the dreamer.

Behind the beauty and the romance of moon imagery flashes the vitalizing idea that woman is the special manifestation of the driving, untiring, *active* force of life. Of this the primitive woman's symbols and musical rites remind her daily. She perceives in everything that flows, that lives and moves and grows, something akin to her own power of growing and giving birth. The very word "rite" means a stream, a flowing, a manner, and a way. All through her life, in company with other women, she is asserting the special "way" of her sex and showing what good for the whole people can come from her work and her thoughts.

The men of primitive tribes know that woman's way in the scheme of life brings good. This conviction comes primarily from the practical results of women's working and thinking, which in simple societies relate directly to the fundamental needs of existence.

When the various rites of the mother's religion with its music and dance ceremonies are pieced together, a kind of composite woman emerges—strong, wise, creative by right of her womanhood. She cannot be seen anywhere in her perfection, though in fortunate and well-educated tribes like the Maoris there are women who very nearly approach the ideal stature of musician-chieftainess. But even when she seems to a Western tourist to be poor, backward, and greatly overburdened with work and babies, she may still have a kind of inner spiritual assurance that the educated and pampered woman of our civilization lacks. For hers is the inestimable privilege of *authority* in religion and song. And so the chief priestess of the Kwakuitl Indians sings, as she fancifully catches superpower from the air and throws it among her people:

> "I have the magical treasure,
> I have supernatural power,
> I can return to life!" [14]

CHAPTER II

BRINGERS OF LIFE

1.

*B*EHIND the music of women, in the simpler societies outside our present "civilized" culture pattern, there is a truly grand idea. It is an idea so obvious that it seems to have occurred to women everywhere, almost as soon as they were able to think in general terms and imaginative symbols. It is so fundamental and so universal that much of it has been incorporated into all the great religious systems.

This is the idea: that the process of birth offers the key to the understanding of everything else in life. As St. Paul wrote the Romans, "For we know that the whole creation groaneth and travaileth . . ." As Christ said, "Except a man be born again, he cannot see the kingdom of God." As Buddha said, "The life of an individual on this earth is but one link or cycle in an endless chain of births and rebirths."

One cannot understand the relation of women to music in our culture today until one understands in detail how the primitive woman centers music, with its ritual and healing, in what is to her the primary fact of human existence—childbirth.

The circumstances and associations of childbirth set the pattern of the music and inspire other rites of the life cycle, such as puberty rites and wedding ceremonies. By a process of symbolic thinking, simple, profound, almost inevitable, music that has definite associations with childbirth becomes the music for death. For except as a seed fall into the ground and die, as Christ said, it shall not live. And beyond this death, there may be birth if she who gives birth will sing in the face of death the song she made out of the struggle of birth.

Marina Núñez del Prado has expressed this idea of rebirth in a

21

powerful statue. (See Plate 7.) The Bolivian mother Aymara prays to the Spirit of Life for her dead baby:

"Give back the smile of my dead son in the waving wheat!
For his flesh, flowers in the strengthening grain of my fields!"

From this faith it is a short step to the belief that everything good and desirable may be thought of as birth into a new condition. So the song of birth becomes a magic for the fertilizing of the fields, for the protection of men at war, for well-being and success of all kinds.

2.

For the woman, childbirth is a profoundly religious and spirit-bearing experience.

Where there are no physicians and hospitals to take over, anesthetics to be administered, and trained nurses to preside with impersonal routine efficiency, a woman must depend on spiritual rather than mechanical aids. Nothing mechanical and scientific stands between her and the dark glory of the moment when in labor and pain, face to face with death, she battles for the new life. But all the unseen mysteries of the universe are involved. Evil ghosts hover to inflict pain. Good spirits may be invoked by incantations and ritual. And over all presides the great, brooding mother spirit. So, as a woman's time approaches, there are preparations as for a supreme religious rite.

Almost everywhere, women banish men during childbirth. They resent any interference and have been known to kill men who spied upon them. But in some cases they compel a husband to remain alone in a hut and cry out, as if in pain, while his wife, on her part, bears her baby in silence. Whatever the local custom is, a professional midwife, who is often the high priestess or shamaness or a magician, takes charge. The mother or other feminine relatives and the woman's neighbors and friends gather round. In societies where the girl leaves her own home and joins her husband's family, the mother-in-law and her relatives are called in.

Midwives and relatives busy themselves loosening hair, unlocking doors, and untying knots in the effort to remove any impediment against birth. They swing and dance to keep in the rhythm of life. Among the Fans of Africa, the business is so important that a special enchantress hides in the bushes near the place of confinement and chants an elaborate melody for hours. Even the pregnant woman sings. And, over and above the human song, goddesses imitate with divine melodies the "low-lying" mother's voice.

A Fox Indian woman says of the birth of her son:

The child could not be born. The women who were attending me were frightened. They said, "We shall pray for help." My mother-in-law went to a woman skilled in birth. She boiled some medicine. She made me sit up and she spat upon my head. She gave me the medicine to drink. She began singing. She started to go out singing and went around the little wicki-up singing. When she danced by where I was, she knocked on the side. "Come out if you are a boy," she would say. And she would sing again. When she danced by she would again knock the side. "Come out if you are a girl," she would say again. After she sang four times in a circle she entered the wicki-up. "Now it will be born." Lo, sure enough, a little boy was born.[1]

In the Fiji Islands today women are famous as poetess-musicians and use their talents to help a woman in childbirth. At this sacred event they allow no man to be present. Escorting their friend to the bank of a river, they place her against a wooden support erected for the purpose. The chief midwife, who is also the high priestess of the tribe, kneels with palms upturned in magic gesture, as in Greece Eileithyia, the goddess of childbirth, is always depicted. She invokes the child about to be born. Around the two central figures the other women stand in a semicircle. They wave their arms to and fro in rhythm to her pains and sing with a sighing, wailing sound. The low notes are given first and then the sound swells up to a high tone. Another wail begins on the high note and drops down, to rise again in rhythm with the effort of birth until the child is born.[2]

Here is the model for that rite of symbolic birth which is to be found in so many religions. The wooden supports and the woman in labor suggest an altar on which is laid a token representing the re-birth—the bread and the wine, the flesh broken and the blood spilled. Here is not the derived symbol but the act itself—the agony of struggle for the perpetuation of life in the divine presence. For the mother looking up in her struggle to the soft tropical sky may feel that out of it an all-comprehending mother spirit supports her—an infinite mercy, who like the moon knows what it is to wax and wane, to go down into darkness and after three days to rise again. So nature, in this quiet place, makes of the birth chamber a church. The fronds of the coconut palms meet overhead like the intricately carved arches of a great cathedral. The still waters of the river amidst the jungle undergrowth are the baptismal font. The rich tropical odor of growing things—of ferns and flowers and ripe bananas and of the fertile earth itself—rises like incense. (See Plate 8.)

And because they believe that in themselves they have power to invoke life universal, these women have something of sacerdotal dignity. Clean-limbed and strong, authority in every line of her straight backbone and high-held head, dignified and formalized by the gold-tinted circle of hair, the high priestess is the intermediary between the real and the mystery. The attendants form the liturgical choir chanting the eternal affirmation of life.

3.

Unless deliberately stifled, as it is in the Fiji Islands, some audible expression of the muscular effort involved in child-bearing accompanies labor pains. In an Indian tribe of Northwestern America, the sounds made by women in childbirth are a kind of irregular crying or singing, half way between a whine and a melody. But whether a whine, a cry, a shriek, or a suggestion of a melody, the generic term for these sounds is "wail."

In the effort to insure propitious delivery, every power of invention is brought to bear upon the childbirth cry. For this is the cry of life, the woman speaking in her critical hour to the universal life. The proper management of the wail is thought to be so important that it is often strictly controlled by social and religious usage. The mother's sound may be re-enforced by the beating of drums, timed to strengthen the rhythmical contractions of birth. Sometimes the mother makes no sound but, instead, her friends or her husband cry out in her behalf. In Thrace and in some Celtic countries, the attendants, the husband, and all the family cry aloud when the child is born. In certain African tribes, women even pretend that a spirit mother is wailing when her child departs from the land of ghosts to become a human baby.

Everywhere in the world, women make their music by imitating all kinds of natural sounds—the songs of birds, the soughing of wind, the rippling of water. But the sound of the birth cry is the natural

Courtesy of Charles Scribner's Sons

1. Carl Lumholtz photographed native women for his book *Through Central Borneo.* The Dyaks believe that beating drums and singing attract good spirits. (See page 3.)

Courtesy of Edward Arnold and Co.

2. A photograph from Routledge's *With a Prehistoric People* shows Akikúyu women in a great assembly. According to the customs of this musically gifted people, solo singers improvise and the group responds. (See page 8.)

3. In a Russian painting, girls can be seen going from house to house, singing Christmas carols and *kolyádki*. (See page 9.)

4. A contemporary Pueblo woman of New Mexico depicts her companions performing the Wheel Dance, an ancient war ritual. (See page 11.)

Photograph by Melville J. Herskovits

5. Wearing silver ornaments like the horns of the moon, these singers of the Dahomey tribe of Africa represent the army of 10,000 women warriors, famous in former times. (See pages 13 and 40.)

Courtesy of Alfred J. Swan

6. Chorus of Russian mothers in the Esthonian village Gorodische sing their wedding ritual. The men listen but do not sing. (See page 13.)

7. Graven in stone by a Bolivian sculptress of today, Aymara is the symbolic mother raising her hands in the gesture that magically brings about birth. (See page 22.)

Courtesy of Marina Nuñez del Prado

Courtesy of Virginia McCall

8. Under the direction of an eyewitness, a Philadelphia artist has sketched a childbirth scene in the Fiji Islands. (See page 24.)

sound most distinctive of women, the most intimately associated
with that supreme experience which is the climax of their physical
life and the source of their religious thinking. The Fiji Island women
—notable musicians as they are—bring to their incantations considerable technical skill and base their music accompanying childbirth upon a sighing, wailing sound.

In transforming the wail into melody, women have a great variety
of methods. A musician may herself build a musical phrase around a
recurring wail. Or she may make a recitative alternating with wailing
by other women in unison. In Corsica, a chorus of women intone a
chant. The leader leaps suddenly into the center of the group and
wails: "Woe! Woe!" as was the custom in performing Greek tragedies. At death ceremonies, Iroquois women formerly divided into
two choruses, one of which gave the long-drawn out sobbing wail
while the other sang a melodious chant.

In this manner, women's dirges in primitive music were born. As
an art form, they evolved from the cry of childbirth, and for musical
existence, depend upon a sound natural only to women. Dirges and
laments are noticeably absent from the repertoire of primitive men.
It is the mother's business to bring life, even in death.

And for this purpose of bringing life women have also stylized the
wail itself. One magician may give it a regular form with a crescendo
to a climax, followed by a relapse into a slow, dragging drawl. A
Nubian woman begins on a high note and drops her voice by thirds
to a twelfth below the original note. Wailing may be considered an
art distinct from singing and a wailer, often an official of high standing, may be praised for her appealing, or her grand, individual style.

The wail, in its stylized form, is used now by many primitive people and was used in ancient societies. It was developed by women
for a particular purpose as an independent art but it is not music
and never became music. From the simple wail, women also evolved
the wail song. In company with melodies derived from other inspirations, this did become music and was employed with endless variation by countless women musicians for those many practical purposes
for which primitive mothers need music.

4.

According to the imagery of women, all life is a series of births
and rebirths that they are empowered to bring about. Sickness can

be transformed into health; adoption can symbolically render a person a blood relative. Puberty, or mating, is birth into maturity; death is rebirth into another world; the annual growth of vegetation, or the new moon, is birth for other forms of life.

One kind of birth is similar to another, so that in some cases the imagery of the three great crises of a woman's life—birth, marriage, and death—become interchangeable. A dead Russian maiden is dressed in her wedding garments and her burial is attended by friends who come as if the ceremony were for the wedding. In a poem by a Greek mourner the bereaved parents implore their daughter to return to them but the girl answers:

"Nay, I may not, dear father mine and mother deep-beloved,
Yesterday was my marriage day, late yester e'en my wedding.
'Hades' I for my husband have, the tomb for my new mother." [3]

The human mother's womb changes into a tomb and death becomes a form of marriage. The idea of the poem was clearly inspired by womb imagery and derived originally from the reality of childbirth.

It is easy for us to misunderstand these primitive wail songs because, with our overintellectualized and overdepartmentalized approach to music and to life, we have lost the simple yet profound consciousness of the oneness of joy and pain, of birth and death, that is in them.

The wail alone, or in its elaborated form of lament and dirge, sounds mournful in our ears. To observers of primitive women who sing with tears streaming down their faces, as in the Maori *tangi*, it may seem an expression of inconsolable grief. But its intent is actually to ensure rebirth. The very word "dirge" comes from the Latin *dirigere*, which means "to direct." The dirge directs the vanished life on its way.

The peculiar mournfulness of this primitive wail music is due to two factors. Even for sophisticated audiences sadness is more artistically moving than joy. It touches deeper levels of the unconscious. It induces a more complete sense of release. The primitive woman early learned that an orgy of weeping brought relief—an idea later elaborated by Aristotle in his dictum that the function of tragedy is the purgation of pity and fear through representative pain and death. So the primitive woman artist makes the most of the wail song, prolonging it, building it up to climaxes of sorrow.

The other factor that makes the wail songs mournful is that life has in it much of pain, and pain translated by the woman musician becomes the wail. For the woman every change may be thought of as birth or rebirth. And every birth has its memory—or anticipation—of physical and emotional distress. Even at weddings, occasions for joy and hilarity, women sense the coming suffering inevitable to their altered state of life. Mating and childbearing, essential in bringing about fulfillment of life, have for women an aftermath of pain and sacrifice. Estonian bridesmaids sing:

> "Make thyself fine, O lovely maiden—
> and on thy head place the wreath of sorrow
> and on thy brow the wreath of pain—
> Quickly, quickly while still there is light
> gird thyself—for the twilight is coming on." [4]

But, sorrowful as women's wail songs may seem to our ears, they have two characteristics that make them anything but depressing when rightly understood. One is the intent, already discussed, to induce rebirth and the faith that this can be done. The other is the periodicity, the rhythmic alteration of mood, which is of the essence of a woman's peculiar vitality. So women combine lamenting and rejoicing in one rite. It is a common practice in primitive tribes for mourners at funeral rites to wail for hours, even for days at a time, but to break every now and then into sudden bursts of rejoicing. They find the burden of grief intolerable, possibly, and release themselves in the cry of joy. Or they rejoice in anticipation of the rebirth and so hasten it. Some Russian groups today also have the same custom. At the festival of Radunitsa, the goddess Ustara (whose name became converted to Easter) is invoked. The people mourn over their dead, over the decay of life in general. Then they turn toward the east and rejoice.

Women's expression of the mood of rejoicing seems universally to involve the sound of the letter "l." It is often formalized into the phrase al-al-al, la-la, or lu-lu—familiar to us as the "alleluia" of Jewish and Christian worship. In the primitive and peasant world, women give the "l" refrain in their songs of joy. (See Plate 21.) Lully-lu is often incorporated into lullabies, which are incantations to persuade children to sleep and also little proofs of joy in them.

Friends of a Jewish bride in Palestine sing a song of good luck for the new husband:

> "May the eye of God protect you.
> Lu-lu-lu-lu-lesch!" [5]

The high trilling tone they use, often pressing their hands on their throats to achieve it, suggests the origin of the word "ululate." But since "to ululate" actually means "to wail," it is the womb from which the cry of joy and the wail of sorrow both come.

In a remarkable example of the union of the cry of joy and the wail of sorrow, a Calabrian singer pictures death as crouching in a mountain defile and snatching a young girl.

> "Joy, I saw death! Joy, I saw her yesterday!
> I beheld her in a narrow way, like unto a great gray hound and I was very curious.
> 'Death, whence comest thou?'
> 'I am come from Germany—I have killed princes, counts, and cavaliers, and now I am come for a young maiden so that with me she may go.'
> Weep, Mamma, weep for me, weep and never rest—no more shalt thou await me." [6]

The idiom of the wail song, varied to suit the occasion but essentially the same in all primitive woman's music, is associated with a great variety of symbols and symbolic gestures. When the woman makes her rituals, she finds a thousand objects to reinforce with sympathetic magic the power of word and movement and tone. For almost everything about her tells of birth and rebirth. Everywhere she finds flowers—flowers that are buds, like little girls, and open and bloom like a girl into womanhood. They fade, but in fading set fruit, and out of the fruit comes the seed, which, when planted, grows and flowers again. In every way flowers are symbols, even to the many strange ways in which, in their shapes and their colors and their folds and secret places where the honey lies, they seem to be modeled after those organs which the primitive woman often looks on proudly as the seat of her power. So flowers are everywhere used in women's rituals. The Hawaiian girls, greeting the big ocean liner with song and singing it on its way out of port, wear great wreaths of fragrant flowers called leis, and hang wreaths about the strangers' necks as a symbol of loving greeting. In the Andaman Islands a young girl is given a flower name from the time of her first menstruation until her first pregnancy. And in Persian folklore, if a girl dies before her marriage she becomes metamorphosed into a flower.

Lights and water are, like flowers, full of meaning. Torches symbolize the light of the moon, which must never be allowed to die, for as the moon comes back, so life comes back. Mirrors imitate the still surface of a lake in which the moon can be reflected. Water flows from the mother's body. When the membranes rupture the child is born—hence the water of baptism and of other rites of rebirth. When the child is born, first comes the water, then the blood. Broken pots filled with red ocher symbolize the blood of the mother sacrificed at childbirth. Plumes and jewels are the child. That queer little figure which is the peculiar mark of the Maoris, with its eyes of gleaming blue-green *paua* shell, is the unborn child with the moonlight in its eyes. In shape, bells suggest the womb. Flutes blow the breath of life. Drums give the beat for the rhythm of the universe.

The movements of the dance often frankly glorify the seat of the woman's power—with that circling movement of the pelvis and rhythmic rotation of the hips which is the distinguishing technique of the woman's dance in the Pacific islands and southeastern Asia. Susceptible young men often find these dances seductive, and so, when danced by young girls, they are often meant to be. For it is the right of woman, young and ripe for motherhood, to attract her man. Yet the real concern of the girls is often only to perform the traditional movements well enough to escape the artistic criticism of the older women and often of the older men, who become connoisseurs in these women's ways. So many hours of tiresome practice have usually gone into the acquisition of this hip and belly movement that it often seems to the girl a chore the elders expect her to perform, with very little relation to her own personal desire, which is naturally to attract a lover.

So the Roratongan girl, clad only in a brief skirt of shredded bark, a brassière, and a flower, lifts her pelvis as high as she can and then keeps it circling to the accompaniment of her chant. It is as if her pelvis were an instrument on which she were playing. It is a kind of invisible music similar to the visible and complex patterns of movement with which the Maori girls often accompany their songs.

Whatever conscious seduction there may be in the girls' dancing, there is none in that of the real experts in the pelvis technique. When one of those middle-aged or really old women who greatly excel the girls in the skillful manipulation of pelvis or feet performs the dance of the pelvis, she has no notion of attracting any man's eye. It is to her the lusty assertion of the glory of her womanhood, the triumphant flourishing of the seat of her power. And when under the fantastic gold lacework of the Shewe Dagon pagoda, on those marble courts smooth as glass, the Burmese women dance with circling movements of hip and breast, while the torchlight flickers on their smooth, earnest faces and the scent of trampled flowers and fruit rises like incense around them, they are dancing not to please men or women or even the impassive gold Buddhas sitting in golden shrines, but rather to realize something greater—their own part in the rhythm of the universe.

Out of the importance of birth, which is the center of the woman's religion and the source of her power to invoke rebirth, grow the various rites of the woman's life cycle—puberty, marriage, family or tribal celebrations of birth, and, finally, death. Since a woman has such important functions to perform, she must be carefully trained and provided with spiritual aids in all the crises of her life. So the little girl learns her pelvic dances. It is even more important for her to have this seat of her power well exercised and well trained, flexible, powerful, rhythmically responsive, than it is for her brother to learn to flex his muscles, clench his fist, strike straight from the shoulder, brandish his weapons, or leap and jump in the war dance. The tribe might get along very well if men did not go to war. It could not get along at all if the women did not bear children. So the girl must learn to move her pelvis freely and powerfully and dance the pelvic dance as the sign of her fitness for womanhood.

5.

When a girl becomes physically capable of womanhood, she needs spiritual instruction, a ritual induction into her new responsibilities, a new attitude to herself. Running around, often playing with her little brothers, she is sexless, immature. These traits she must now shed as the snake sheds its skin or the butterfly its cocoon, and emerge a true woman, with a woman's personality.

Girls' puberty rites are held at new moon and the initiates dance all night and every night while the moon is waxing. Dancing, instrumental music, and special songs quite generally accompany the rites.

Just as for childbirth, women have their own hierarchy. The mother, the eldest sister, and other female relatives play their part. High women officials lend dignity to the ceremonies. The queen of the Ashantis, for example, has a silver stool modeled on the type of stool used by women in labor. Seated on this throne, she presides at the rites of the rebirth.

In some parts of Africa, puberty rites are controlled by the women's secret societies. The Bundu, in Sierra Leone, is one of the most powerful of these associations. Women called "Soko" know the secrets of life—of which music is one—and pass them on to the next generation. (See Plate 9.)

Certain musical instruments are associated with the girls' puberty rites. According to local custom, girls play drums, rattles, xylophones, horns, and musical bows. The Bavenda girls, who belong to a very musical race, have an orchestra made up of different instruments. They perform at the Phala-phala Dance, one of the initiates' rites.

Whenever women assume responsibility for the girls' initiation into womanhood, they have also the incentive to invent the rites, the dances, and the songs. They make the ceremonies a time for chanting long stories in which heroines abound, a time for singing incantations, invocations to deities, a time for lamenting the loss of their little daughters and rejoicing that a new woman has arrived in their midst. The time, the occasion, and the symbolism inspire creative musical imagination.

A typical ceremony of puberty, interpreted as rebirth into womanhood, is that of the Intonjane in Africa. This is usually in charge of the aunts on the father's side, who choose girls and women to help them. When the old moon fades, the initiate is led, with much ceremony, to a small thatched hut that symbolizes the womb, and there she is left alone during the dark of the moon. On the second day girls go out early from the village to cut soft grasses for the ceremony. The women and girls left in the village sing and dance from dawn till sunrise, celebrating the coming of a new woman, invoking all good upon her. On the morning of the third day they dance again.

After sunset on the night when the new moon will appear in the sky, women and girls cover the girl with a blanket, wrap her head in a veil, and surround her in a dense crowd so that no man may see her. They take her with singing and dancing and clapping of hands away to a distant hill. In the dusk, just as the slim, silver crescent of the young moon gleams over the African bush, they come back with her to the village, singing and rejoicing as if a new person were being welcomed to the kraal, and from that night to the night of the full moon she sings and rejoices with them. Both the older women and the girls are musicians. No man has made for them the music they sing to the moon. They have made it themselves, out of their own hearts, with their own skill, for their own woman's need.[7] (See Plate 10.)

Where girls have ritual preparation for womanhood under women's leadership and are adequately trained in music, their poetic-musical compositions are rich in imagery, full of allusions to the various devices employed to bring about the rebirth, especially flowers. The girls liken themselves to a bud, which only the warmth of love can open. Or they look longingly at a meadow and ask who will make them a wedding wreath. The songs are often made in the form of a duet between mother and daughter. The mother asks the girl what is troubling her and the daughter confesses her desire to rest in her lover's arms. Many laments voicing disappointment or loneliness and many love lyrics expressing devotion to the beloved belong to this group. Known as "maiden songs" among European peasants, they form an important and particularly beautiful group of folk music.

6.

Marriage, like puberty, calls for the women's talent in music making. A typical primitive wedding is one among the Pygmies of Africa. These slender little black folk—four feet high, weighing only about eighty pounds—are thought to be one of the oldest races on earth. Though they never arrived even at the agricultural stage of society, and live by hunting and fishing in the great, hot, tangled forests along the equator, explorers have testified that their intelligence is of a high order. They have a rich lore of ceremony and music; they are vivacious and witty, cleanly and fond of decency, order, and beauty in the details of their very simple lives.

When a girl is to be married, the clan of the fiancé comes to her village to take her away. The men set up enormous tom-toms. As the drums begin to beat, the bride retires into a hut with her mother-in-law and as many of her girl comrades as can crowd themselves in. The mother-in-law places in the bride's arms the latest-born baby of the village. The bride says nothing. Silently she gives the baby back

and turns away. At this all the bridesmaids begin to sing and the
bride bursts into tears. Her bridesmaids keep on singing the whole
night through. And while they sing, the bride must weep, even
though to keep the tears flowing after long hours she puts a pimento
seed in the corner of her eye. The songs of the bridesmaids are long,
and among them there are strains of great beauty, in which after the
manner of all ancient poetry the music is of one piece with the verse
form, conceived with it in a single impulse of the imagination.

Song of the Bridesmaids, African Pygmy Tribes

Counting your steps and turning no backward glance,
Reluctant your feet and with the slow tears falling,
Today with a troubled heart, with a heavy heart you are leaving,
The Bridegroom is waiting, maiden, reluctant, advance.

Here is the home you loved, your girlhood companions,
Here you played as a child, here you trod in the village dance,
You must leave it now, turning no backward glance,
With a heavy heart you must say farewell to your loved ones.

The Bridegroom is waiting, maiden, reluctant, advance.

Counting your slow steps, go, but keep with you ever,
Keep in your heart the treasure, the sandal flower
Plucked from your mother's garden, it will tell you:
"There they love me still and will love me forever."

Counting your steps and turning no backward glance,
Maiden, reluctant, maiden, reluctant, advance.[8]

There are tears throughout these wedding songs, like the soft
rhythmic sound of falling rain on the awakening earth in spring.

At a Russian bride's farewell party—her *devíshnik*—which she
gives for her bridesmaids the night before the marriage, the leader
starts to sing in a low voice and the others pick up her melody:

"Why are you here, my sisters? Why are you here, my white swans?
You have come, my sisters, for my last girl's party.

"My dear friends, maidens fair, the golden crown will be taken off
    my head, the red ribbons will fall out of my fair braids,
My freedom will cease to be." [9]

The bride herself, seated in the center surrounded by the bridesmaids, repeats the words of the song, but instead of singing she wails —the stylized wail that is one of the earmarks of women's expression from time immemorial.

Bridesmaids' songs are both numerous and beautiful. There are the flower songs, sung while the girls are picking flowers and greens to decorate the house and to make the bridal wreaths. In the Cyclades they sing:

> "Adorn the crowns with pearls and flowers,
> The bride and bridegroom are the moon and stars." [10]

There are songs ridiculing or extolling the bridegroom; songs praising the bride's beauty, songs rejoicing over the bride's new estate; and always songs lamenting the passing of girlhood.

> Happy she may be again,
> But never more a maiden.[11]

The older women and the professional song leader have their opportunity, too, for musical expression. Songs are sung while the food for the wedding feast is being prepared, while the bride's bed is made, while she is swinging and dancing her way into her new life, while they are waiting for the bridegroom to come, while the house is being decorated, while the bride is being washed and dressed. In Syria, when the professional hairdresser has finished her work she beats her little drums and sings:

> "O bride, be silent, your mother weeps,
> And your bridegroom and his friends rejoice!" [12]

Finally, the bride herself must sing, and in her song her joy is tempered with unfeigned grief and longing. A Greek girl realizes that her family will miss her as she will miss them—especially at the hour of waking, at mealtime, and at family celebrations. She sings:

> "I leave my blessing on my home!
> Neighbors and friends, adieu!
> Three vials filled with bitterness,
> Mother, I leave to you!
> The first to drink at dawn of day,

The next in noontide heat,
The last and worst in festive scenes,
Where all but one will meet." [13]

Wedding music is women's music, made by the bride, her bridesmaids, her feminine relatives, professional attendants, and the special singers. In any age, in any culture, including our own, music to
accompany the marriage is a comparatively unimportant category of
men's compositions. All wedding songs by Greek and Roman men
were modeled on those of Sappho. Among primitives and peasants
today—especially in Russia—men rarely sing during the long-drawn-
out marriage ceremonies but are satisfied to listen for days to wom-
en's endless repertory. (See Plates 6 and 11.)

7.

When the woman feels the first sign of new life in her body, she
rejoices, again often with elaborate and interesting rituals. After the
child is born, women have a series of celebrations at which they
dance, play on instruments, and sing.

The desire of parents to present their offspring in some formal
manner to other men and women of their group and to whatever
deity they worship seems to be universal. In primitive societies the
mother, who has admittedly played the larger part in this new creation, participates actively. Sometimes the ceremony is a joint affair
between men and women. Often women exclude men and conduct
the rites alone, according to their own interpretation.

The Pygmies have both types of ceremony. When a son is born,
the fathers celebrate and sing their own songs of rejoicing. The
women join in the refrain with their cries of jubilation. The young
mother herself is, however, the most important person of the group.
Custom decrees that she perform the dance of life, not only for the
purpose of giving life to her own child but to bring symbolic regeneration to the whole tribe. To the accompaniment of the shouts of
exultation given by the other women, she dances into the center of
the open plot and imitates every movement of her recent experience.

For every child, son or daughter, the musically minded Pygmy
women have a special ceremony to present it to the moon, the symbol of the rhythm of life. Among the Pygmies, the moon is feminine
—Generatrix, She Who Creates. To unite the mothers with the moon

spirit, the women paint their bodies white and yellow and dance the dance of life. They sing their sacred songs to Mother Moon—songs that have never been heard by men, even by those of their own tribe. This is a secret ceremony, women's own business to make the life they have created secure on earth.

In the Baltic States—Estonia, Lithuania, and Latvia—antiphonal choruses of women welcome the newborn child. Among the Latvians, two groups of girl singers vie with each other and compete for the praise of the guests. Sometimes two girls sing sitting face to face and holding hands. The listeners accompany them. These choruses are renowned for their excellence and represent the most finished type of peasant art. (See Plate 12.)

One of the most common ceremonies for women after childbirth is the rite that reintroduces her to her normal life. As practiced in primitive tribes, it is associated primarily with the idea of a mother being a potent manifestation of the life force. At the time of childbirth the life force is believed to be present in such power that it might injure other people. Like a live electric wire, it is dangerous. Primitive people have a feeling that they must detach themselves from the supernatural after any event that seems to suggest supernatural agency. When, for instance, strangers insist upon photographing them, they hurry afterward to bathe in flowing water. Most primitive women have a special ceremony to detach a mother from her close contact with the life force. At such ceremonies they employ the customary rebirth techniques—drumming, dancing, and singing magic songs. Owing to the distortion of these particular rites in "civilized" societies, the original significance of the idea behind them should be understood by everyone interested in women's spiritual growth and in her opportunities to be a creative musician.

A mother in the state of confinement, and even a menstruating woman, is often called "unclean." This word is used in the sense that she has disturbed the ordinary course of events. Butchers are also "unclean," because they handle live blood; those who tend the dead are "unclean"; men and women who have just had sexual intercourse are "unclean." All of these people and their actions have had contact with the life force. But a woman giving birth has had the closest contact and has the most profoundly disturbed the normal course of events. It is a general custom, too, to allow a longer period of time to elapse between the birth of a girl baby and the ritual detachment of the mother from the life force than in the case of the birth of a boy.

This is probably because a girl baby must derive added strength from her mother in order to carry on with women's business. But in any case, the word "unclean" has not the significance of an unhygienic or dirty condition, nor does it have any connotation of evildoing. The rites of primitive women, invented by them and presided over by them, are definitely associated with the holiness of woman as the bringer of life.

8.

It is in the presence of death that a woman's singing is called to its highest functioning. To the primitive mind, death is rebirth into another world. Because women bring life, they are needed to assist the spirit along its destined path. Without their ministrations, a soul might be lost and remain suspended in mid-air without rest forever.

Mothers, sisters, wives, midwives, priestesses, and especially the professional singers are in demand as purveyors of life. In the Hebrides the midwife is called upon to close in the sleep of death the eyes she opened at birth, and to sing her incantations for the rebirth. According to locality, the professional mourner has different names. In Russia she is "the sobbing one" (*voplénitsa*); in Corsica, *praefica*, like the ancient Roman woman mourner; in Calabria and Sardinia, *reputatrica*, or the one who tells the story of the dead. The Irish women's leader takes charge and, calling her companions around her, begins the chant: "Cease now your wailing, women of the soft, wet eyes." [14] (See Plate 13.)

In many places men are excluded from death rites. In others, men participate but without the authority of women, who are generally called upon to beat the drum of life, to act out the mimicry of birth, to pour the libation, to swing, to dance, to wave flowers and green branches, to tell the history of the departed, to wail, and especially to create and sing the dirges.

Mourning ritual usually includes dancing and often swinging. Death is the principal one of those events in human experience that disturb the even flow of life. Affirmation of the will to live is therefore important. Swinging and dancing keep one in touch with the rhythm of the universe, and at the same time can be employed as devices to bring about the rebirth. Among the Dyaks of Borneo the professional wailer sits on a swing near the corpse and begs the spirits to guide the soul in the right direction.

The dance is capable of infinite variation and has been developed into many forms by the fertile imagination of primitive women. Among the Baronga, when a chief has been dead for three months the oldest woman of his family connection is called in as leader of the ceremonies. The men demolish the hut that was the former home of the chief and prepare a flat place for dancing. The old woman then dances the womb dance and imitates every movement of generation and childbirth in order to deliver his soul. Likewise, on the shores of the Gulf of Carpenteria (Australia) certain relatives of the dead person have the duty of performing the mourning dance around the body. Weeping and singing all night until they fall exhausted, the women stretch out their arms as if to lay the body in the earth and thud their feet upon the ground in rhythm. (See Plate 14.)

Of all the devices to bring about rebirth, the wail is the most important. In the Jabo tribe of eastern Liberia the wail is developed into a long and elaborate composition by the mourner, who is an official of very high rank, lawyer and historian of the tribe. She stands with the white sunlight and black shadows of this equatorial land playing on her polished black body. She is stately and tall, full of poise and dignity, for in her land women are persons of power. In the absence of written records, the vast store of tribal information is kept in the head of this woman official—historian, lawyer, and singer at funerals. Since she knows the background of all present events, what she asserts becomes the law of the land. No funeral of a man of property can be conducted without her.

At the funeral this personage presides while a chorus of women wails for hours. Then she takes the stage and, performing solo, builds around her own wail an elaborate composition. She chants the virtues of the deceased, describes the status of his family, enumerates its prerogatives, and reports on the extent of his property, modifying her wail and transforming it into a melody. She sings the names of the living men and women of the tribe; she sings the names of the ancestors, both men and women, from the beginning. She sprinkles the many proverbs in which the life wisdom of the tribe is concentrated at appropriate intervals throughout this musical discourse, and always she builds out of the wail her melody. To her, as to Fiji women in their childbirth rites and the Russian women at the *devishnik* or bridal ceremony, the primitive wail is an inspiration to musical composition.

In the effort to make the wail a living and developing art form,

satisfactory to their artistic instinct while performing its more practical purpose of invoking the rebirth, women are stimulated also to
poetic imagery. The best performers try to avoid stereotypes and to
make words and music specifically apply to the one who is mourned.
In Albania, when they mourn an unmarried girl they sing:

> "O joyless woman who hath never known joy,
> Who hath never fulfilled thine own life." [15]

When they mourn a mother they sing:

> "O spirit of the house within the very walls where you sat—
> There you left shining glory!" [16]

In Dahomey (Africa) the oldest member of the family has the
duty of watching the dead body with the widow. It is also her duty
to compose the burial song at the grave and another special song
when the grave is later revisited by the family.

> An old woman weeps, amidst the leaves;
> A white haired woman—O—weeps amidst the leaves of the forest,
> And she says, the birds in the bush,
> The life of these birds is to be envied.
> How is it that man born into life has no more generations?
> He has no more! [17]

Laments return again and again to the imagery of the rhythm of
life. An Arabian mother mourning for her son slain in battle sang of
days and nights endlessly alternating. A famous Polynesian poetess-
musician, when two hawks bore her tidings of her son's death, compared him to the moon:

> "Thou art a moon that ne'er will rise again,
> O son of mine, O son, O son of mine!" [18]

The poetic imagery includes the representation of divine feminine
beings who sing and wail. In the Hebrides a goddess called Grainne
personifies the "Love of Women." She it was who kept the death
watch over the hero Dearg and made the famous lay, still considered
a masterpiece of its kind:

See, O God, how I am—
A woman without heart forever,
A woman without son, without husband,
A woman without gladness or health.[19]

This is the model for the many songs of sea sorrow in the northern
isles, always composed by women when their men are drowned at
sea. Like dirges the world over, its air has the form of a wailing
chant.

Beautiful and touching as these individual songs may be, the
meaning of them is missed entirely if one thinks of them as lyrics of
personal sorrow. The grand fact is not that the woman weeps, but
that she has the privilege of a representative position at death for her
family and her community. And she has this because, in herself, as
the bearer of life, she is the symbol of life. This is a position to call
out any woman's talents, to give spiritual power and cohesion to
the women functioning in groups or choirs at a state funeral or memorial service.

In Dahomey, for example, an important occasion for music is the
memorial ceremony held before the tomb of a former king. A
woman's choir of fifty singers officiates. It was heard by Dr. and Mrs.
Herskovits in 1935. (See Plate 5.)

From the point of view of musical style [writes Dr. Herskovits],
the most striking songs [of the Dahomean culture] are undoubtedly
those which glorify the names and deeds of the dead kings and
living chiefs. Here is no impromptu performance, but rather singing
of a quality that can only result from long periods of rehearsal . . .
the leader conducts very like a choir master in our European civilization conducts his singers. Songs are sung in unison to the accompaniment of only a gong, and, to the European ear, the tessitura is
almost incredible, particularly in view of the length of the skips
which take the singers abruptly from the highest to the lowest
tones of their range. The training of the chorus is also to be re-
marked, for judged by any standards of *a cappella* singing the technical proficiency of these groups of women in unison of attack and
in dynamics of shading is of the highest.[20]

Such singers have technique. But they have something more—a
deep spiritual composure. For there is something in death that
brings out a woman's talent and peculiar quality of imagination.
And to the communal celebration of death, to the great concourse of

9. While her husband made anthropological investigations, Frances Hall painted a Sherbro tribe initiation rite. (See page 31.)

10. For his book *Sex, Custom, and Psychopathology,* Laubscher photographed Bavenda mothers inducting girls into womanhood. (See page 32.)

From G. Buschan, Illustrierte Volkerkünde

11. On an old cloth painting, Norwegian bridesmaids swing the bride into her new life. (See page 35.)

12. A seventeenth-century miniature shows professional women singers called "Domin" performing songs of congratulation to an Indian princess and her newborn son. (See page 36.)

Courtesy of the Boston Museum of Fine Arts

13. At a wake in nineteenth-century Ireland, the men listen while women perform the ritual wailing and singing that brings new life. (See page 37.)

14. In an article on certain Australian mourning rituals, Ursula McConnel describes how women dance, sing laments, and make gestures as if to bury the dead. (See page 38.)

15. In Borneo, mothers swing their babies to sleep. (See page 43.)

16. Stone figurines from archaic Greece represent women bakers, led by one playing the flute. (See pages 43 and 101.)

men and the gathering of official personages, they bring their natural authority. Having created and practiced their wail songs of rebirth in rites from which they exclude men, for their own spiritual support, they are in a strategic position to be called in, in power, under their own leaders. Theirs is the privilege of adapting their own music to the high occasion when their community as a whole wishes to make the woman's natural affirmation of life in the face of death. Other songs they may make for themselves; many of their dances and rites may never be known except to other women. But here they are called to perform a public duty for the spiritual reassurance of all. So the dirge, as elaborated by women out of the childbirth wail and out of their faith that all life is one, becomes women's most important and distinctive contribution to music.

CHAPTER III

WORKERS AND DREAMERS

1.

THE great moments in the woman's life are not many. Rituals may be called for only once in a year or once in a lifetime. But a woman's work goes on all the time. If she did not work, her family could not live. In many primitive societies women work too hard. The hours are too long, the work often heavy and monotonous, performed against the discomfort of extreme heat, extreme cold, or, as in the rice swamps, in a perpetual state of dampness.

But whatever the work is, it goes more quickly and easily if a woman sings. Most primitive people sing at their work for the practical purpose of easing the burden, as all who have watched—and heard—the coolies unloading the cargoes of steam liners in Shanghai or Calcutta or Singapore know.

In the African community of M'Komis, women are known to be poor and inefficient workers if they do not sing. Among the Bantu, the organization of groups for communal work is definitely stimulated by the opportunity to sing in chorus. Tibetan women work harder and longer when they lighten their labor with songs. In Lithuania, where the lyric poetess-musican flourishes, a young man in search of a wife will spy upon the girls while they are working to find one who can sing especially well, so fixed is the idea among these people that a good singer is also a good worker.

Spirits and goddesses who reflect woman's power and woman's activity are often singers and workers. When Tibetan women draw water at the wells, especially during the ceremony of the Great Prayer, the Goddess of Government incarnates herself as one of them. In the guise of a working woman, Pal-den-Tha-mo teaches her companions the topical songs. Holda, a Teutonic goddess, was a spinner who sang loud and long as she sat at her spinning wheel. Those feminine spirits that appear in so many myths representing fate, destiny, and fortune are always spinning and singing. Men workers are apparently not deified as singers.

Women's work songs are legion. Though they frequently rise out of the patterns and rhythms of a woman's work—as in the case of spinning songs, for example—their real inspiration are the associations and symbols centered in the woman's deepest personal experience. All art is the unleashing of the unconscious. Save as the unconscious is released, there is no true inspiration. And the primitive woman deftly fits the words and musical tones that come spontaneously to her lips to the pattern of what her hands happen to be doing. In this process she has one great advantage over her civilized sisters. She works in her own time, in her own way, under the leadership of women. So no male philosophy stops the welling up of emotion from her woman's unconscious, and the same musical idiom that has been developed for the rituals of birth and rebirth serve for the work songs.

In some kinds of work, women sing alone. In others, they sing and dance together. Since most mothers rock their babies in solitude, lullabies are solo songs. The work of grinding corn at a hand mill is also customarily a solitary task. The songs sung at this occupation are solo and, as a rule, sad. But when women work in groups at tanning hides, making pottery, milking cows, making butter, harvesting grain, mowing, gathering nuts and berries, washing clothes, spinning, weaving, fetching wood and water, and many other tasks, their songs are gay and spirited. (See Plates 15 and 16.)

Often the workers enliven their task by a singing game. In some European districts, for instance, the spinners sit in a circle with the best singer, who is usually the most expert spinner, in the center. She improvises a verse and then throws her spindle to one of the girls, who must add another verse to the song started by the leader. Whatever the mood and the form of the songs, however, they are women's own production, flowing freely from a natural ability for self-expression in terms of music. (See Plate 17.)

It is a general custom for the work leader and the song leader to be the same person. Sometimes strangers are brought in with the idea that they will suggest new songs and, by imparting new life to the music, will also speed up the work. Mary McLeod, a famous seventeenth-century singer, used to row around in her own boat from one little island of the Hebrides to another in order to assist the women with their "waulking." In the islands today, women are still waulking, as the task of tossing and circulating the cloth that comes woven from the loom is called. Descriptions of the business show how Gaelic women combine work and music.

At this waulking we were women only. . . . An old woman, one of the two song-leaders, began to croon softly. And, as one listened, a quaint refrain shaped itself, a theme fashioned in strong rhythmic and melodic outlines, calculated, like a fugue subject, to impress itself easily upon the memory. This was caught up and repeated by the workers *tutti*. A verse phrase of more recitative-like character, perhaps consisting of only eight notes to eight syllables, was then intoned by the leader, and this was followed by a second refrain, longer than the first, but again of a strongly rhythmical character. This, in its turn, was caught up and repeated in chorus. And now the leader sang the alternating verse portions only, leaving the refrains to the other women. But the musical interest was not yet exhausted, for the leader skilfully varied the verse themes, and I have tried in vain to catch and note all the changes sung on a few notes by one of these capable, practised folk-singers of the Isles.[1]

Women of the primitive and pagan cultures are remarkably rhythmical in their movements. It has been noticed that they walk more steadily than men and that they move with measured motion while engaged in work. In Madagascar, for instance, women working in the field, making long furrows for planting rice, move all the time evenly as if to a fixed beat. In the majority of primitive communities women work under their own leaders apart from men, at tasks that are their own by custom and tradition. The pace they set is their own pace. The movements are convenient to them. The tempo adopted by men in marching and rowing, for instance, would not suit women, and the tempo of songs sung to accompany marching or rowing would be different for men and for women, and therefore quite individual for each sex. Every work song takes its form from the rhythm of the work. The leader's signal is often incorporated into the text of the song. Words like "ho" or "oi" or the repetition of numbers—one, two, three, four—mean that the leader is setting the pace for the work.

To make the work go well, it is wise to have a verse that is the charm, or rune. Meaningless words like *ko-ko-ko-ko, ninna, ninna,* or *lully-lu* constitute the magic added to the verbal and musical command. Women use these charms for everything that they do—for quieting children and sick people, for healing wounds, for bringing milk into the breasts, for tattooing, for building, for making and washing clothes, for tanning hides, for making baskets or pottery, for bringing their men home safely, and finally, most important of all, for charming the good and evil spirits believed to be perpetually hovering about.

The charms and incantations that a woman may employ are sometimes enumerated in stories of supernatural women who guard the incantations and bring them out on occasion. When the hero Siegfried woke Brynhild from her magic sleep, she gave him a reward in the form of a magic kit containing her incantations. "This enchanted box," she said, "is full of secret power; full of enchantment, of prayers, and of joyous words. With it, you can learn the runes to bring you victory, the runes of the philters which will ensure you the fidelity of the captive wife, runes to bring about pregnancy, runes for plants which will heal wounds and cure sickness. Such are the runes whose power will endure until the day which puts an end to the reign of the gods." [2]

2.

Many different types of song are created by women as they work. There are the lullabies; the satiric songs, in which women make fun of men; the lyrics, either love songs or nature songs; the laments; and the ballads and epics.

Lullabies and other songs to entertain children form one of the largest groups of women's songs. They are composed not only by mothers but also by nurses and elder sisters, who in many societies are charged with the care of babies while their mothers do more productive work. Songs to induce sleep invariably take an even, rocking rhythm and often associate the rocking with swinging on trees.

> Rock-a-bye, baby, on the treetop,
> When the wind blows, the cradle will rock.

Dyak mothers actually suspend their babies on the branches of trees, where they swing to and fro and listen to their mothers' voices blending with natural sounds of wind, water, and the trilling of birds.

The subjects selected by women for the lullaby poems are usually directly related to the child or to themselves. Some mothers and nurses praise the baby and assure it of undying affection and protection. A Hottentot mother touches each part of her baby's body and commands it to grow strong and big. Many mothers compare the child to a flower or to a jewel or to the moon. Some sing of their own experience at childbirth:

"Peace, my child, be still and sleep, my love, my tiny one.
Pain I learned from you, learned such pain as only God and I can
     ever know, and she who stayed beside me and saw you born.
Peace, my child, and cease to weep. Peace, my child, be still." [3]

In describing Eskimo music in Greenland, Thalbitzer refers repeatedly to the drumming, dancing, and singing of the women. And when he gives an example of the musical aptitude of these interesting people, he uses a woman and the song she sings to her baby as an illustration.

Much more art is required in the rendering of a little children's song than one would think from looking at the notes or words. The whole of the singing is marked by the deepest feeling in the voice. The singer makes use of the finest modulations in appealing to the fantasy of the listening child. . . . A bewitching charm lies in the East Greenland's mother's lullaby tones which she hums as she rocks her child. She sways her body and croons a simple song of two notes, one very long and one short which is higher—the most primitive song in the world which may have remained unchanged from the earliest childhood of humanity. Generation after generation has been introduced with those tones which have formed themselves in the soul of the Eskimo woman out of the loneliness and wild monotony of the desert land.[4]

The Pygmies, too, have a rich spiritual and musical life with fully developed rituals for the life cycle. As we have seen, Pygmy customs provide incentives for both men and women to develop creative musical imagination. But nothing that the men produce in music has impressed the historians of these extraordinary people as favorably as the women's songs. The high point of musical achievement stands out in the lullabies created and sung by the sisters and mothers.

Satiric songs form another large group of women's musical expression. An illustration of good-natured raillery can be seen in a Serbian folk song that describes girls and boys at work gathering in the harvest. After the work is done the boys fall asleep exhausted, only to wake hours later and to find the girls knitting and singing, not tired at all! Songs sung when women and men work together are usually gay and cheerful, with sometimes a suggestion of sarcasm or playful derogation. The satiric songs of bridesmaids often insinuate that the bride is superior to the bridegroom or that the new husband will not dare to mistreat his wife on account of the loyalty of her family—a fact in many primitive tribes. In Dutch Guiana an established form of social criticism is maintained through poetic-musical compositions. Women publish their opinions of men by means of song. The fact that society gives a name—*lobi singi*—to the custom endows the women's music with importance.

Laments of various kinds are sung by women while they work. In the Cyclades the professional mourners practice their dirges and plan the improvised verses they expect to sing at the next funeral. Or a musician may express her own sorrow. An Osage Indian woman has a special lament she sings while weaving the rush mat that is to be used on the new shrine. Softly and flowingly she gives her cry of longing for her dead relatives:

> "You have left me to linger in hopeless longing—
>   Ah; the pain, the pain!" [5]

In India, women have a set of laments that they sing while grinding corn. These belong to the group of incantations known as *raga* and *ragini*, which are believed to have a direct influence on the weather, the change of night and day, and even the shift of the seasons. In these laments, called *Bārah-Māsas*, the singer mourns the absence of someone she loves and devotes each verse to a month of the Hindu year, describing the particular kind of woe she feels at that season. In this way she lightens the labor of her work, and by causing symbolically the rebirth of the year, hastens the return of her beloved.

Work is a time for storytelling. The world over, women are famous for their ballads and epics, which they usually chant with interludes of song and instrumental music. Russians are particularly adept at this type of musical expression. On the huge Lake Onéga in the far north, women rowers are employed by the government for mail delivery. While making their rounds, which take many hours, they chant long sagas. Long ago other women like them were symbolized by Wotan's daughter Saga—divine storyteller.

The topics of these song-stories vary in accordance with varying folk customs or folk experiences. In a lovely Russian folk song a girl describes how she makes a flute:

> In the field, a birch tree stands,
>   *Lyóuli*, it stands,
> I will cut three sticks from the birch tree,
>   *Lyóuli*—
> I will make three pipes—
> The fourth one will be the balalaika.[6]

A Chinese tea picker sings the whole story of her life—how she is awakened by the sun, goes to work in the fields, looks forward to the evening, and so on. A large number of the ballads and epic poems sung by women refer to historical events such as battles, floods, famine, and to the deeds or love affairs of ancestral heroes and heroines. The whole of peasant life is portrayed in the Lithuanian lyrics (*daina*). Songs of the family cult have a name of their own in Russian—*semeíniya*. Songs relating to the ways of the people also have a name—*bitovíya*.

Another type of story is pure fantasy. Whenever an African Valenge woman starts to improvise, she says, "*Karingani was karingani*," which means "Story of stories." The audience repeats these words over and over, as if to remind themselves that the tale is only make-believe. These are the legends in which mythical creatures appear. We call them myths or fairy stories. Flowers, trees, and animals talk. Heroes and heroines become identified with them or with supernatural beings and then perform incredible deeds. In the stories, the superhuman and the human women too are continually singing in the most beautiful way imaginable.

The Ibibios have a legend in which the naiad of a pool sacred to women came to the help of one of these skillful singers. There were certain days, so says the legend, when no one was allowed to go near the spring. But a mother was forced to break the taboo in order to get fresh water for a sick child. She was blocked on the way by the spirit of the trees. She made a song appealing to the tree to let her pass: "I pray you, open the road, and let me pass to the spring!"

When the spirit heard her lovely voice, he swept his branches aside. She hurried on but was stopped by a leopard. She charmed him, too, and induced him to move out of her way. At last she came to the spring, and she sang again more sweetly than ever, entreating the goddess to forgive her for breaking the rule. Moved by the magic singing, the naiad guarding the pool rose from the water and gave the mother permission to fill her pitcher.[7]

A favorite fantasy appearing in all parts of the world is the bird-woman, who may be either a wailer, a warrior, a dancer, or a singer. She is always endowed with magic power. It is common for mourners in myths to turn into birds. In Lithuania the verb "to cuckoo" signifies "to lament." In Africa the honey bird, or *schneter,* is said to be an old woman who, wailing, pursued her lost son until she was changed into a bird. Among the North American Indians there is a myth of a girl who, grief-stricken over her lost lover, became a song-bird. In Russia the bird-women Sírin and Alkonóst rejoice and lament. Feathered creatures, half women, changing miraculously from one state to the other, have different names. In Russia they are called *vili.* They perform all kinds of superhuman feats and are akin to the Valkyrie, who, in Teutonic myth, bear the dead warriors to Valhalla. *Vili* steal the apples (symbols of fertility) from the magic trees that grow golden fruit. They have long golden braids; they dance, sing, and always love music. (See Plate 47.)

Other spirit women live in faraway lands where men can never go. On the mythical island of Tuma, near the Trobriands, there are hundreds of women ready to dance all night. In the Hebrides, the beautiful Binnevale, who was called the "Mouth of Music," lived in her own specter world where the sun never set, the wind never rose, and singing never ceased.

These mythical retreats for women have actual counterparts. Many primitive women have their private islands and mountain haunts to which they retire at times of menstruation, puberty rites, and child-bearing. The fantasy is an idealization of primitive custom.

3.

After the work of the day is finished, people everywhere turn to recreation and entertainment. Especially on holy days and at festival times, men and women congregate in the public place. There they play games, dance, swing, tell stories, and sing. Village dances in the

Hebrides are often accompanied by an old woman singing the *port à beul*. This is a type of vocal music that the Gaels find more exhilarating to dancers than any instruments. Often as the merrymakers dance around a May pole or a bonfire, drums are beaten and gay songs are sung. But always music of some kind is indispensable.

Choral singing or instrumental playing by women frequently entertains men. (See Plate 18.) The Trobriand Islanders, who are devoted to music, have song festivals called *kamroru*. Women dress themselves gaily and sit on new mats spread out in the central plot of ground. Swaying rhythmically, they sing all evening while the men look on and listen admiringly. In Kamchatka, too, the women were once wonderful singers. A traveler, Stellers, who visited the peninsula during the eighteenth century, noticed that the women had unusually musical voices, that they made extraordinary modulations while singing, and that they sang in parts. He described how the women sat on the rocks, like sirens, and sang to attract traders coming from other tribes. Stellers was so much impressed with the women singers that he said their arias could be favorably compared to those of Orlando di Lasso. "As they sing, they become very calm and well-poised. From this can be seen their special genius for music." [8]

Swing festivals are another type of amusement enjoyed by girls and boys together, but with girls taking the lead. Wherever the swinging games are played, girls and women are the chief celebrants and the creators of the songs. In Lithuania, especially, where the poetess-musician is so conspicuous, the lyric poetry contains a large number of girls' swing songs.

Swinging is, with many people, a rite performed at times when a symbolic threshold is being crossed. The bride swings into her new life, men and women swing at funerals, when seed is being planted, when rain is needed. The Dyaks of Borneo use swinging in connection with both daily life and religious ceremonies. Mothers swing their babies on trees; professional wailers swing at a burial and sing the songs that will direct the soul to its heaven; old women swing at the planting season in order to secure the soul of the rice.

Even if the swing festival is dedicated to amusement, it is usually a seasonal affair, suggesting its ritual origin. In India the women swing during the rainy months. (See Plate 19.) In Korea swing songs are sung on the fifth day of the fifth moon of the year. In the Cyclades the swings are put up in Lent. In the region of the Seven

Mountains (Germany) flax harvesters swing at the end of October and the girls play a singing game:

> Where does the moon rise?
> Blue, blue, little flax flowers!
> It rises over that linden tree.
> Flowers in the valley,
> Maiden in the dwelling,
> O, gallant Rosa! [9]

This verse is repeated as many times as there are girls present, and the home of each one is indicated as the rising place of the moon, thus connecting the song with the moon rituals common to so many primitive and peasant societies.

Another set of swing songs incorporates the wail into the even, rocking rhythm. In Karpathos, Greece, a festival is celebrated on each of the four Sundays preceding Easter. Swings are suspended between the windows of the houses bordering the narrow streets and on them the women sit. The whole village watches, but only women and girls swing and sing the death wails for the crucified Christ.

Primitive women and girls also have their own amusements apart from men. Beginning at an early age, the little girls play singing games similar to our "ring around a rosy," or the pantomimic type like "Here we go round the mulberry bush." Those invented by the young Pygmies are quite remarkable. Some are imitations of the mothers' work, such as fishing. One especially fine exhibition of talent is a singing game imitative of a partridge calling her young.

Older women, too, play, dance, and sing for each other's amusement. They frequently have secret societies, or women's clubs, where they meet with their friends. Bushwomen entertain each other for hours dancing the *kokucurra*—flute dance—and playing their flutes. In Dutch Guiana the women celebrate with dancing and singing at birthday parties—*mati*. Formerly, specialists made stirring toasts of congratulation, using this incentive to develop their poetic-musical talent. In many societies women are famed as storytellers. Among the Valenge Africans the relating of both true and imaginary events is one of women's chief pastimes. The Baronga are particularly good at it and begin singing tales and legends when they are little girls tending the babies of the family. Names and photographs exist of more than one "distinguished historian." Primitive women often act out their stories like a play. The women of the Caroline

Islands have a mock war, when they paint themselves red, brandish spears, and dance, not as if in sympathetic magic to help their men to victory in battle, but as if in a drama.

In the peasant groups there is the same kind of play and entertainment. The Russians have their *besédi* and their *posidélki*—words meaning "conversations" and "sit-down parties." These are always gay affairs at which the girls spin, embroider their trousseaux, and play games. With infallible memories and boundless enthusiasm, thousands of songs are sung.

Games played by older girls generally involve courtship, love, marriage, and ideas relating to rebirth. In Russia they tell each other's fortune on Christmas Eve. They place a dish (*blyóudo*) on the table and put in it their rings, earrings, bread, salt, and three pieces of charcoal. The charcoal signifies the house spirit and sacred flame of the domestic hearth. Then they sing the dish songs (*podblyóudniya*) and take one object out of the dish with each refrain. If the ring is drawn out first, it means marriage. If the charcoal, it means death. Another game song (*igorniya*) describes the hiding of the gold. "I am hiding, hiding the gold," sings the leader as she places a gold ring, which symbolizes the sun hidden in the winter. A girl in the center has to find the ring and bring it to life again. From Easter until midsummer, Russian girls perform their rebirth rites. In one of these, Kastróubonka impersonates the sun. To imitate the natural decline in the sun's vitality during the winter, a girl falls down pretending to be dead. She is buried in a mock burial by the other girls and bewailed by them. They move around her in a circle lamenting. After a time, the dead girl comes to life and they all rejoice with special songs.

Where there are games and singing, there must also be a leader, and in the women's groups the leaders are women. One singer mentioned by a collector of Russian folk tales in 1934 was Dóunya, a young girl twelve years old. Her repertory consisted chiefly of fairy tales which she told to two little children of whom she took care. Dóunya inserted songs, spiritual verses, and dirges into her stories. Anna Antónovna was another song leader. This old blind singer had no home of her own but went around to the different houses in the village to help the housekeepers. She earned her board and lodging by spinning, but it was her singing that made her welcome in the morning while the work was going on and in the evening when the games began.

Here are the keepers of traditional lore, re-creators of the musical heritage of the past, composers of new rhythms and melodies in their own right—artist folk singers in the making. They might well serve as guide and inspiration for some of the new social and artistic stirrings of our own day. Theirs is a kind of music that women might well bring back, in a great fertilizing flow, into the music of tomorrow.

CHAPTER IV

VICTIMS OF TABOO

1.

*W*HAT has happened to the women of our civilization? Why are we not matching in creative output the simple women of cultures much less developed than our own? Everywhere in the world, outside the highly civilized centers of Western culture, there are women whose participation in music is active and creative. Women's contributions in the form of love songs, lullabies, dirges, ballads, and epics are among the musical treasures of an art that itself has recognition in the annals of human achievement.

Are we less women than these singers and musicians? We love, work, play, bear children, seek reassurance in a sense of oneness with the life force. We inherit a magnificent art of music. Why, then, do not women as composers make, on the level of our highly developed culture, symphonies, requiems, songs, dances equivalent to those that are created by women everywhere in other cultures? Why are we so inhibited?

Before we seek the answer to our own specific problem, we may look again at the primitive and peasant cultures. Even there we can see that women are not everywhere performing their own rites and making their own music. Tradition or custom determines what forms of ritual, dance, and music shall develop. Frequently, customs seem to be followed without reason. They are fixed by what is called "taboo"—a social habit that, once established, becomes absolutely binding. Taboo means that something or other "just isn't done."

Primitive people all have the same general approach to life, the same conception of what the right relation of men and women to the laws of the universe ought to be. Their customs, their ways of living, however, vary radically from group to group. Some, for instance, believe in monogamous marriage. Others permit a man to have several wives, or a woman to have several husbands. In some communities the birth of twins is regarded as a sign of good luck. In others it signifies some evil influence at work and the mother is forced by unwritten law to leave her husband and her other children and to go to a settlement where only women who have borne twins may live. Custom determines what kind of work is suitable for men and for women. In some societies women milk cows and make butter. In others only men tend the cattle. Sometimes women do all the fishing; sometimes they neither fish nor eat fish that is caught by men. Everywhere people abide by local custom, local taboo.

2.

In the large majority of societies both men and women make music and dance. Both have their ceremonial dances, songs, and instruments in connection with the work and the rites customary to any given group. It frequently happens that certain instruments are played only by men and certain others only by women—taboo being equally strong against either group. There are some tribes, however, where *only* women are the musicians. Because men are *not* of the female sex, they have an inferior status with the spirits, and are therefore not in the class preferred to make affective music.

Such a tribe is the Tuaran Dusun of British North Borneo. Among these people, women only are the priests. Upon them alone falls the task of performing the rites that, with music, are thought to be capable of propitiating evil spirits. Priestesses conduct ceremonies at the planting of rice, for producing rain, and for blessing the villages. Dividing themselves into two groups, the women danc forth as in an antiphonal chorus and sing songs in a se In a neighboring tribe the women use a sacred rattl bamboo receptacle at the door of each house. O handle it. The men are actually afraid to touch dinate part in all religious ceremonies, the accompany the songs and dances of t drums. Although these particular me capable as men of other races, the riers imposed by custom.

The Wanyamwezi in Africa are tural level from the Borneo tribes, distinct musical disadvantage. The word Wanyamwezi signifies "Land of the Moon," and this tribe is part of the great Bantu family in which women in general hold high position. Wanyamwezi women are very strong physically and from a distance can hardly be distinguished from men. They have the right to be elected chieftainesses. They have the right to be magicians and witch doctors; and as wives of chiefs, they have great influence on all public matters. Religion with the Wanyamwezi consists in worshiping the spirits of the dead mothers and fathers. It is the women's business to keep the living tribe in contact with these unseen powers. This makes them important and necessary in the spiritual life of the tribe, and out of their spiritual function grows their music.

Wanyamwezi women sing more songs than the men and institute more ceremonies at which music is required. They celebrate secretly at puberty rites with songs and dances. Men have no corresponding rites. Women make music for the marriage ceremony, music for funerals, and music for prayers in which mother and father spirits are invoked. They sing lullabies and have special songs to celebrate the birth of twins. As women do most of the work, they have many work songs, especially for the preparation of the beverage *pombe*. Choral dances for war, for traveling, and for the greeting of visitors are particularly beautiful. Moving their bodies back and forth, waving green branches, clapping their hands, these magicians charm the assembled company. Only predestined women are poet-musicians. Famous as composers of songs, some of them are very influential and richly paid by the chiefs. Women alone rank as official songsters and lead other women singers in chorus. Accordingly, they are encouraged from earliest childhood to cultivate their natural talent. There is obviously no reason why men should not have the same high musical status, but they do not. Men never attain the status of official poet-musician and do not compete successfully with the women. In every branch of music making, women excel.

In other tribes where men are in no competition with women, they frequently raise barriers between their musicians and a free expression in music. Among the Omaha Indians, for instance, men singers ...ned to adhere rigidly to a rhythmic model for the chants of ...e-wachi Festival. Since the Omahas are a very musical ... capable of inventing new melodies and rhythms, this ... arly a taboo and has nothing whatever to do with

From *Ján Hála, Pod Tatrami*

17. A contemporary writer and artist has sketched girl spinners of the Slovak village Vežee at work. Boys, waiting to walk home with the girls, listen to the spinning songs. (See page 17.)

18. Nineteenth-century Cambodian women of the royal household play orchestral music to entertain the king and his guests. (See page 50.)

19. Swinging is universally a rhythm to insure life. A miniature of the Kangra School depicts a seventeenth-century lady on a swing and her companions playing musical instruments. (See page 50.)

20. Arctic explorers see women musicians in action. A Koryak mother of northern Siberia beats her drum to protect her family from evil spirits. (See page 59.)

21. "Al-al" or "lu-lu" generally express rejoicing as in "alleluia." While hunters drag in a white whale, Koryak women dance on the beach and sing, "Ah, a guest has come, la, la, la, lo." (See pages 27 and 59.)

22, 23, 24. Rock paintings from the preliterate age depict women performing ceremonies similar to those in many primitive tribes today. (See pages 62 and 63.)

Courtesy of Methuen and Co., Ltd.

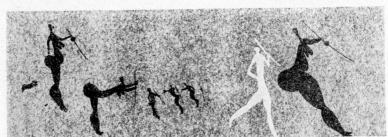

Courtesy of The Clarendon Press, Oxford

From L. Frobenius, Mdsimu Dsangara

Taboos of all kinds surround women and can often be traced to fear of their supposed contact with the supernatural. In some tribes women are officials, such as queen, chieftainess, priestess, shamaness, blian, doctor, rain maker, or magician, wielding real power, both temporal and spiritual. In others their responsibility is limited to the women's group and they are not called upon as public officials to translate their feminine power into benefits for the whole society. In still others women's organizations are comparatively weak. Women and girls have but little opportunity to work together in symbolizing their experiences.

Customs for women and music also vary greatly from group to group. It is frequently the custom for women to sing the songs in honor of ancestors. In other places they never sing them. Sometimes there is a taboo upon their playing the flute, or the particular type of drum used by men in secret ceremonies. In Surinam, for instance, women, the principal singers, never play drums. They believe that if they break the taboo their breasts will grow down to the ground. On Manam Island (New Guinea) girls are called upon to sound the single death beat but do not use drums at any other time.

The Caraja tribe of Bananal Island, Brazil, places a complete barrier between women and music. In this tribe it is the custom for women not to sing at all—not even lullabies for their babies. According to the cultural definition of singing, men only are the singers. When women wail and keen over the dead, the Caraja describe the sound—which we would call singing—by a word analogous to "croaking," a word used by them for the raucous calls of unmelodious birds. The Caraja word parallel to our word "sing" is used for the singing of men and of songbirds. Occasionally when women are working in the fields they attempt to imitate the men singers, but generally end by joking and granting that women cannot sing. Yet they have larynxes like other human beings and the same natural ways. Simply because they live in a society that does not expect them to be musicians and that deliberately discourages them from receiving training in music, they are forced by custom to pretend that music is outside women's sphere.

3.

Barriers arise from various causes. In some tribes, occupations around which music formerly developed have fallen into disuse and the accompanying songs are forgotten. "Meta, the Rikatha potteress, has given up the manufacture of pottery. All her pots cracked because, she said, she was the only woman practicing the art. In her former home, everybody made pots and the potteresses strengthened each other. When a pot was heard cracking in the furnace, somebody ran to the hut and collected a little of the dust on the floor and threw it on the other pots. It was too far for Meta to run to her old home." [1] And so no more pots are made. No more pottery songs are sung.

Or a taboo may be in force against introducing innovations in a traditional musical form. Such a restriction does exist among some of the African tribes where, although a woman has authority as a priestess over initiation ceremonies, she is under the prescription of a native law that deadens her imagination.

In other tribes particular types of song are never needed. Rowing songs, for instance, are not made by mountaineers. War songs are not necessary to peace lovers. Bridesmaids' songs are never sung where people make light of the marriage ceremony or omit it altogether.

Restrictions on sexual freedom before marriage naturally prevent a girl from composing wooing songs. When sexual freedom is allowed, however, girls may become the aggressors in courtship. In this role they create courting songs. In the Trobriand Island groups of girls with their faces tattooed make ceremonial expeditions to a neighboring village and, singing a ritual courting song, give signal to the boys of the village to approach. The two groups mingle and smoke and sing all night. Obviously, these courting girls, with no inhibiting tribal tradition of sex passivity, have incentives to compose love songs of their own.

Marriage is often a barrier that prevents women from either creating or performing music. The moonlight dances of the Akikúyu girls (east Africa) are never danced by married women, who express great surprise when the suggestion is made that one of them do so. A husband might say: "I have bought you and you want to go to dances!" Among the Annamites, girls are professional singers and dancers and are very much in demand at banquets or festivals, where they improvise for hours at a time. But opportunity for such performance disappears the day they marry.

A more formidable type of barrier between women and music in particular primitive tribes arises because women in those tribes are not in positions of authority and responsibility. It may be that men only are the chiefs, the priests, the shamans, the magicians, or the doctors. Men, therefore, have the incentive to invent appropriate songs and dances for the occasions where music is required. Among the Mescalero Indians, for example, priests rather than priestesses do all the singing at a girl's puberty rites. The same prohibitive factor operates in Bali, where the girls, although famous dancers, are taught and directed by men. Bali women are expected to perform, but not to create. Loss of leadership, or lack of a chance to lead, is a barrier to creative work that ranks second to none. The value of leadership to the composer cannot possibly be overestimated. It is the musical leader who has the opportunity to display artistic ability. It is the leader who can select significant poetic and musical phrases out of the many expressed by the less talented. It is through the leader that incoherent, incompleted utterances of immature artists are filtered and refined until they become art forms, acceptable to the whole group. Free and active participation in music making is, of course, a necessary condition to the possibility for leadership. But the mere singing, dancing, and playing of instruments in a group will not of themselves result in substantial creative achievement without the added opportunity of commanding the situation.

In the shamanistic cults authority may shift back and forth between the sexes. Shamans are individuals especially endowed with supernatural power to control the good and evil spirits. Shamanism is often identified with mothers, who, as chief guardians of family welfare and as chief interpreters of the supernatural, have the responsibility for controlling spirits who might harm or benefit their mates and offspring. Among the Koryaks of Siberia every woman has her own drum and her own individual drumbeat. Whenever any untoward event threatens to disturb her family affairs, she beats her drum and chants her magic formulas to frighten away the evil spirits. In this same tribe women are the official shamanesses, notable for their ability to keep in contact with the spirit world. Their primeval ancestress, Miti-Miti by name, brighter and more glorious than her husband, Big Raven, excelled him in cunning inventions and especially in the making of incantations. The real and the ideal women correspond. (See Plates 20 and 21.)

Among the Maidu Indians today, women are still the only shamans, and with their drums officiate as doctors and magicians. There are many other places, too, in which women are the shamans, notably in Kamchatka, where they are such fine musicians. Even in civilized Korea today a sorceress called Mu-Tang goes from house to house and by means of charms and music benefits the sick. Frequently both women and men know the art and are qualified to perform magic and to sell their musical formulas as we would sell medicine. In some places men have usurped the power of women, have taken over women's functions, and have become professional magicians. When shamanism becomes an affair affecting the welfare of groups larger than the family, men often exclude women from the professional group. They confess the higher qualifications of women for dealing with spirits, however, by dressing as women and by even imitating women's voices.

The North American Indians are an example of a large cultural group that regard music as the function of men rather than of women. There are many exceptions to this general rule, in the case both of individuals and of tribes. North American Indian women often dance, sing, and create music, but not to the extent that men do. When women are musicians, their music equals men's in quality and is often reproduced or mentioned by musicologists. There is no lack of musical ability, therefore, in North American Indian women, but a certain type of taboo prevents them from developing native talent. This taboo may be traced to the general custom of receiving dreams from the spirit world. These Indian men are expected to have contact with spirits, especially at the time of their initiation into manhood. When they fast and pray in solitude, they conceive music. These women, on the other hand, are not expected to receive messages from the supernatural. They are capable of it and frequently do, but just as frequently they are actively discouraged from such contacts. Among the Papago, girls who begin to show signs of mantic powers are forced to have their "shamans' crystals" removed. In this manner, a girl is directed away from developing creative musical imagination for no reason except that she is not a man.

How the different traditions for capability in music originated no one knows. Both men and women, however, made the customs in the first place or allowed certain prescribed manners to develop into tradition. Women, for instance, are not compelled by men to carry out puberty rites, which in many tribes involve some practices definitely damaging to the individuals concerned. Mothers and girls submit to being shut up in a cage for months after the first menstruation or after the birth of a baby. Nor is the separation of men and women in work and worship a state forced upon women by men. Women at times are aggressively antagonistic toward men and have been known to maul men unmercifully and even kill them for daring to intrude upon childbirth or other rites.

In connection with music, women sometimes themselves uphold customs that deter them from being musicians and probably often establish such customs. The Iroquois Indian women, for instance, who have a remarkably high status as mothers and tribal leaders, call upon men to be the singers at certain of the women's dances. Before the men begin to sing, they say: "We do this for our mothers." It has been suggested that long ago women needed the men's protection from enemies during the performance of the religious dances, and secured the men's services as watchmen by allowing them the privilege of singing.

Without the consent and approval of women, no cultural pattern could endure for generation after generation. Nevertheless, women often uphold cruel and senseless taboos that could be removed at will but which, while they are sanctioned, act as a bar to the free use of human energy.

The natural aptitude of men and women for musical expression is self-evident. But whether or not this natural aptitude is allowed to develop or to lie dormant depends upon local custom. As flowers flourish in bits of soil between rocks, so will musicians grow where even the least incentive exists; but where tribal custom dwarfs and obstructs, neither men nor women can create music, any more than flowers can grow under the shadow and weight of stones.

Has tribal custom dwarfed and obstructed the musical talent of the women of our society? Let us go back to the beginning of human records and allow the unfolding pages of western European civilization to tell the tale.

CHAPTER V

THE FIRST MUSICIANS

1.

*T*HE day that men and women danced the first dance, sang the first song, and beat the first drum will never be known. Who the first musicians were, where they lived, what motives and incentives led them to make rhythms and melodies, will forever remain a secret.

When the last of the great glaciers that had covered Europe for thousands of years was melting away, the warmth that came into the sunshine and the green that grew in the valleys made that age the real beginning of our history. The oldest monuments of human achievement that have survived are the paintings and carvings on rocks. Found in many parts of Europe and Africa in caves and on rock surfaces, protected by overhanging ledges, the finest ones date from about 10,000 B.C. Not all, however, are so ancient. Some, in Africa, are of quite recent origin. Yet the recent ones are so like the old that only an expert can tell the difference. A remarkable similarity in custom between very early peoples and those living in the same region today can be deduced from the illustrations and also from the testimony of the people themselves. The Bushmen of Africa, for example, interpret one rock painting as representing their Dance of the Blood—a charm against sickness. (See Plate 22.)

In some paintings women without men can be seen performing ceremonies of the sort that in present-day primitive tribes is accompanied by women's music. The women might be conducting a puberty rite or initiating a priestess. (See Plate 24.) One African rock picture seems to correspond accurately to a myth of the Australian Wikmunkan Ghost Clan, in which only the women know how to sing the mourning songs. According to legend, the ancestral husband and wife came to a tragic end and assumed the form of ghosts.

The wife sat weeping by a lagoon and made laments that her women attendants heard and passed down to generation upon generation of women.

The habitual secrecy with which our primitive contemporaries conduct their rites and the recognized authority of women in matters of birth and rebirth indicate strongly that designing and painting were also an evidence of women's magic powers and that many of the rock paintings were women's work. In certain North American Indian tribes of today, girls who are secluded during their puberty rites occupy their time painting pictures on the rocks. The midwives of Malacca, too, trace mystic designs—mainly flowers—on the bamboo tubes that hold the water they use for washing their patients. Only the erroneous notion of many nineteenth-century scholars that women do not function imaginatively has established the fiction that the pictures were all the work of men artists. (See Plates 22, 23, 25, and 26.)

2.

Everything that we can deduce by working backward from the present to these rock paintings suggests that the art of music may have begun in the singing of magic by women, and that women were the first musicians, and perhaps for some time the only ones. In general, the earliest forms of human society seem to have resembled those of the tribes that today have the least developed cultures. Some of the most primitive people today are very musical people— the Pygmies, the Bushmen, certain of the primitive Siberian tribes, some of the North American Indians, the Semangs in the Malay Peninsula, some of the Australians, the Tierra del Fuegans, and the now extinct Tasmanians. Semang men do not dance but are content to watch the women repeat their very primitive dance steps. Among the Seri Indians, only the women perform music. They have been heard singing simple melodies as they construct their rude huts of branches. They beat drums at puberty rites for girls and at death ceremonies. Bushwomen make drums and beat them. They play flutes and compose songs—especially lullabies and flower songs. The Kamchatkans and the Pygmies, as we have already seen, stand out conspicuously as creative musicians. Women of the Ona tribe (Tierra del Fuego), led by their own "kloket mother," perform a dance accompanied by a chant that is considered one of the rare examples of genuinely primitive music.

It is a striking fact that the women of the simplest cultures are more interested in religious ceremonies than are the men. In some tribes women only are the religious officials. In many, puberty rites for girls are conspicuous while corresponding rites for boys are lacking.

Again, observation of these primitive tribes today confirms the opinion now generally held by scholars that the earliest form of religion was moon worship, and the earliest religious ritual was a dancing and singing magic performed by women, with a view to influencing the potent power of the moon over life on earth. Today among the Pygmies the moon is feminine and is thought of as Generatrix, or initiator of life. The women of the Ona tribe (Tierra del Fuego) believe that Kra, the Moon Woman, came down to earth, lived with them, and taught them the ways of all women. This myth suggests that formal worship of the moon originated when women first observed that their own monthly cycle was synchronized to that of the moon and that the term of pregnancy could be counted by lunar months. There is, indeed, no explanation of the similarity of women's rites in all parts of the world except that they sprang from natural causes, common to all women.

Several myths represent a forcible determination on the part of men, at some point, to take over the women's magic moon rites. The Ona tribe has a myth that appears also in many other places. According to it, women had originally a pre-emptive right over the life of the spirit and over music. They once possessed the secrets of birth and death and spent their time discussing rituals and organizing choral dances. Often they dressed up like ghosts and deceived the men into thinking them supernatural beings. Finally, the men discovered the ruse and killed the women's leaders. Ever after, the men performed the women's ceremonies, excluding women from the stolen rites.

While this type of myth cannot be taken in the strictly historical sense, it reveals a state of envy—by no means limited to the primitive level—on the part of men for women's closer association to natural forces. Where men are known to have taken over mimetic rites that were originally the activities of women, as well as in many other cases where the history of the rite is not known, men often dress like women and imitate women's voices. This constitutes a clear recognition by men that they had adopted the magic devices, including the music that is inseparable from the rituals.

Just as religious music was probably made by women first, so the form of work songs probably originated with women. Such a development of musical imagination may be assumed from the fact that women are believed to have worked in groups long before men organized themselves for pursuits other than hunting and fighting—neither of which adapts itself to rhythmic action.

Whatever men may have done with music to suit their own needs in these earliest times, there is no question that all evidence points to the complete independence of women in music and ritual and to the general recognition of their special authority as life bearers in the making of singing magic.

3.

After the rock paintings, the next historical evidence of human activity is found in pottery vessels used for domestic purposes, mortuary urns, and little idols of men, women, and children. These have been excavated in the Indus Valley, in Sumer, in Egypt, and in Europe. They are frequently decorated with male and female symbols. The umbilical cord as the life line is a favorite design. Others are the triangle and spiral, which are also feminine symbols. Often vases were made in the form of a lyre—one of the oldest of the moon-woman symbols—or in the shape of a woman actually giving birth to a child. There are many figurines of women holding musical instruments—clappers, drum, cymbals, or flute. Other figurines represent women weeping or wailing. Most significantly, the images of musicians are generally female. Scholars suggest that the people of those times believed the images, when placed in a grave, to be capable of bringing about the rebirth by means of magic music.

These are often the earliest remains of truly civilized society, which began to be firmly established about 5000 B.C. in a few great river valleys.

Between 10,000 B.C. and 5000 B.C. the last ice melted in Europe. The shores of the Mediterranean were like a great garden. Where now there are only deserts in the Sahara and in parts of the Near East, there were meadows and flowing streams. And in Asia and Africa, as the earth settled into the warmth of our present time, great rivers built wide flat areas out of silt brought down from the mountainous centers of the continents. On these rich flats great numbers of people could live together and grow food for all. So in these river basins the early primitive tribes, each clustered around its tribal mothers, combined into large societies. These societies began to develop all those skills and comforts that are possible only where there is a pooling of the power of many people for the needs of subsistence and a specializing of skills. Instead of one primitive woman cooking and weaving and raising food, people began to have cooks and bakers, weavers, herdsmen, and farmers.

Between 10,000 and 5000 B.C. such great communities were forming in four great river basins—in Egypt, where the Nile River brings the black silt of the far-away mountains down to the sea, making there the flat lands of the Nile delta; in the Near East, where the two largest rivers of western Asia, the Euphrates and the Tigris, roll down their topsoil and spread it in a great reedy, marshy swamp and plain called Mesopotamia (or "Between the Rivers"); in China, where the clayey yellow mud is brought down by the Yellow River from the high peaks of central Asia and spread for hundreds of miles, making soil of inexhaustible fertility; and in the Indus Valley, where the earth from the Himalayas is rolled westward to the Arabian Sea. Here the tribal families of the primitive mothers began to coalesce and to build on a larger and larger scale, in more enduring materials. The dried brick made of the river mud (what we call adobe) took the place of reeds and wood; and then stone brought a long distance down the rivers from the mountains took the place of adobe. By 5000 B.C. people were making things so enduring that one can find today the remains of large cities and societies. In the same period several forms of writing began to develop, and from that time we know more and more about the past.

But what happened in those years when the primitive mothers were uniting and linking their families to make cities and states? Did they keep on singing to the moon and weaving songs of lamentation and of triumph? Did the primitive mother evolve with evolving society into the queen and priestess? And when there began to be great religious ceremonies, with thousands of people participating in vast temples with massive pillars of carved stone and hundreds of lights at the altar, was there still a singing to the moon? And were women as priestesses leading it? We have every evidence that this was so, even in some cases down to Christian times, for in the first picture writings, statues, and paintings there is the Moon-Mother-Musician goddess in the full flower of her glory.

4.

This goddess, as she appears at the time when written and pictorial records become numerous, is the climax of a long development. She sums up and crystallizes what women did, what they wished to do, and what men believed they could do in the preliterate period when ancient mythology was being elaborated and handed down by word of mouth.

When about five thousand years ago unknown scribes began to write the first histories (in the form of stories designed to be sung), they told about superhuman beings who created the world, founded civilizations, and performed heroic deeds. In these epics women played a lively part, frequently a greater part than that attributed to men. To many people these deities of ancient times seem to be creations of poetic imagination with no relation to actual conditions. Gods and goddesses were ideal images, it is true, but the ideals expressed in them indicated existing values. A goddess standing on a crescent moon, for instance, represented the close association of women with new life. But at the same time the deities were generally reflections of the people—real men and women being prototypes of gods and goddesses.

The great driving energy that is the fount of all life was to many Hindus a female force. They gave it a name—śakti. In later times, in this section of Hinduism, every god had to be acompanied by his śakti and was often so depicted. Her energy manifested itself with particular power in the persons of the Great Mothers. They were sevenfold—the Seven Mothers, whose cult exists among many of the more primitive groups today. The large number of female figurines that come from the Indus Valley civilization suggests that a goddess-mother was worshiped three thousand years ago. In Egyptian history no time is known when four of the mighty mothers were not already there. Néït, the Weaver, thought to be of Libyan origin, had for title "The Old One Who Was When Nothing Was," or "The One Born before There Was Birth." Cat-headed Bastet had a name that meant Love. Nekhbiyet—Eileithyia to the Greeks—was the goddess of birth. She was the moon, the bringer of life. The Egyptians honored her by calling one of their towns after her. Hat-hor was "The Great One; eye of the sun-lady of heaven; mistress of all the gods." With the same authority, the Sumerian Innanna carried civilization and the arts to new centers. And under another name, the Great Mother in Sumer created the world and everything in it. The idea that woman gives the final touch which endows human beings with capability is also found in primitive tribes. It is an exciting one for a girl to realize and might well be incorporated into the teaching of history.

These goddess-mothers were generally represented as giving speech, music, and the art of gesture to humanity, and as being themselves dancers and musicians. The reason why the mother was thought of as the giver of speech and music may be easily understood if we again work backward from what we know of simple societies today. For where life is very simple, the baby is almost inseparable from the mother until after the age when it can speak and can begin to sing and imitate patterns of gesture. Mothers often carry their babies on their backs while working or while dancing and singing in religious ceremonies. The child drinks in speech and music with its mother's milk. So Bhāratī and Sarasvati, divine representatives of the dark-eyed women of early India, were thought of as giving all their people speech, music, and ritual. Sarasvati gave poetry and music and arranged musical tones into scales. Bhāratī taught the union of dancing with singing and is often called the Mother of the Bards.

In certain ancient invocations to deities, these two goddess-musicians were summoned with Ilā, goddess of the rite itself, and were spoken of as a group of three. Since they were deities of speech, gesture, music, and ritual, it seems clear that poetry, dance, and the occasion were enhanced by music and that they were integrated then, as they are now in India when the temple dancing girls add songs to their rhythmic gestures. The fact that these ancient deities were goddesses, not gods, implies that before their time women had been active in the making of rites, dances, and songs.

In Egypt, cat-headed Bastet held the sistrum and delighted in dancing and in music. Hat-hor, the Great One, was "mistress of the dancing, lady of music and wreathing of garlands, mistress of songs." They were matched by Innanna in Sumer, who was described as organizing rites, wailing to bring new life, lamenting over the dying year, and rejoicing over the rebirth. "She of the Beautiful Voice" made the lamentations and the incantations for the magic rituals. "O singer" are the words with which people began their appeals for mercy and compassion. The link between the real woman and the ideal in these representations was such a goddess as the Chinese Nukua. With her fine gold-tinted skin and tilted eyes, she has been identified as an empress, wife of the emperor Fohi. About 2500 B.C. these two interested themselves in making musical reforms, and to the Empress is attributed the creation of a tonal system for the use of musicians. In legend, the real woman became a goddess who mythically performed what the good Empress had already achieved.

5.

These oldest goddesses, spirits, symbols, and even names represent the type of woman normal for the period *before* written history begins. The women of the ancient world of seven and eight thousand years ago—in China, India, and on the Mediterranean shores—were themselves the prototypes of the deities. The hierarchy of divine and semidivine spirits represented the institutionalized role of women in that type of society. If a goddess was supreme in her circle, a queen and high priestess had previously had authority in her tribe or clan, settling a new territory, perhaps, selecting a sacred grove, finding times and places for the cult dances and songs. As the goddess Isis did, so might a queen have led the people to abandon cannibalism and to eat the bread she taught them to bake. If a goddess was able to help a woman in childbirth or to make grain grow by means of her incantations, then women had previously been skilled in medicine and in agricultural magic. If many goddesses danced and sang, lamented and rejoiced over the waxing and waning moon, or over decaying and sprouting vegetation, then many more priestesses had contributed to the development of those elaborate rituals and had been singing and dancing in choirs. There can be no doubt that women were creative musicians in that age which preceded the epoch of written history. Superhuman or human, women had economic and spiritual authority and could do what people expected to be done with music.

Women's religion, women's customs in primitive tribes, traditions handed down by men's secret societies, and the symbols of divine women in early mythology all point directly to the conclusion that men had not yet seriously put their minds upon the development of rituals, domestic work, and music until after women had established their own conception of a life of the spirit, including expression in music.

CHAPTER VI

QUEEN AND PRIESTESS

1.

FROM about 5000 B.C. there are more and more indications of the way in which women were functioning as musicians. In the two greater river civilizations from which we draw our social and religious ideas—Egypt, whose culture was filtered to us through Greece, and Sumer (including Babylonia, Assyria, and Chaldea), whose heritage came to us through the Jews—the woman chieftainess and priestess-musician retained her high power for many centuries.

The spirit of the great civilizations of antiquity was the spirit of the primitive world, not of our modern world. Like simple people today, the ancients worshiped nature in its various manifestations as moon, as sun, as plants and animals, as the life-giving power of their great rivers. And like primitive people, also, they used music in a practical way to control their environment with sympathetic magic. Above all, they revered the special harmony of women with the rhythm of nature.

As civilization developed, religion, music, and the functions of women in connection with them were elaborated and refined. The forces of nature were personified by many goddesses and gods. Chief among them were the great goddesses, representative of woman's unity with the life force. When communal storehouses for surplus foods were built as a primitive form of social security, it was natural that the music and ritual for invoking the life force should center in these food houses. Gradually they developed into great temples, keeping down to Christian times some traces of their original structure and function as food houses.

Since woman's place in the scheme of life had purpose and dignity, public institutions were built around her natural functions, as well as around those of men. Women then represented in an official capacity the principle of female energy. Priestesses with their choirs of dancing, singing votaries functioned in the most important temples and in the most important rites, worshiping nature's rhythmic laws and striving to keep in touch with them by the techniques of primitive times, particularly by the dance and by music. But whereas in primitive times women appear to have carried on their rites separately from men, as civilization developed the tendency was for men and women to carry out their rites together. Many depictions of religious ceremonies represent a procession of men advancing from one side and of women from the opposite side, meeting before the altar in perfect equality.

2.

It is fortunate for our understanding of the early Mediterranean culture, in which our own civilization began, that its spirit and way of life have survived to this day in a mountainous region of the Sahara Desert. Here live the Tuareg tribes, thought to be the descendants of the once mighty Libyan nation, and believed to retain customs formerly prevalent in Egypt, in the Near East, and in Crete.

"She walks with her head high" [1]—a native proverb thus characterizes the strong-minded, gifted, and intelligent Tuareg woman, who is respected by the men of her nation in a manner that has no parallel in the Western world. These women have complete authority over the home and the rearing of children. They own property over which the husband has no rights. It is the custom for them to take an active part in public life, to be asked for advice in the tribal councils, to rule as chieftainesses, and even to lead the warriors into battle. Women are the preservers of tradition and learning. Where the ancient script, which has a similarity to the old Minoan script of Crete, is still used, women are more versed in it than men. Before marriage, girls enjoy great freedom. They are the wooers and often ride all night on their camels to visit their lovers. No household tasks are expected of them, but rather dancing, making poetry, and singing.

Music pervades the life of Tuareg women. When the explorers Denham and Clapperton visited the tribe over a hundred years ago, they reported: "In the evening, we heard numerous bands of females singing . . . this custom is very common among the people and is one of the principal amusements in the mountain recesses. They go out when their work is finished in the evenings and remain till near midnight singing and telling stories. The males seldom sing." [2]

At the present time it is the custom for noblewomen to organize the meetings at which songs are performed and judged. The texts of these songs are extremely varied, ranging from the love lyric to ballads of war and travel and to hymns of thanksgiving. Although men and women both create the music, women are the more famous. Some of them are known throughout the Sahara as the great creative artists of this region. Women are at the center of these *ahaals* and have evidently taken the lead in establishing them, just as the famous *salonières* of Europe attracted the brilliant men and women of the eighteenth century to their own private houses. An *ahaal* often takes place in the moonlight under a large tamarisk tree. The company gathers around the great fire. The women, clad in graceful veils and heavy ornaments that might have come from the Bronze Age, sit in a circle. Young men stand behind them and camels loom in the shadows. A stringed instrument called *amzad* is played by the women as they sing haunting melodies in a rhythm unknown and indefinable to Europeans.

"The heart thou lovest, and which loves thee not,
Whatever thou do to strain towards him, he flieth.
A sad torment for a thing it were better not to ponder.
But if two hearts meet, it is heaven!
It is better than all friends;
It is better than the whole world!" [3]

The status of the woman musician and the attitude of men and women toward the poetess suggests what musical customs were actually in force in an age when goddess, queen, and high priestess had a pride and spiritual independence comparable to that of the present-day Tuareg poetess-musicians. (See Plate 34.)

3.

Protected by mountains and living off the main highways of aggression, the Tuareg probably represents a survival into modern times of a fairly typical example of the light-brown race of northern Africa that appears to have given our Western civilization its earliest institutions. This race was widespread both in north Africa and in

From L. Frobenius, Mdsimu Dsangara

25. On the extreme left of this prehistoric rock painting, a woman holds her arms in the conventional pose of mourners. The Australian Wikmunkan Ghost Clan believe that the first lament was made by a wife for her drowned husband. (See pages 62 and 63.)

26. One hand of the prehistoric priestess rests on the seat of her power. The other holds a bison horn shaped like a crescent moon. A similar instrument is used today by the musical Valenge women to deflower girls. (See pages 62 and 63.)

Courtesy of The Hispanic Society of America

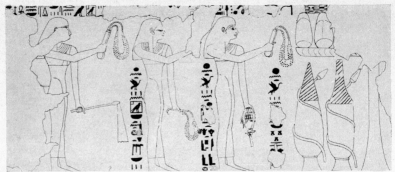

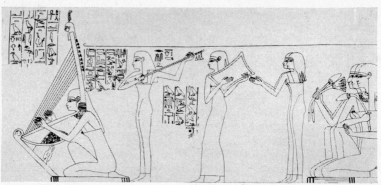

27, 28, 29. Egyptian wall paintings represented scenes of real life. Women musicians can be seen officiating at religious ceremonies. On the extreme right of Plate 28, the choirmistress holds her hand before her mouth, probably making the ululating trill. (See pages 76 and 78.)

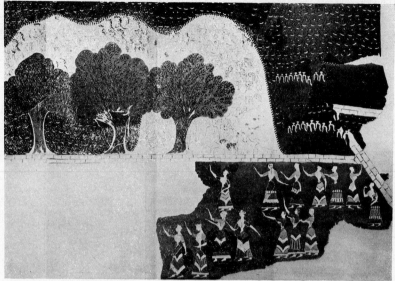

Courtesy of The Macmillan Company

30, 31. Cretan priestesses perform a religious dance before a great concourse of people, possibly invoking a feminine spirit to ensure the continuation of life. (See page 85.)

32. Cretan frescoes, like the Egyptian, reveal ancient customs. These choristers are boys, dressed like girls and led by a priestess. (See page 84.)

33. On a Greek vase, a chorus of women stands enveloped in a cape, the leader holding a tambourine. (See page 92.)

such Mediterranean islands as Crete. To it belonged the Egyptians, who have been called Hamites and are assumed to have been of the white race.

No civilization, not even that of China, has had a longer continuous existence than the Egyptian. From about 4000 B.C. to the conquest by the Moslems in the seventh century A.D. it had not only a continuity of life but a relative harmony and freedom from internal disturbance that indicated something very sound in its social organization. Egypt was distinguished for the high degree of comfort and beauty attained in household furnishings. All the arts of daily living were brought to a state approaching perfection. In some kinds of manufacture the Egyptians have never been surpassed, and rarely equaled. On the bodies in the Egyptian tombs there is linen of an exquisite sheerness. There was cloisonné of exquisite delicacy and perfection of finish. There were beautiful glazes on tiles and pottery of many colors—green and blue, purple, violet, red, yellow, and white. The manufacture of glass and the artistic use of it in inlays and mosaics was remarkable for skill, beauty, and originality. The same high standard may surely be assumed for music, especially since music was regarded by them as a direct and powerful magic for influencing spirits.

Egypt was also distinguished for the very high status of its women. As if reminiscent of a former matriarchy, royal power was transmitted through the female line. Every daughter of the Pharaohs was born a queen and possessed the prerogatives of royalty from the day of her birth. A man became king only by marrying a princess. In the later days of Egypt none of the sons of the royal house, however powerful, was allowed to forget that he held his right through his queen.

The custom of matrilineal inheritance made the queens legal and spiritual heads of the people. From the earliest times they undoubtedly had a large share in government and in affairs of the external world. As high priestesses, queens were identified with a local goddess, homage being paid to them in death as well as in life. Upon the death of the beloved Egyptian queen A'h-mose Nofret-iri (Eighteenth Dynasty), a special priesthood was organized to burn incense in her honor and to recite the formulas of prayers used in addressing the gods. When her mummy was excavated it was found to have dark-blue skin, the attribute of Hat-hor and Isis, goddesses of life and death. Immediately below the queen in rank were the other women whose husband was also the king. Custom allowed the king and other important men a number of lesser wives, who were princesses from neighboring countries. Some of the great kings had as many as three hundred concubines in their royal households. But these women were in a very different position from the concubines of later times or of some Oriental societies, for their relation to the queen as assistant priestesses gave them an institutionalized role in religious ceremonies and therefore a certain state dignity that can be acquired in no other way.

The position of ordinary women, who did not partake of the divinity of the women of the royal house, was, on a smaller scale, a replica of that of the priestess-queens. In the many legal documents that survive from ancient times in Egypt, this is emphasized again and again.

I acknowledge thy rights of wife [so runs one of those contracts]; from this day forward I shall never by any word oppose thy claims. I shall acknowledge thee before anyone as my wife, but I have no power to say to thee: "Thou art my wife." It is I who am the man who is thy husband. From the day that I become thy husband I cannot oppose thee, in whatsoever place thou mayest please to go. I cede thee . . . [here follows a list of possessions] that are in thy dwelling. I have no power to interfere in any transaction made by thee, from this day. Every document made in my favour by any person is now placed among thy deeds, and is also at the disposal of thy father or any relatives acting for thee. Thou shall hold me bound to honour any such deed. Should anyone hand over to me any moneys that are due to thee, I shall hand them over to thee without delay, without opposition, and in addition pay thee a further twenty measures of silver, one hundred shekels, and again twenty measures of silver.[4]

"Thou assumest full power over me to compel me to perform these things,"[5] declares a similar contract.

It was the custom for women to mingle in the general life of town and country, taking part in industry and agriculture as well as in trading. One of the boasts of Rameses III in the period of prosperity about 1200 B.C. was: "I let the woman of Egypt walk out to the place she wished, no vile persons molested her on her way."[6]

From the spiritual point of view, woman was generally regarded as being close to the invisible powers behind life and death. She could see and hear that which was beyond the perception of man. She could control the spirits with her flexible and piercing voice. Without a wife to influence the spirits, a man could not enter the gates of the future life. Many women, and not merely a few, therefore, played an active part in public festivals and in religious ceremonies. During the period of the New Kingdom (*c.* 1800 B.C.) scarcely one could be found who was not, or had not once been, a priestess or at least a minor official in the service of the deities.

The queen, as leader of women, was followed by an independent hierarchy of women—prophetess, spiritual teacher, priestess-musician, and choirs of dancing, singing attendants. The prophetess was regarded as divinely inspired; the priestess was the actual embodiment of the goddess she represented.

The priestess served both goddesses and gods. If priests served too in a goddess cult, they ranked lower than the women officials. It was the custom for priestesses to receive salaries from temple property and to be members of societies of scribes. They did not live in seclusion but attended to other normal duties. Many of them had titles such as "Worshiper," "Clothier," "Mother," "She Who Suckles." These names denote a high antiquity, an identity with the natural woman, and a precedent for the descriptive names frequently given to goddesses.

While the Egyptians were building their great civilization, making life stable, beautiful, and comfortable, they were never allowed to forget that the end of life is death and that beyond death is rebirth. Their genius and their wealth spent themselves lavishly on the tomb. Their religious feelings were expressed chiefly in rituals, incantations, and musical ceremonies intended to direct the soul on its way and to invoke the rebirth.

In conducting the rites for the rebirth, the indispensable priestess used the magic devices common to women the world over—holy water, the sacred ear of corn, incense, flowers; musical instruments, especially the sistrum; dancing, wailing, and singing. (See Plate 35.)

That the priestesses were trained musicians can be seen from their titles. A Fourth Dynasty name was Mrt, meaning priestess-musician. Another name given the woman conductor—Hnyt—signifies "Chief of the Female Musicians." Still another name was Phylarch, used in the time of the New Empire, when the priestess-musicians divided into *phylae*, or watches, for the purposes of attending to the music of the temple. From the time of the New Empire on for many centuries,

chantresses increased in number and importance, being mentioned
more often in the records. There were the "Great Players with the
Hand"—always the hieroglyphic for singing; there was the "Great
Chantress." Throughout Egyptian history she never failed to "content Amun with her voice." One of the most important, as well as
one of the oldest, of the rebirth rites was the celebration of the Osiris
mysteries. For this, priestess-musicians had special hymns of mourning for the death of Osiris in which his resurrection was anticipated.
The priestesses impersonated the goddesses Isis and Nephthys—
divine composers of all laments. They carried tambourines and sang
both solo songs and duets.

Another important rebirth ceremony took place during the Sed
Festival. This was celebrated for a dead king or other prominent
man. According to an old custom practiced before the days of mum-
mifying, a statue was made in the image of the deceased. While the
statue was still in the workmen's shop, before it was dragged
through the streets with crowds of wailing, mourning people, the
priestess-musician was summoned to perform the rite of "the opening
of the mouth" by means of her magic incantations.

A festival to ensure the continuation of life was the one named
after Hat-hor. On the day chosen for its celebration, a choir of priestesses marched in procession, holding out emblems to bring health
and wealth, blessing the people within their houses. In wall paintings these priestesses were depicted and designated especially as "the
female musicians of Hat-hor, Lady of Dendera, Mistress of all the
Gods." The inscriptions also convey the words they were supposed
to be singing: "I offer to thee the *menat* necklace, the *sistra*, in order
that they may give to thee a fair and long-lasting life." (See Plate
27.) Many religious ceremonies were conducted by priests and
priestesses together. In the temple at Karnak bands of men and
women musicians are depicted clapping hands and singing. Choirs of
male and female musicians who daily sang hymns in the worship of
Berenike are mentioned in a decree of Canopus. Celebrating the
accession of Rameses IV is a line in a poem: "Maidens rejoice and
repeat their songs of gladness. . . ." [7]

Throughout Egyptian history there is evidence in written documents, in pictures, and in statuary of women participating to the full-
est extent in the religious ceremony and in the music accompanying
it. As goddess, as priestess, as magician, as wailer, as choir leader, as
choral singer, as dancer, and as instrumental player, women were

there in the temples on an equality with men and often in a superior position to men. Often, indeed, the great temples, with their thick walls and massive columns, reproduced in stone the pattern of those huts made of reeds tied together that African women everywhere still construct with their own hands for their homes. And the elaborate ceremonies conducted in them retained a homely memory of the household life of women. More than one scholar has quoted the hymn:

> Awake in peace, thou cleansed one, in peace!
>
> .   .   .
>
> Thou sleepest in the barque of evening,
> Thou awakest in the barque in the morning [8]

as an example of similarity in practice in ordinary living and in temple service. These are supposed to be the words sung by the women of primitive Egypt for the purpose of rousing their chief in the morning. In later centuries, when the king impersonated the sun god in the temple, the same hymn was used by the priestess-musicians in the "House of the Morning" as a ritual for the ceremonial morning rebirth.

A similar association between the temple service and home practice can be seen in childbirth rites. In the pyramid temple of Sahuri —where the pyramid form itself resembles the female symbol of the triangle—priestesses impersonated Nekhbiyet, goddess of childbirth like the Greek Eileithyia, with whom magic formulas and incantations for aid in childbirth were immemorially identified. Egyptian women must have made such incantations, just as primitive women do today, or royal births would not have been described in legends in which Isis, the cunning magician, and three other deities appeared disguised as musicians to assist the queen in her need.

Songs sung by women in connection with other home events have been preserved and show the same belief that characterizes all primitive music in the magic properties of an incantation:

> Keep away from his teeth—they will bite you!
> Keep away from his navel—it is the morning star! [9]

Every part of the little body is mentioned in this long charm to protect a baby from evil spirits.

In personal as well as in the symbolic life of the spirit, the wail and the incantation were required to bring about the rebirth after death. A funeral was a great religious ceremony at which women, whose particular and unique function was mourning, always participated. They followed the bier in a procession, throwing ashes on their heads, waving green branches, scratching their cheeks, holding tear cups to their eyes, and screaming themselves hoarse. The wailers were sometimes members of the family, but they could also be professionals who made wailing a specialty distinct from the musical lament or dirge.

Often the dead body was borne on a barge across the Nile, followed by other barges carrying wailers and choirs of women singers. Statuettes of Isis and Nephthys, goddess composers of both wails and laments, might be placed at one end of the boat and surrounded by women performing the rite of wailing. At the other end another group of women led by a choir mistress might officiate as singers. (See Plate 28.)

At home, the funeral feast was accompanied by music. Women played the lyre and the flute, beat their drums, and clapped their hands to the rhythm of songs invoking the blessing of a goddess whose function it was to receive the dead. "Put balsam in the locks of Ma'et; for health and life are with her. . . ." (See Plate 29.)

In old Egypt both the love lyric and the song-story reached a high point of development. There is a flower song in one of the famous collections similar in imagery to other women's flower songs in all parts of the world. A maiden is weaving a wreath. Each flower she adds reminds her of her love:

> Blush roses are in it [the wreath], one blushes before thee—
> My life depends upon hearing thee.
> Whenever I see thee, it is better to me than food or drink.[9]

Did not some woman there use her musical talent to express her personal emotions and to compose "the beautiful gladsome songs of thy sister whom thy heart loves"?[10] Penthelia, we know, was one who described in song and story the events of the Trojan wars. Her technique is said to have inspired Homer, or other Greek bards, to imitate her treatment of this epic material.

As a priestess of the god Phtha, Penthelia may be regarded as a

symbol of the woman who was both a religious official and an entertainer. She was only one of many Egyptian women musicians
trained for service in the temples who was also expected to use music
upon other occasions than the temple ceremony. The large groups of
women living in the palaces danced, played, and sang at banquets
and other entertainments, employing the same musical ideas and
idiom that were appropriate to the rituals. A certain Rahonem was
at one time the chief woman manager of the lesser wives, and in her
capacity as directress of the female players of the tabour (drum)
and of the female singers, had the same title as that given to the
priestess-musician.

The princess-musicians were assisted by girls drawn from social
classes beneath the rank of royalty and trained in regular music
schools. Many pictures show graceful dancers and instrumentalists
playing lyres, flutes, and drums in combination. During the Eighteenth Dynasty these professional women musicians competed successfully with the blind harpers. In singing, the trained musicians
had an undeniable advantage over men. Their voices, believed to be
so potent in affecting spirits, combined also the clarity and flexibility
for making subtle and delicate melodic variations. Ideals in religion
and art converged to bring the woman musician forward in a manner unparalleled in the modern world where women and music both
have different values.

Women's association with music in Egypt reached a brilliant
climax in the Eighteenth Dynasty and continued to be a vital one
until the priests converted religion into an organized system of sor-
cery from which all but they were excluded. Women's music can be
traced back to the earliest days of Egyptian history. In the beginning
it was chiefly dancing and singing, especially lamenting, in which
they excelled. The oldest goddesses symbolized these early women
musicians. In instrumental music women apparently did not participate extensively until about 2700 B.C., after the passing of the Old
Empire. Men are depicted as the usual performers on instruments.
Some kind of a taboo evidently existed preventing women from being trained in a field in which they later showed so much proficiency.
Significantly, the oldest goddesses hold the sistrum but not other
instruments. If this negative reflection of women's musical activities
has verity, so then must the positive reflection be true to life. And
the predominant part taken by these old goddesses over gods in

dance and song strongly indicates that real women, whose interests and activities became integrated into divine characters, were in fact leaders in ritual and in music.

4.

Simultaneously with Egypt, peoples of the Near East, allied to the Jews in language, customs, ideas, and physical type, were building another great civilization in the low flat land between the Tigris and Euphrates Rivers. The most southern part of this region, where the rivers come down to the Persian Gulf, was called Chaldea. The northern section, composed of the lower slopes and valleys of the high mountains whence the rivers came, was called Assyria. The great central area—lying low and flat between the rivers—was called Babylonia and was dominated by its great city, Babylon, whose ruins are about seventy miles south of the medieval and modern city of Bagdad. The three sections of this great region are referred to together as Sumer.

The life of Babylonia was the life of merchants and small farmers, busy, prosperous, with widespread education and general comfort and luxury in the arrangements for daily living. It was regulated by an elaborate system of law that guaranteed justice and, in general, favored women and especially mothers. For example, if a free woman married a slave, her children were guaranteed to her and could not be made slaves by the father's master.

Almost everybody in Babylon, both men and women, learned to read. Writing was done with a pointed stylus on tablets of wet clay and baked. Women even had the first woman's college mentioned in history. In the district of Cappadocia, tablets have been found that mention a lady's college in a "women's city." The studies appear to have been arts, letters, and crafts.

As in Egypt, princesses were priestesses and women carried out religious rituals with music and incantations in which the wail was made the basis of a great variety of music. Both men and women played instruments and gave the chants. In Akkadian, the language of north Babylonia, the word for the liturgical psalmist and chanter was *zammertu*, of the feminine gender. Convents of women religious officials called "virgins" were attached to the temples. Though said to be vowed to chastity, actually, under Babylonian law, they were allowed to marry. They were not supposed to have children of their own but might give their husbands a concubine, whose children were regarded as their own. Possibly there is some misunderstanding of the various laws regulating the women religious officials who had a high status and many prerogatives. Possibly the word virgin as applied to these married priestesses means only that they were expected to be persons of decorum or good character. The statement that they were to have no children but might give their husbands a concubine whose children were to be regarded as their own means merely that their duties to the temple must be set above those to their home. In compensation for which they might very properly get another woman to manage their households!

Temples were great storehouses of surplus products under the administration of the state, for which people in privation might make application. A tenth or tithe of all products was contributed to the temple—whence comes the practice of tithing in the Jewish and Christian churches. A similar plan of making the temple the storehouse of surpluses to help the people in famines was followed in early Persia. It seems a natural expression of a mother's forethought.

In the temples there was an elaborate music by women, under the direction of the queen and princesses as priestesses. Queen Shu-bad of Ur made music on harp and tambourine with her ladies in waiting or with professional musicians. In her society, too, the word *nartu*, meaning "chanter," is feminine. Lipushiau, the granddaughter of King Naram-Sin, was appointed player of the *balag-di* drum in the moon god's temple at Ur. This drum was used not only for the liturgy but at feasts. Its other name, *balag-lul*, has a connection with singing. We can fancy this girl of 2380 B.C. drumming and making incantations to hasten the rebirth of the moon and then dancing and singing with her companions in the palace.

In Ishtar's temple at Erech, troops of dancing priestesses chanted their laments in a dialect used only when a female deity was supposed to be reciting. Although the word "wailing" is repeated in every line, the tradition of Ishtar as "She of the Beautiful Voice" and other references to "sacred music" point to some form of singing accompanying the utilitarian magic of the wail. Choral dancing in connection with national victory or defeat was a widespread custom. When the Sumerians and Akkadians were being oppressed by their Gutian conquerors during the third millennium B.C., the women of several towns assembled to mourn their fate. Dividing into two choruses, they gave the lament antiphonally, each group singing, in alternation, appropriate verses. At a much later date a document from Babylonia records that a certain group of women musicians were to assist in the celebration for a victorious army. Such performances, of which many other examples could be given, were by no means an impromptu or an individual expression of emotion but an organized, studied affair demanded by public opinion.

The tendency of all this religious and musical ritual under the leadership of singing women in Babylonia was toward an intellectual and monotheistic religion that had an influence for many centuries over religious thought. But the soul of the universe, as the Babylonians saw it, was not the male warrior god on which the monotheistic imagination of other near-by Semites, the Jews, later fastened, but was instead an all-encompassing mother principle, generally personified as Ishtar. Ishtar was Life—the teeming life of the rich Babylonian plain. She was in the waving grain, in the figs and the olive trees, in the fat cattle and sheep, in the inexhaustible waters from the high mountains that watered the garden lands the Sumerians had made for themselves. She was in the bright fostering sun by day and the moon and stars by night. Ishtar was not a goddess like the other gods and goddesses of Babylonia. She was something above and behind them, the ultimate explanation, universal being, life itself.

Between the superhuman woman-being and earthly men and women the imagination of the Babylonians created not only a pantheon of deities, but a host of intermediary spirits. Spirits were everywhere. The unseen world was full of imagined beings, both female and male, local and specialized representatives of the ultimate life, who might be influenced by the singing magic or incantations. Women had their special wisdom, which was revered by men. The oracles at Arbela were always regarded as being divinely inspired. And always the singing women continued to invoke the fertile power of Ishtar. If her power appeared to fail them, they created lamentations that sometimes have great poetic beauty and remind us of many passages in the Bible. The intention of these, as in all wail songs of women, is to invoke the rebirth.

The wailing is for the plants, the first lament is, "they grow not."
The wailing is for the barley; the ears grow not,
For the habitations and the flocks it is, they produce not.

For the perishing wedded ones, for perishing children it is: the dark-
headed people create not. The wailing is for the great river: it
brings the flood no more.

.   .   .

The wailing is for the forests; the tamarisks grow not.

.   .   .

The wailing is for the garden store-house; honey and wine are
produced not.

.   .   .

The wailing is for the palace; life unto distant days is not.[11]

5.

The mountainous island of Crete, only a hundred and fifty miles
long and from seven to thirty-five miles wide, is a small place to have
been the seat of a great civilization. Though its lower valleys are
well-watered and fertile, the land growing lemons, oranges, pears,
grapes, and olives to perfection, it could hardly have sustained a
large number of people. But, from about 3000 to 1200 B.C., the
Cretans traded far and wide with people on the shores and other islands of the Mediterranean Sea. They seem to have made these
contacts without much fighting. Few civilizations of which we have
record are so unmilitary or have lasted so long. The culture was, in
every way, an example of a beneficent type of matriarchy, with
women as goddess-priestess-musicians.

The immense and remarkable remains of its "hundred cities" reveal that artistic and engineering talent were devoted, not to temples
and tombs, but to details of household life. In the palace at Knossus,
there was plumbing such as Europe did not know until the nineteenth
century. The town of Knossus was crossed by a well-paved street
with a stone sewer and was flanked with fine private homes. The
frescoed walls show women dancers and gymnasts, as well as priestesses in costumes similar to those in the rock paintings of Spain. (See
Plate 37.) Yet in other pictures, the clothes are surprisingly modern.
In their flounced skirts, trim waists, and decorative sleeves, these
Cretan women seem to move and sing. No other ancient paintings are
as lifelike.

Crete, like Egypt and Sumer, illustrates the principle that in that
period of history, women were the inspirers and the chief ministrants

of spiritual life. Gods were rare and inconspicuous, goddesses numerous and important. This society, which has left such charming records of polished and refined daily living, shared with some African tribes (especially the Bantu) many of the regular female symbols. Among these, either wholly female or combining female and male characteristics, were the moon, the double axe, pillars, rocks, trees, flowers, shells, snakes, and birds.

In the service of the deities and other symbols of life, priestesses predominated. Many frescoes depict women conducting a sacrifice attended by men porters. When the men attendants carried musical instruments, they dressed like women. When youths joined a choir, they were led by a priestess and imitated the dress of maidens, as if to deceive the spirits into believing them members of the stronger spiritual sex. (See Plate 32.)

The spiritual superiority of women was manifested also in the small images of musicians made for the purpose of accompanying the dead in their graves. The manufacture of these figurines— invariably feminine—was a regular industry, especially in the nearby Cyclades Islands.

It is a striking fact that nothing remains of an overemphasis in the glory of man as king, priest, or husband. Polygamy evidently had no vogue in Crete. Monogamous marriage was the custom. In a betrothal scene, depicted on an ivory cylinder near Knossus, the man and the woman, both the same height, raise their right arms for a handclasp. They stand as equals.

The presence of small chapels in the women's quarters of the palace indicates that informal and formal rites were indistinguishable. The queen—high priestess—probably burnt her incense, poured out holy water, lit her torches, and arranged her flowers in vases of her own making on her domestic altar. Being both a normal mother and a representative of a goddess, such a worshiper would repeat at home her incantations for protecting her family and for controlling spirits.

Girls had their swings hanging between pillars topped by the sacred doves, symbols of love and fertility. At their first pregnancy, they may have been called to their rites by a mother blowing a seashell trumpet as girls today in South Sea islands are summoned by the priestess in charge. (See Plate 36.) When rain was needed, women sprang in ecstatic motion around the great rock which represented Rhea, spirit of flowing water and goddess of the dance. The fame of such dancers spread far beyond the borders of their own land and long after their own time. Sappho sang: "Thus of old did the dainty feet of Cretan maidens dance pat to the music beside some lovely altar, pressing the soft smooth bloom of the grass." [12]

Public religious festivals were probably staged out-of-doors in an open stadium. Plate 30 shows a ceremony conducted by priestesses and attended by a large assembly of women and men. The object of adoration is unfortunately missing, but Sir Arthur Evans suggests that it may have been the day-spring from on high in the shape of a tiny goddess. (See Plate 31.) One can imagine hearing the voices of the priestess-musicians chanting hymns, songs of praise, laments, and joyful songs of the birth. Hymnos, paen, elegoes, and dithyrambos are Greek terms for poetic forms which, with the skillful use of melodic norms, derived from Crete.

This choral dance on the "Isle of Women" seems to be the forerunner of the Greek tragedies in which men dressed as women and acted the part of women characters. What would give clearer evidence of the fact that men first imitated, and then developed for a purpose of their own, rites which had been invented and utilized for centuries by women in the mother's religion?

6.

No names of individual creative musicians have survived from those far-off times. There is no way of knowing whether men or women excelled in the invention of dances and music. But women's relation to music and to a religion, based on the sense of the glory and power of woman's function as life bearer, was very different from that of the woman of today, outwardly free but spiritually devitalized, with no faith in her womanhood to inspire her to song.

All these ancient religions were based on the primitive woman's grand idea that she who gives birth can invoke the rebirth—that, as mother, she has authority over life and death. And this authority she exercised by making music. The intimate relation in ancient societies between goddess, queen, priestess, and ordinary woman meant that the collective body of women was drawn into a musical life that had its origin in connection with institutions and occasions planned in previous centuries by women themselves. It meant that the woman with creative musical imagination had behind her a long tradition of capability on the part of women and that she started composing on an already high plateau of experience and achievement.

Occasions for the development of musical talent had already been formalized in the regular events of living—in the birth of a baby, rebirth at adolescence, marriage, death, and springtide, in the work of feeding, clothing, and manufacturing needed articles, in caring for children, and in amusement. All the ancients recognized and valued woman's bond with the life force. There was no denial of the imaginative faculty. Institutions existed for the purpose of directing her beneficent power into the proper channels. Music was regarded as a direct extension of the functions of women. As in primitive tribes, the barriers between women and music were merely local limitations upon specific occasions when women were expected to function as musicians. As long as there were goddesses, queens, and priestesses, as long as there were women leaders holding positions of responsibility in musical life, women were adapting and arranging the inherited songs and dances, or creating variations on them for new occasions. And they were doing this on their own inspiration, in the proud consciousness that, as women and mothers, they sang with voices that the great powers of life would be bound to heed.

CHAPTER VII

THE LYRIC POETESS

1.

SOME time between 2000 B.C. and 1000 B.C. our modern world began. For on the great plains of Russia, north of the Black Sea and the Caspian, another people—the Aryans—began stirring. During the next centuries they moved outward in all directions, traveling great distances, riding on horses, and driving their cattle before them. They went down into India, pushed back the older Dravidians into southern India, took over the north of India, and began to tell their own story in the *Rig-Veda*. They came down into the Near East and established Persia, whose present name, Iran, means Aryan. They spread westward into Europe and gave their language and customs to whoever was living there at the time when they arrived. Above all, they took over, one after another, the isles and peninsulas of the eastern Mediterranean and put themselves to school amidst the Cretans, choosing and modifying and usually simplifying the charming civilization they found there. Greek civilization did not originate as a single country or culture. It began among little groups of rather rude, hardy people who settled in amidst the decaying luxury and splendor of richer and brighter days, and who in their own plain way civilized themselves by borrowing from their betters.

The one bond among these early Greeks was that they spoke the same language. This was a bond, more or less, among all Aryan peoples, from the misty shores of Ireland to the sunburned banks of the Ganges. This was and is the only bond. Aryan does not refer to a race or a color of skin. It refers only to a kind of language. An early Chinese writer who saw these Aryans in India mentioned their distinctive appearance, however, as well as their widespread language and their attitude to women. "From Wan westward to An-si the languages of the people, though differing slightly from one another are generally similar so that they may understand one another when conversing. All these people have deep eyes and a rich growth of beard. They hold their women in high honor, for whatever a woman says, her husband invariably agrees to it." [1]

Wherever people speak the same language, they tend to have common ideas and social attitudes. The first of the Aryans to write down their ideas about life were those in India. In the *Rig-Veda*, written perhaps about 1200 B.C., there are references to women and to their authority in religion, music, and social life. "From of old comes the wife to the public sacrifice and to the festive gathering; as orderer of the sacrifice comes the noble woman attended by men." [2] This record from the sacred books indicates that the wife was essential to the ceremony.

An especially beautiful service was one performed at the hearth-altar. "O gods," says the *Rig-Veda*, "the married couple, who together intend to present to you libations—who together come on the grass to place there the sacred food—[grant that] this couple, surrounded by little children and growing sons and daughters, pass a happy life. . . ." [3]

At the marriage ceremony, the company chanted hymns to Agni, the fire god, invoking perfection of the well-knit bond between husband and wife. One such hymn, in which only feminine adjectives appear, has been ascribed to the poetess-musician Visvavara, a member of the priestly family of Atreya.

Show thyself strong for mighty bliss, O Agni,

. . .

And overcome the might of those who hate us! [4]

With these Aryan people, marriage ensured the mother and her children protection from the native enemy hordes but apparently did not limit her personal liberty beyond the natural prescriptions of physiological laws or pervert the relationship into a degradation of woman's natural powers. In ancient India a boy was thought to be blessed eightfold if his mother presided at his initiation into manhood. Institutions through which woman's authority in matters of re-birth rituals could be maintained continued to hold people's respect.

As Pandy says to his wife, Kunty, in the Indian epic, the Mahab-

Courtesy of Ernest Benn, Ltd.

34. Raishallala of the Tuareg tribe of northern Africa, photographed in front of her tent, is a modern example of the ancient Mediterranean poetess-musician. (See page 72.)

From C. Sachs, Die Musik der Antike   *Courtesy of The Macmillan Co.*

35, 36, 37. Women musicians of ancient Egypt and Crete.
(See pages 75, 83, and 84.)

38. On a small bas-relief from ancient Greece, the goddess Eileithyia protects the mother in childbirth. (See page 96.)

39. In ancient Greece, the swing festival was a woman's rite associated with the rhythm of life. (See page 100.)

From Perrot-Chipiez, Histoire de l'art dans l'antiquité

From O. Benndorf, Vorlegeblätter fur Archaelogische Ubungen

Musee de Louvre

40, 41, 42. Greek artists often decorated their pottery with representations of women working, rejoicing at weddings, and mourning at funerals. (See pages 98, 99, and 101.)

From A. Furtwängler. Griechische Vasenmalerei

43. Greek girls learned their religious dances from women musicians. (See page 103.)

Courtesy of G. Routledge & Sons, Ltd.

44. Sappho, honored by her pupils, sang, "Mark me, the after days shall see, those that will still remember me." (See page 107.)

harata, which reflects the life of a later day, "I shall tell thee about the practice of old indicated by illustrious Rishis fully acquainted with every rule of morality. O, thou handsome of face and sweet smiles, women were not formerly immured in houses and dependent upon husbands and relatives. They used to go about freely enjoying themselves as best they pleased." [5]

The next records we have of the way the early Aryans felt are the poems of Homer, which began to be sung (perhaps as early as 1000 B.C.) all up and down the islands of the Aegean, and the shores of Greece and Asia Minor, where the Greeks were settling. All these Greeks traced their ancestry to Helen, the daughter of the moon. The hero of one of the two great Homeric poems, the Iliad, is Achilles, grandson of the lunar goddess Doris, the Engenderer. Doris had fifty daughters known as the Nereids. One of them, "silver-slippered Thetis," was the mother of Achilles.

These early Greek stories concern the kidnaping of their beautiful Helen by the Trojans, also Aryans, who carried her away to Asia, and the attempts of the kings of Argos and Mycenae and innumerable heroes, sons of goddesses, to get her back. Woman is such an all-pervading, all-protecting spirit in the Odyssey, the other great Homeric epic, that it is not unlikely that the poem was fashioned by weaving together lays earlier composed and sung by women.

2.

Throughout Greek history until about 400 B.C., when the drama began to absorb public interest and the theater usurped the mimetic rite, singing, dancing, and playing on instruments had the same significance and the same utility that they have today for our primitive and peasant contemporaries. Music was deemed by them a thing divine, the breath of life, a tremendous power for influencing the thought and actions of people, for controlling nature and supernatural beings.

Like other ancient peoples, the Greeks placed a high value on the art of the dance, which they regarded, like swinging, as a means for keeping in the flow of life and for ensuring equilibrium to the soul. Many of the dance movements had come from magic gestures intended to awaken life. The high leap and the wide sweep of the leg won immortality for the dead or made the corn grow tall. Scooping imaginary dewdrops with the hands, arching arms like the moon were techniques to stimulate growth. Holding hands and forming a circle conveyed the strength of the group to each individual.

With the art of manufacturing musical instruments capable of fine gradations of tone still in its infancy, the voice was naturally the favorite medium for musical expression. In the golden ages of Egypt and Crete, emphasis was placed upon melody—a development that the Greeks later carried far toward perfection. But behind this art was practical magic, revealed by words in several of the ancient Aryan languages besides Greek. In Sanskrit, for instance, the word *mantra*, which means a verse of praise to a deity, comes also to mean a magical invocation to compel that higher power to grant some human appeal. The old Indians had charms known as *rāga* and *rāginī*, Aryan words that have survived in the Lithuanian language as *ragana*, meaning one who makes magic formulas or incantations. In Latin, the words *carmen* and *ode* both have the double meaning of "song" and "charm."

Music, indeed, to the Indians of former days, was regarded as being conformable to cosmic laws when it was brought into juxtaposition with certain seasons and hours. Were every rule about the performance of music strictly obeyed, the six male *rāga* tunes and the thirty female *rāginīs* were then considered capable of producing some desired effect. Should they be used in defiance of tradition, a calamity, such as the turning of day into night, might ensue. (See Plate 45.)

In Greece, the conception of the universal life force operating through music was given a beautiful expression by the fifth century B.C. philosopher Pythagoras and his wife Theano, a poetess-musician. They taught that the spheres and the stars of heaven move to music in an eternal song and dance. And so they organized rites for their followers, to the end that each person, by taking part in the music and the dance, might achieve an inner harmony of spirit.

Later Greek educators and philosophers employed the various musical "modes" which had developed through centuries of musical experience to induce a state of mind or "mood." A certain arrangement of tones in a scale was believed to be capable of inspiring soldiers with courage; another was used to inspire worshipers with reverence; still another stimulated passion. Plato later proposed that music for young people should be limited to those modes that would strengthen their characters. He desired to imitate the Egyptians in the creation of melodies that had the capability of calming human passions and purging the soul. The seriousness with which he advanced his theory shows that the most highly educated men believed in the *affective* power of music and of music as an accompaniment to the other arts.

Of such social and religious uses for music, professionalism and the training of professional performers of music were by-products. For many centuries the important music of that great Greek culture remained in its primitive milieu—in the religious rite, for the purpose of placing the worshipers in accord with the life force; in the home, for work, recreation, and magic; at the banquet and formal social gatherings, for entertainment. Consequently in early Greece women were at the center of these three types of music. They danced, sang, and played instruments, especially flutes and cymbals and drums. From childhood to the grave, at home, in small group gatherings, and in formal public ceremonials, early Greek women had opportunity and occasion to use music, and incentive to compose it. The result of such a setting was a rich musical experience for women in general and a great wealth of songs composed for women and by women.

Throughout the period of ancient times until the Christian Era, and even long after, the Greeks like other ancient creators of music usually followed the primitive custom of associating their songs, dances, and instrumental playing with a specific occasion and purpose. Musical art reached its climax when it enhanced the emotional value of some event—a victory over enemy armies, defeat in battle, a wedding, a funeral, a religious festival, a public or private entertainment. The same musical idiom served for all occasions and purposes; one cannot tell from the picture whether a religious rite is being celebrated or whether an entertainment is being staged. This is because the function of music had not changed since the most primitive times. People believed that music was for the purpose of heightening emotional reactions. No matter what the occasion, the artist employed the same techniques.

3.

As in all goddess-worshiping cultures, priestesses in Greece were valued and respected members of their communities. They usually came from noble families and held their offices by hereditary right. Priestesses were assisted in their duties by the so-called *hierai*, sacred women, and the girl choristers. These remained an integral part of the religious and musical life of Greece until long after the beginning of the Christian Era. Members of the choir received training in their youth for the proper performance of the dances and religious songs, often spending the year before marriage within the precincts of a temple under the guidance of a priestess.

Priestesses assembled in societies or hierarchies. Some of the best known were the Oleiai of Orchomenos, the Dysmainai of Mount Taygetos, and the Dionysiades of Sparta. Most renowned of all were the Thyiades, a society whose origin is shrouded in the mists of antiquity. Its members claimed descent from Ino, mother of the Danoi, who, legend tells, brought women's rites from Egypt to Greece. Ino herself was the Horned Cow, like the crescent moon. The Thyiades had colleges in several different places, notably Elis, Pisatis, Sparta, and Delphi. They served both Hera and Dionysos; and when celebrating rites for the rebirth of Dionysos, they were led by the mythical mother of Dionysos, Semele. Though Dionysos was the god of wine and later was worshiped by drunken votaries, his rites in Crete and old Greece were not orgiastic in the sense of intoxication from drink. The women who belonged to these important religious institutions sang their hymns and danced their dances in sobriety. Their ecstasy was a ritual, performed in imitation of the maenads of immemorial tradition and for the same immemorial reason—to become one with the rhythm of all life. (See Plate 33.)

The cult of Dionysos, which was widely and enthusiastically accepted throughout the classical world in the pre-Christian centuries, represented a religious idea that seems to have had an extraordinary popular appeal—the idea that a woman might bear a child without the interposition of a human father, in ecstatic union with a god. This child might be a son or a daughter, and in some cases the divine infant was thought of as of both sexes. But whether son or daughter, the young divinity born like a human baby, nurtured at a human mother's breast, growing up as a human being, beautiful and beloved, demonstrated that through the woman's body alone, with no help from the human male, the universal life force might be incarnated in a young being who was both human and divine. This idea, which appears in various forms in Greek mythology, was best represented by the young god Dionysos, son of Semele and Zeus.

It is important to emphasize the fact that in the earliest times all Dionysiac cults were exclusively women's cults and that they came from the Cretan culture where only women were the priestesses. The

song of the birth (dithyramb) was the song of the mothers, and by
tradition the women choirs of the tribe of Akamantis had used the
primitive cry of joy—alleluia. Priestesses of Elis, probably the distinguished women who belonged to the college of the Thyiades
priesthood, sang the oldest dithyramb preserved in Greek literature:

> In springtime, O Dionysos,
> To thy holy temple come,
> To Elis with thy Graces,
> Rushing with thy bull-foot, come,
> Noble Bull, noble Bull! [6]

From these symbolic mothers singing their dithyramb invoking the
divine child to birth, back to the midwife chanting her incantations
to hasten the arrival of the human child, we see the extraordinary
continuity of Greek ritualistic practice, the carry-over of personal experience to group emotional expression.

The most usual name for the worshipers of Dionysos was the
Bacchae or the bacchantes. Both words mean "the mothers." With
Dionysos were associated also ancient mythical women called
maenads. We know much about these singing, dancing societies of
women and their secret rites in the mountains. For in a later century
an inquiring and sensitive man named Euripides happened to escape from the rather conceited circles of the male intelligentsia of
Athens in his day and to catch a glimpse of them. He was profoundly
stirred and wrote a beautiful choral drama, *The Bacchae* (or *The
Mothers*), about them. Had Euripides known more about the primitive origins of his own civilization, he might have avoided a groping
indefiniteness in his beautiful verse. But he believed, in his poet's
soul, that these women, with their ringing cry, "Oh, wild white
maids, to the hills, to the hills!" [7] had something men might well try
to understand.

Their rites, he thought, came from Crete, and he represented the
Bacchae as singing:

> "For thee of old some crested Corybant
> First woke in Cretan air
> The wild orb of our orgies,
> Our Timbrel; and thy gorges
> Rang with this strain; and blended Phrygian chant
> And sweet keen pipes were there.

"But the Timbrel, the Timbrel was another's,
And away to Mother Rhea it must wend;
And to our holy singing from the Mothers
The mad Satyrs carried it, to blend
In the dancing and the cheer
Of our third and perfect year." [8]

Casting an interested masculine eye over their attire, but not apparently aware of the age-old meaning of their symbols, Euripides noted that the Bacchae wore long white dresses and had fawn skins flung over their shoulders, and that some of them carried wands with serpents wound around them. "The Songs of Serpents sound in the mazes of their hair." [9] Perhaps he had never heard that the snake is from immemorial time the symbol of rebirth. All the maidens carried oak wands wreathed in ivy. Most of them had ivy wound in their hair. They had outposts to warn all onlookers away. A maiden went ahead of the procession chanting:

"Who lingers in the road? Who espies us?
He shall hide him in his house nor be bold.
Let the heart keep silence that defies us;
For I sing this day to Dionysos
The song that is appointed from of old." [10]

And when the women, seeking the still dell of the Muses, had climbed far into the hills (as primitive women in Africa do to this day), a shepherd saw them in the dawn, sleeping after their nightlong songs and incantations.

"Our herded kine were moving in the dawn
Up to the peaks, the greyest, coldest time,
When the first rays steal earthward, and the rime
Yields, when I saw three bands of them. The one
Autonoe led, one Ino, one thine own
Mother, Agave. There beneath the trees
Sleeping they lay, like wild things flung at ease
In the forests; one half sinking on a bed
Of deep pine greenery; one with careless head
Amid the fallen oak leaves; all most cold
In purity—not as thy tale was told
Of wine-cups and wild music and the chase
For love amid the forest's loneliness." [11]

While there were a few mysteries in which men and women jointly participated, most of the secret rites were conducted by women alone, and only by initiated women. Those that concern women's mysteries have never been fully understood since their meaning was not disclosed to any uninitiated person. The whole subject of the women's hierarchies—their secrecy, their mythical association with goddesses and with the moon—takes us back into the farthest realm of primitive times and shows the force of those old beliefs even among people as highly educated as the Greeks.

4.

The expression of religious feeling by means of rites was an integral part of Greek daily life. The Greeks had inherited belief in the power of magic, and they placated their numerous deities at every turn—in their homes, at wayside shrines, in sacred groves and caves, and later with formal ceremonies in the great temples of the classical age. Before a meal a Greek family would place on its hearth a few bits of food in offering to Hestia, goddess of the hearth, and would pour a few drops of unmixed wine on the floor to placate the good daemon of the house. Women made obeisance to Eileithyia and to Hekate, goddesses of life and death, at shrines erected at the thresholds of their homes. In his "Ode to Theron," Pindar tells of the maidens who danced and sang before his door through the night.

Divine protection was particularly required for the special events in human life—for birth, presentation of the child to society and to the spirits, puberty, marriage, and death—and for the normal changes of nature—the birth and decay of vegetation. In the main, Greek religious rites centered around these rhythmical crises. The character of the rites varied all the way from simple house cult practices of primitive times to elaborate festivals involving many people and lasting for days.

The most striking aspect of Greek religious practice is the continuity of its expression—the constant carry-over from the real to the ideal; from actual experience to a deity who symbolized the experience. To women, this constant carry-over was extraordinarily important. All their activities, all their physiological crises had feminine impersonations to whom they could voice their needs. In these symbols women projected their own strength and capabilities, their own value in the life scheme. In the worship of the goddesses, women had opportunity and compulsion to express with ritual and music their own deep emotions, their own creative urges. Help for a woman in childbirth, for example, was not confined to incantations sung by a midwife to ease and speed her actual labor. In congregation, at shrines—such as the shrine at Olympia that Eileithyia, goddess of childbirth, shared with the snake-child Sosipolis—women sang formal hymns to their protectress. At the great festival of the Thesmophoria, sacred to married women, it was customary on the third day for the women votaries to sing a hymn of invocation to Artemis Kalligenia, or Prothyraia, to her who would grant an easy birth to mothers. (See Plate 38.)

To Artemis Prothyraia

Hear me, O most majestic goddess, spirit of the many names,
Deliveress from the pangs of birth, sweet presence to those in travail,
Savioress of women, you who alone love children, goddess of the
     gentle mind,
Giver of a birth that is rapid, deliveress from mortal sorrows,
Prothyraia, you who are before the Door!
Who hold the keys, beautiful to meet, kind to all,
     who love to feed and keep animals,
Of the homes of all you are mistress, you rejoice in the gladness of
     feasts,
Loosener of girdles, invisible, yet manifest by your works to all!
Through sympathy you suffer along with women in travail,
And with those who bring forth easily you rejoice,
Ilithyia, goddess of childbirth, releaser from the throes none can
     escape!
On you alone they call in travail, O resting-place of the soul,
For in you the pains of childbirth are forgotten.
Artemis Ilithyia, and Prothyraia, hallowed in beauty,
Hear, blessed one! Give the fruit of seed, coming as a deliveress,
And saving us, even as you were born eternal Savioress of all! [12]

The woman's singing magic of birth and rebirth was used in the various rites of the life cycle as it still is among primitive peoples. At puberty, Greek girls were inducted into maturity with various minutiae of ceremony. As with primitive tribes, flowers, the holy bath, games, foot races, festivals at the new moon, and always dancing and singing were characteristic features of these ceremonials. For example, girl initiates serving Hera, in whose cult flowers were always used, would gather spring blossoms and twine them around a statue of the goddess as they danced to the music of flutes and invoked the holy one in song. In ceremonies of Artemis at Sicyon, where the Crete-inherited feminine influence was especially strong, a statue of the goddess was annually carried down to the sea and dipped into the water for the sacred bath. The most beautiful girl initiate was chosen to impersonate the goddess, and a choir of dancing and singing girls led the procession to the sea. In the rear followed a choir of boys, also dancing and singing. These boys probably represent a relatively late addition to a ritual in which originally only women and girls took part. The great festival of the Heraea, held under the direction of the Thyiades in the month of Parthenos, when the moon was new, was also a puberty rite, a festival of games for girls like the Olympic games for boys, and probably of older origin. The music for the Heraea was made by the Thyiades. Under their organization and leadership, two choirs of sixteen women sang the sacred hymns.

Little is known of the Heraea, but it is not difficult to guess the character of the rites or to infer the leadership of women. These women's rites are alike the world over. Among the Tusayan Indians in New Mexico, for example, the La-la-konta Festival lasts for ten days and has a deep religious significance for the whole tribe. Its chief purpose is to induce the germination of seeds. The girls run a race, a common practice at puberty rites and certainly a feature of the Heraea. There is a procession to the spring—water is always the source of life—and a dance. The priestesses hold their office by heredity. After ceremonially calling the women together at the shrine, they lead them in wonderful choral singing. As we have seen in many places in the primitive world, as well as in Egypt, the priestess is also musician. Undoubtedly in Greece, women with the same status also composed their own music for their own rites.

Marriage rites in Greece, like those of puberty, were rites of transition from one state of life to another, celebrated both at real and at symbolic marriages. Real weddings usually took place just before full moon. Before the ceremony, sacrifices to the goddesses were made and the bride was given her sacramental bath. At the festivities the bride was veiled to signify rebirth from a symbolic womb and also to signify dedication to her new life. The two mothers lit the torches that symbolized the light of the life-giving moon. Accompanied by flute players, the wedding procession marched to the bridegroom's house. The wedding feast was the ideal time for felicitations. (See Plate 41.)

Bridesmaids greeted the bridegroom:

> "Raise high the roof-beam, carpenters,
> Hymenaeus!
> Like Ares comes the bridegroom,
> Hymenaeus!
> Taller far than a tall man,
> Hymenaeus!" [13]

The hymn-call was to bring forth the daemons of fertility. It was always shouted at weddings as a kind of good-luck motto by the friends of the bride and groom. Bridesmaids at a Greek wedding always lamented the passing of the bride's girlhood. In Sappho's words they sang:

> "Maidenhood, maidenhood, whither art thou gone from me?
> Never again will I come to thee, never again." [14]

Then groomsmen would praise the bride: "O fair, O lovely!" and the wedding guests would praise the bridal pair:

> "Hail, bride!
> Noble bridegroom!
> All hail!" [15]

It was the bridesmaids' duty and pleasure to prepare the bridal bed in a bower garlanded with flowers, and to conduct the bride to it. The epithalamium, accompanied by dancing, was sung outside of the bridal chamber at night by bridesmaids and youths. At dawn came the last benediction of the friends:

> "Farewell the bride,
> Farewell the bridegroom." [16]

In temples and at festivals, sacred marriages, symbolic of the union of the sexes, were performed on many occasions, often with other rebirth rites. At the Heraea festival, for example, the girl victorious in the foot races, olive-crowned, would be married symbolically to the boy winner of the Olympic games. At the rites of Dionysos in

Athens the wife of the second archon officiated regularly as bride to a symbolic Dionysos. Sometimes, as in the cult of Hera at Samos, the rites of the sacred marriage were performed without men, but they were never performed without women—a fact that clearly suggests a feminine origin of the marriage rite as a *"rite de passage"* for a woman about to enter a new state of life. In Greek religion the rites of the sacred marriage and of the birth of the holy child or of some symbol of the rebirth were indissoluble and represented the central mystery of religious ritual.

Greek funeral rites, like other rites of the rebirth, were held for both real and for symbolic deaths. When a person died, the family and the professional women mourners would gather around the bier. It was the business of the professional mourner to give the wailing necessary to hasten the rebirth of the dead soul into the spirit world. The mourner was expected to remain for several days, during which time she sang one dirge after another. A mourner was not worth her pay if she repeated herself. She probably behaved very like the present-day professional singer at funerals in Mykonos. In old Greece the group of family mourners burst out with a refrain. The men exclaimed in their own characteristic fashion and the women gave the *evoe*, "Alleluia," similar to the cry of joy given by priestesses in the bacchanals. Sometimes a flute player, also a woman, accompanied the cortege. There was a great demand for these women artists and they had consequently a strong incentive to create music that would be considered good among professionals. (See Plate 42.)

Part of the funeral ceremony was often conducted very like a drama. The cortege consisted of a chariot, or men, bearing the coffin, of women walking in front, at the sides, and in the rear. It was the custom to display grief. The women beat their breasts, wailed for a time, then walked in silence, then wailed again. When the procession halted, the mourners grouped themselves in dramatic attitudes. Sometimes there would be formal choirs. Following a very old custom, the people of Megara used to send fifty maidens and fifty youths to Corinth whenever a death occurred in the Bacchiad family. In all types of death ceremonies women played their classic role.

At the symbolic deaths, mourning for the dead vegetation of the year, or for a hero, a heroine, or a god, a goddess took the place of mourning for a real person. During the Thesmophoria, married women stood at the crossroads and lamented in spirit with Demeter, goddess of the grain, who was searching for her lost daughter, Kore.

In the Adonia, women wailed on their housetops for Adonis, a vegetation god. At all the festivals, after the lamenting came the cries of joy in anticipation of the resurrection, be it of nature, the moon, or the deity.

5.

Religious festivals in Greece showed many traces of a matriarchal origin. In the great periodic rites known as the Thargelia for transferring the force behind vegetation to the new harvest, men and women celebrated together, as do those of many primitive tribes in similar fertility festivals. Men and women both joined, too, in those for Adonis as well as in the requiems, from which our idea of All Saints' and All Souls' Days came. Connected with the rites of the Anthesteria were the Eumenides or avengers of a mother's wrongs. Women sang as they walked along carrying flowers and green branches. In Aeschylus' drama *The Eumenides* is a description of what was probably the actual rites:

> Pass to your house thus augustly estated,
> Come, O mysterious maidens, come, offspring of night!
> And silence all for our sacred song.
> Come ye with sacrifice offered, with worship and with rite.

Some festivals celebrated by men were modeled on women's festivals. The Apatouria—Festival of the Same Fathers—was, for example, an adaptation of a far older form, Festival of the Same Mothers.

Many rites of rebirth were practiced by women alone, or with men playing a secondary role. Korythalia was the women's version of the various May-pole dances (*eiresione*). The Aiora, or Swing Festival, was distinctly a women's ritual, bound up with the moon and the rhythm of life. (See Plate 39.) Besides the Heraea, which had the primitive girls' puberty rites in the race at new moon, there were other festivals of Hera. One was the Anthesphoria, celebrated with flutes amidst bowers of greens. Various Artemisia belonged to women. In them the features were processions to a sacred spring, bronze tympani, and laments called *oupingi*. At the Hersephoria the dew-carrying maidens refreshed the bloom of their own youth. The Tithenidia was a festival for the nursing mothers of Sparta, who danced and sang to Artemis as they ate loaves of bread shaped like a woman's breast. Like the Eleusinian mysteries, the Thesmophoria concerned agricultural magic—woman's ancient prerogative. It was conducted by married women.

Many festivals of Dionysos belonged to women originally, as well as the Adonia, in which Aphrodite's son, or lover, was first mourned for as dead and then rejoiced over as resurrected. Three festivals made up the Ennateric group. The second of this group was the Herois, in which the women invoked Semele, mother of Dionysos, and called upon the dead heroines to return and help them in their colossal task of bringing life to the earth. The third was the Charila and involved carrying out death, preparing for new life. At Orchomenos, where the Thyiades had one of their colleges, the priestesses sang to the Charites, the gift-bringers of plenty.

Greek songs, both religious and occupational, were divided into categories and had generic names. There were songs of winnowing, songs of reaping, mill songs that women sang as they ground grain, songs of the water carriers, and rope songs sung at the well in imitation of the gurgling water. (See Plate 40.)

Nursing mothers had songs of their own—*katabaukaleses*, which means literally to lull to sleep. The bakers sang to Demeter: "Send forth a sheaf, a plenteous sheaf, a sheaf send forth!" [17] (See Plate 16.)

6.

Out of the rich musical life of Greece, with its many opportunities for women to sing and to make music, came a substantial number of poetess-musicians whose fame has carried down to our own day. A Greek compiler lists forty such poetesses by name. These women won numerous prizes in public competitions, had statues erected to them, and some were likened to the Muses by their men competitors. Phantasia, who came to Greece from Memphis, Egypt, in pre-Homeric times, was one of the early story-singers. It was the custom in those days for men and women to gather after supper in the great hall of a dwelling and to amuse themselves by chanting and listening to stories. Phantasia, being a skilled storyteller, like many women in primitive tribes today, entertained her companions with music. She and her friend Themis are reputed to have invented the heroic meter, the hexameter. Certainly they made a compound measure out of two lines of the Linus, that song of lament for Adonis sung by so many choirs of women.

Individual women artists sang laments in public not only in pre-classical and classical Greece but long afterward. In one of his most charming idylls, Theocritus mentioned a skillful singer from Argos who sang in the market place of Syracuse at the festival of Adonis. Two members of the audience, Praxinoe and Gorgo, are speaking: "Silence, Praxinoe! She is preparing to sing the Adonis—the girl of Argos, the skillful singer who carried off the prize of Sperchis, she is preparing to sing the lamentation. She sings, I know well, with talent." The singer modulates the hymn, and Gorgo exclaims: "It is more beautiful than I ever thought; fortunate woman to be so well informed! Altogether fortunate that she sings so softly!" [18] This professional musician was carrying on a custom of immemorial antiquity. She was giving the wail that would hasten the rebirth of Adonis, the god who personified the vegetation of the year. And, according to the way of the woman artist-musician, she had converted the wail into an art form—the musical lament.

Perhaps the two most important categories of women's religious songs were the hymns of invocation composed and sung by the hierarchies of priestesses—notably the Thyiades and the Elean priestesses—and the lyric poems sung by the girl choirs, known as *parthenia* or songs for maidens. The girl choirs were famous for the excellence of their performance. Pindar wrote of them: "Round Parnassus high cliffs, the bright-eyed Delphian maidens enter the fleet chorus and sing a sweet song with clear voices." [19] And Alkman spoke of his delight in the Spartan "maidens of honey voice, so loud and clear." [20]

The songs that the girl choirs sang usually had for theme some myth or legend of god or goddess, hero or heroine. As the girls sang, they would dance and gesticulate and more or less act out the story of the legend. Obviously, this was simply a development of the age-old mimetic rite and a forerunner of the later complicated Greek drama. About the seventh century B.C. a form of choral dance developed, called the *hypercheme*, in which the dancing and gesticulating chorus was reinforced by a stationary group of singers. In this way, more difficult and more complex music could be performed and more attention paid to the melodic element in the music. Favorite subjects for *hyperchemata* were such tales as Bacchylides' myth of Ida and Marpessa, a kind of wedding cantata, or the myth of Theseus' victory over the Minotaur of Crete. In the latter, dancing boys joined with the girls of the dancing chorus. The participation of girl choirs and of actors in this type of ritual dance drama—definite precursor of Greek classical drama, in which only men were allowed to sing or to perform—illustrates the extent to which women took part in the musical life of the preclassical Greeks. (See Plate 43.)

A Greek woman artist—this one distinguished for her singing, her dancing, and her lyric poetry—was Megolastrata of Sparta. Called the beautiful blonde, she led the Spartan girl choirs and composed music for their performances. Unfortunately, not one of her compositions has been preserved, but her fame as a leader and as a composer has come down to us from the seventh century B.C., a time when the girl choirs were especially active and important in Greek life.

Telesilla of Argos was a heroic figure, one of those courageous militant women who through quick decision save their countries in moments of great danger. When the Spartans threatened her city-state, Telesilla is said to have gathered weapons from homes and temples, to have given them to the women of Argos, and to have led them against the enemy. A poetess-musician as well as a warrior, Telesilla is especially famous for her hymns and for her political songs. Only two verses are left from her poetry, a call to maidens, obviously part of a hymn.

Corinna, a poetess-musician of Boetia, was Pindar's teacher and won five times over him in poetic competition. So lovely were her songs that the poet Antipater named her as one of the nine women whom he selected as earthly muses. Corinna's work consisted of epigrams, lyric poems, and choruses for women. Unhappily, only a few fragments of her poetry are extant and none of her melodies. As she herself explained, she sang of native myths and legends, of heroes and especially of heroines—"But I, I am come to sing the prowess of Heroes and Heroines, in fair old-wives' tales for the white-robed daughters of Tanagra!" [21]

Sicyon, a city-state that kept on conspicuously with Cretan customs and in which women played a leading part in both religious and musical life, was the home of the poetess-musician Praxilla. She was famous also for her *skolias* or table songs—later called drinking songs—sung at banquets, sometimes solo, sometimes in chorus; for her dithyrambs; and for an epic poem entitled "Adonia." Praxilla's songs were so well thought of in Athens that they were compared with those of Alkman and of Sappho, and were sung at banquets of the nobility.

Of all the poetess-musicians of Greece, the most famous, the one whose very name is almost synonymous with the words "lyric poetry," is Sappho of Lesbos (seventh century B.C.). Lesbos is a triangular island, lying a few miles off the shore of European Turkey— one of those garden islands of the Aegean, full of mountain dells and fresh streams rushing down to the sea, where the small gray olive trees cling to the hillsides, fruit grows sweet and ripe in the valleys, flowers bloom, birds sing, and the sun shines most of the days of the year.

In the seventh century B.C. Lesbos had built up quite a trade with the other Greek islands and the half-Asian, half-Hellenic cities of Asia Minor. And since it was so prosperous, its talented citizens found time and opportunity to bring the art of singing to the lyre to a very high perfection and to take great pains with the music and ceremonial of religious processionals led by women. Here in this tiny island city-state of Lesbos, women had the high social, political, literary, and religious status then common in the Aegean world. They owned their own property and were free to come and go as they pleased. Well educated, especially in poetry and music, they enjoyed the companionship of both men and other women, taking part, as a matter of course, in political and literary discussions. As priestesses in the temples of Lesbos, they served especially Hera, Aphrodite, Demeter, and Artemis. Perhaps no place in all of Greece was more favorable than Lesbos for the flowering of a woman's creative talent, and in this environment Sappho was born, matured, and asserted her leadership.

A woman of independent wealth, highly respected and greatly admired, not only in her own community but throughout Greece, Sappho lived all of her life, with the exception of about five years, in the beautiful surroundings of Lesbos. After her return from her period of political exile in Syracuse she founded a girl's college, or art school as we would call it, to which young women came from far and wide to study poetry and music.

The most gifted of these girls was Erinna. Erinna's mother is said to have chained her to her spinning wheel in order to make her spin rather than sing, or perhaps only to spin while she was singing. But Erinna appears to have found a way to study with Sappho with such

45. The Rāginīs of India represent the ideal graces of womanhood. Bhairaveen, a beautiful maiden, places her flowers on the altar of "Linga" at dawn, when Rāginī Bhairaveen may be sung. This, and other symbolic paintings showing the relation of women to old Indian music, were recently done by Fyzee-Rahamin for his wife, who can sing the six Rāga and the thirty Rāginī melodies and who knows the history of their power of enchantment. (See pages 47 and 90.)

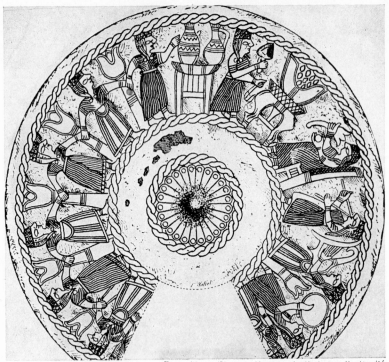

From Perrot-Chipiez. Histoire de l'art dan l'antiquité

46. On a decorated goblet from old Cyprus, the goddess Astarte can be seen with her priestess-musicians. (See page 117.)

Courtesy of Alfred J. Swan

47. A modern Russian painter has portrayed the music of his country as personified by two birdwomen: Sírin and Alkonóst. (See pages 49 and 118.)

48. In Latvia, where women's songs enrich the musical literature, the pagan goddess Laime is represented on a wood-cut receiving a woman's sacrifice. (See page 110.)

C. Lenormant, Elites des monuments céramographiques

E. Gerhard, Auserlesene Griechische Vasenbilder

49, 50. History is told on pottery. Artemis, accompanied by the dog as symbol of healing power, played magic music but was superseded by Apollo. (See pages 120, 122 and 142.)

success that when she died at nineteen, her poems were already known and admired. It was even said that she could write hexameters better than Sappho. Only one fragment of her work remains, a beautiful lyric song in honor of a dead girl, also a singer—Baucis. Improperly entitled "The Distaff" by later critics, this poem is really a lament, written in hexameter with no refrain but with recurring cries of sorrow.

There appears to have been much affection and pretty displays of endearments among these girls and between them and their slight dark-haired leader and teacher, Sappho. These ways, which are natural enough in any group of girls, later received an unpleasant interpretation among the fourth-century male intelligentsia of Athens, who were openly carrying male homosexuality to a high degree of refined exhibitionism and celebrating it even in works as dignified as the dialogues of Plato. Most modern scholars believe the so-called "Lesbianism" of Sappho and her girls to be only the gossip over wine cups in Athens, where middle-aged literary gentlemen and men about town toasted their own boy flames.

The actual records of Sappho seem to indicate a normal woman's life. She had a little daughter named Cleis. She did some social and poetic sparring with the other most famous poet of Lesbos, a man named Alcaeus. What she and Alcaeus seem to have done is to sing between them a *tenso*, which is a sort of poetical dialogue between kindred spirits. The *tenso* has been an art form from earliest times all over the world, among the Chinese in the pre-Confucian age, among ladies and lords of the medieval court of the Japanese emperor in Kyoto, and among the Tuareg today. The Song of Solomon in the Bible is a *tenso* representing King Solomon's dialogue with Arabian queens whom he courted.

So Alcaeus sang to Sappho: "violet-weaving, pure, sweet smiling Sappho, I wish to say something but shame hinders me."

And Sappho replied, in song: "Hadst thou had desire of aught good or fair, shame would not have touched thine eyes, but thou wouldst have spoken thereof openly." [22]

No one has ever questioned Sappho's genius as a lyric poet. Her fame has lasted for more than twenty centuries. Plato called her the Tenth Muse and Ausonius named her the Muses' Sister. Unfortunately, only a few fragments of the poetry upon which Sappho's fame primarily rests have come down to us; and all of the music with which she accompanied her songs has been lost. But from her own poetry and from relatively contemporaneous accounts in Greek literature, we know her high reputation as a player and singer. She was called "a nightingale of hymns." Her favorite instruments to accompany her songs were the "golden lyre" and the "sweet-toned flute." "Come now, O lyre of mine," she herself sings, "lift up thy voice divine." [23]

Besides accompanying her songs with lyre and flute, Sappho is reputed to have developed for her own use a special kind of stringed instrument called the pectis and to have introduced into musical usage the plectrum, or quill, for striking the lyre's strings. Her creative genius is further illustrated in her invention of new melodies, new forms of music. She is credited with having evolved the mixolydian mode and with having invented a new style of music by breaking up the meter. "This feature," writes one modern admirer, "the Greeks called 'contrast of accent.' In her verse it was like silver things clashing against each other. She buckled together these clashing feet by the golden bands of rhythm and by this means made havoc of emphasis. . . . But when she chose to make symmetry of emphasis, she could. The sapphic meter is a woman's hexameter. It is the feminine heroic." [24]

Sappho and her pupils officiated at public religious festivals as well as at weddings, and Sappho herself may even have been official conductor of the temple choirs. "Come to the splendid temple grounds of Hera of the gleaming eyes, you girls of Lesbos," she writes, "and trip lightly with whirling measure, performing a beautiful choral dance for the goddess; and Sappho shall lead you, her golden lyre in her hand." [25] We have fragments of the beautiful wail laments that Sappho and her girls sang to hasten the rebirth of the child god at festivals to Adonis:

Maidens: Tender Adonis lies adying,
    O Cytheria, what were best to do?

Cytheria (Leader): Go, beat your breasts, ye maids, and crying,
    Rend ye your robes in sign of rue!" [26]

The subjects of Sappho's lyrics were the subjects important to women, the everyday happenings of their lives. She sang of her love for her little daughter; she wrote love songs and marriage songs; hymns and laments to be sung at religious ceremonies. So famous were her epithalamia or wedding songs that Sappho and her pupils were frequently and widely employed as musicians at weddings. And the poetic form of her epithalamia was the model which other writers used for nearly a thousand years in Greece, Rome, and even Europe. Knowing Sappho's authority in one type of art-song, can we not assume the same for the Egyptian poetess-musicians who created the laments and dirges attributed to the goddess Isis?

In order to judge the quality of Sappho's music, it is unnecessary to have samples of it. Her verses, her melodies, and the strains that accompanied them on flute or lyre were regarded by her contemporaries and by critics of the golden age as bearing the stamp of perfection. Her work had the same quality as the poetry and sculpture of the Periclean Age in Athens. Unquestionably, the music composed by Sappho and her companions, while of course very different from that of our times, was creation of the very highest order by trained musical talent.

Sappho was not a "sport"—a woman gone masculine—as many people have considered her, or an extraordinary deviation from type that might never occur again. She was simply an extremely talented individual, a woman with a great aptitude for poetic-musical expression, who lived in an environment peculiarly favorable for its full development. For her there existed a juxtaposition of the three factors *always* essential to the full unfolding of creative musical imagination. She developed in a culture in which music was an integral part of both informal and formal life. She belonged to a class of people from whom, in that culture, music was expected. As a member of the Aegean society, she inherited melodic impulse. Every artist of the islands had the background of Egypt and Crete for musical assertion in lyric song. Finally, Sappho had training and experience in the technique required by the standards of her community—an outstanding woman, it is true, but intrinsically no different from other exceptionally talented women of her own and of many other communities. What made Sappho the peerless lady of music and song was the fact that she had behind her an immemorial past of experiment by women in poetry and music. Hers was the last perfect flowering of thousands of years of women's song. (See Plate 44.)

CHAPTER VIII

ARTEMIS

1.

FOR creative expression in music there must be a free flow between the plane of daily experience and the plane of thought and fantasy. One must be able to transfer into universal and ideal terms one's vital personal experience. To the extent to which the ideal plane is restricted or distorted, the creative energies of the individual are devitalized or even poisoned.

Women in pre-Christian times all over the world had simply and naturally evolved a grand religious idea out of their greatest experience—the experience of birth. And just as simply and naturally, they assumed that the life of the universe could be expressed in terms of a woman's experience. Surely, they thought, the universal life must be a mother. It might unite with a father. But the motherhood of the deity was to them more obvious and more really important than the fatherhood. They were not restricted, as Western women later were for nineteen hundred years, to a single male god. On the contrary, they had a representation of what they, as women, knew of life. They had a means of idealizing and universalizing their own highest impulses.

Women were pre-eminent in the creation of music in these early times. They are not pre-eminent now. For in those days, they were also pre-eminent in the formulation of religious ideas. They did not take their religion from men, or leave it to men to make their music.

To understand what happened to women later, one must understand the kind of religious images that women had as an inspiration for the outpouring of their songs. In all the myths, rituals, sculpture, painting, and literature of antiquity, there is an all-pervading woman presence. Whether she is called Cybele or Ishtar or Isis or Hera, or some name foreign to our ears, she represents woman power as an active beneficent principle in all life, sometimes as life itself, the ultimate being, mother of all living things. A realized truth generates creative power. From these noble images of women, energy flowed back to the individual woman, releasing and strengthening her imagination and her artistic impulse at this deep level where music is conceived.

Behind the rites of primitive people everywhere today, and in all very early religions, there is the woman spirit. In the great early civilizations of Egypt, Babylonia, and Crete, the Great Mother acquired a grand, all-embracing personality, and was loved and worshiped with a passionate faith. In Rome the cult of the Great Mother persisted and resisted the powerful onslaught of the growing Christian Church until the fifth century. In Greece, where the tendency was to bring all gods down to earth and turn them into human beings, the personality of the Great Mother was split up into a number of divine feminine figures and lovingly individualized, by the Greek talent for character delineation, into ideal women, clearly distinguished from each other in temperament, appearance, and the kind of interest they took in human affairs—but all of them noble, benignant, all-powerful.

The great goddesses, by whatever name they were called, had their own rites, in which music and dancing were always conspicuous, their own liturgies, their own myths, and their own insignia. One had the spiral; others carried the plume, jewels, an ear of corn, the three-stalked flower, a musical instrument. One was crowned with the sun's halo, one held the sky cape above her, another a sea shell. One stood surrounded by the swiftly flowing rivers of the world. Many were accompanied by lions—symbols of the strength inherent in womanhood. All the great goddesses represented the rhythm of life and the moon.

These goddesses, in their many beautiful impersonations, with their various symbols, represent three mighty facts of nature, akin to each other in their character and manifestations, which seemed to these early human beings, and especially to women, to hold the key to life. One was the waxing and waning of the moon, its three nights of darkness, its effulgent period of resplendent light making night for the brief period of the full moon a kind of heavenly day full of mystery and magic. The second was the fact that, in nature, death is the prelude to new birth. When the flower petals fall, there remains the seed from which new flowers will spring. And the third was the kinship of the woman—in all those biological details that distinguish her from the male—to the moon cycle and to the something that gives birth throughout all nature. Hence the divine life was naturally and inevitably feminine and woman was its natural priestess. She knew how to speak to it in her incantations; she knew the rhythms, the gestures, and the symbols, the spirit behind all things that would understand and heed. (See Plate 48.)

2.

As time went on and many, many women worked to perfect their understanding of the ultimate woman power, different goddesses, or different phases of the one great woman spirit, came to represent the woman in her different characters and functions—as mate, mother, worker, musician, and "virgin," or free, unattached to a mate, untrammeled with children.

All the goddesses represented to some degree the woman's life span. But there was one great spirit, the Greek Hera, who represented this the most clearly. She had three distinct forms, corresponding to the three phases of changing life. In the first she was the girl-child, young, fresh, free, having not yet come to maturity. In the second she was a woman of the childbearing age, in the fullness of her peculiar power of womanhood, as mate and mother. In the last she was the woman past childbearing age, but not old, free again, in the ripeness of character, in the profound knowledge of life that motherhood and wifehood nobly fulfilled have brought her.

In the beginning, when Hera first came to Greece from goddess-ruled Crete, she was entirely independent of Zeus. Even in the Olympian age she kept her own temples, priestesses, girl choirs, and rites, in which music and dancing were integrated. Hera was primarily the matron, guardian of marriage, mistress of the home, noble, dignified, and wise. A famous artistic representation of her, of which only a description now remains, showed her seated on a throne, carrying the scepter of world dominion in one hand and in the other a pomegranate—symbol of life.

The concept of mate as distinguished from that of mistress of the home received other impersonations. A dignified god symbolizing mating or sex is rare in the ancient pantheons. The Oriental gods usually represent unbridled male energy. The little boy Cupid or Eros was a frivolous conception of late Greek literature dominated by male intelligentsia, and very trivial and silly in comparison with the mighty, all-powerful goddesses of sex in earlier times, who symbolize the *rhythm* of sex desire.

Of these, one of the oldest was Sumerian Innanna, later Ishtar. In her resided the rhythm of sex desire. When she rested, all procreation ceased. Even the urge for it died until she gave the signal for the rebirth. An ancient myth represented Ishtar descending into hell, or darkness, for three days, corresponding to the three nights of the dark of the moon. On the third day she was revived by two goddesses impersonating the bread of life and the water of life; then, clothed in splendor and beauty, she emerged and roused all living things to mate.

Ishtar was one of the mightiest superhuman powers of all time, known as "Directress of Mankind." She was worshiped in many temples by both women and men. Troops of dancing, singing priestesses and many women officials served her. On the monuments and seals of Sumer she appeared in a long robe with a crown on her head and an eight-pointed star in her hand. From this same Ishtar, beautiful Venus in Rome took her name and her characteristics. In Greece, Ishtar and the idea of deifying sexual love were impersonated by Aphrodite, whose real home was the island of Cyprus. Here, where Cretan culture took early root, Aphrodite was a moon goddess and specifically the bearer of the life-giving dew, or mist, which comes at night. This refreshing moisture was thought to be, like the life-giving seminal fluid, the gift of the moon. Hence Aphrodite was the goddess born of the sea, and also the moon, which influenced, in some obscure magnetic ways, its tides and the sexual rhythm in women. Like other Great Mothers, Aphrodite lamented and made songs of rejoicing over the death and resurrection of her son, Adonis. Everywhere in Greek culture the mighty goddess of the rhythm of life itself and of music was the inspiration of festivals at which the whole populace shared her grief and joy.

In most of these deities of sex there was a recognition of the sex urge as the basis for a higher development of the life of the spirit. But without woman's authority in regulating the rhythm of sex life, spiritual life also lay dormant. As if to symbolize woman's life-giving power in affairs of the spirit, one of the old Oriental goddesses was depicted holding the material substance of the world encased in a spiritual essence. This image may be regarded as representing the meaning of all ancient feminine deities—unity of the higher human faculties with the natural and real things of the earth.

3.

Nearly all great goddesses were mothers and often passed on the torch of life to the next generation by their own power. Many of them had names whose roots indicated their function. The last part of the Greek Demeter's name means mother. A present day South Indian word for "nurse" or "mother" is "amma," and it is incorporated into the Great Mothers' names, such as Nukalamma. In representations of the mother goddess, her maternal functions were universalized by associating various symbols of life and the rhythm of life with the figure of the woman. In picture after picture the Great Mother sits on her throne holding, not a child, but the more comprehensive emblem of the phial containing the water of life. She beats a drum, not only because real women use a drum as a magic device to assist childbirth, but because her life is bound to rhythm. She sings, not only because real mothers sing to their children, giving them their first impressions of melody, but because the music of the spheres resounds to human ears only through the door of life she opens for both body and soul.

. With only local variations in the different countries, the Great Mother was the focus of celebrations for changes in the seasons and for the reappearance of the new moon.

The goddess gave a child to the world, fashioned out of her own body and blood. She gave nourishment that her child might thrive—first her own milk and then cultivated foods. The child was sometimes a son and sometimes a daughter. Demeter gave Kore, a beautiful clean-limbed, clear-eyed maiden. Other goddesses had both a maiden and a youth. Cybele's child, Attis, was double-sexed. The offspring of the Great Mother was often identified with the fruits of the earth and became the symbol of regeneration, to be lamented and rejoiced over by the goddesses and their semidivine attendants. Every year or so, at great national festivals, Ishtar mourned for Tammuz, Isis for Osiris, Cybele for Attis, Aphrodite for Adonis, and Demeter for Kore. Rites for the rebirth were the most important rites and they were ceremonies of the goddess-mother, not the godfather. It was the mother's sacrifice, the mother's power for bringing life, the mother's point of view that gave the religion of those times its character and appeal.

As mother, the goddess created the world in co-operation with a male deity, to whom, with a grim feminine realism, the early priest-ess-theologians assigned the lesser part in this mighty achievement. It would have been impossible, in those honest early days, to convince a woman who had borne children that the father's part in projecting life was the greater part and should be so represented in the creation of divine images. Running through all the early stories of the creation there is also the idea that a male god can never do much until a woman puts real life into him or his work. Prometheus once made a youth, but it was Athene who pressed the spiritual substance into his brain. The shepherd boy Endymion led a passive existence on Mount Latmos until Selene, the Full-Moon Mother, embraced him. Inspired by her magic touch, he began to dream of noble thoughts and deeds. Again, in one of the Nile legends the river is a male spirit that flows between two banks represented by a goddess. She stands with outstretched arms, as though begging for the water to come and fertilize her. But the mighty river swelled and flowed only when Isis let fall her tears of mourning for Osiris, the Nile god. The goddess had to make the wailing and the weeping that always brings about the rebirth.

In a hymn of remarkable vigor, Indrānī, one of the Seven Mothers in India, chanted the dogma of her superiority over her husband: "I am the banner and the head, a mighty arbitress am I! I am victorious and my Lord shall be submissive to my will. I am victorious o'er my Lord, my song of triumph is supreme." [1]

The women theologians did not generally assume that even a goddess could create the world without a mate. The oldest company of Egyptian deities consisted of four pairs of consorts with equal powers. Throughout Egyptian history most of the well-known gods had their female counterparts functioning in exactly the same way. The old Babylonian creation myth told of the primeval ocean flood containing male and female elements. Oriental gods still have their *sakti*—their female half without whom they would be powerless.

As mother, the goddess could compel rebirth. Rites for the rebirth were the most important features of early cults, and in them emphasis was placed on women's attitudes rather than on men's. Ishtar rejuvenated her son Tammuz by holding him on her knees. Demeter displayed an ear of corn as the symbol of power to bring about rebirth. The woman's power of self-sacrifice for the sake of others, the mother's authority in regeneration is beautifully expressed in the story of the rebirth of Osiris. This popular Egyptian god, who personified the life-giving river Nile, was murdered by Set, the Typhoon, and cut into fourteen pieces as a symbol of the waning moon, which takes that number of nights to disappear from the sky. His mate, Isis, Creatrix of Green Things, determined to save his life. Alone and exhausted almost to the point of death, she persevered until she had found the scattered pieces of his body. Nūt, the Sky Mother, united and regenerated the dead god. "She gives to thee thy head and thy legs, she joins the limbs together, and replaces thy heart in thy body." [2] Then Isis conceived by Osiris and bore the child Horus. Without her persistence in the face of dire distress and her overpowering love, life on earth might have remained dormant— symbolically speaking—forever.

Of all the goddess-mothers, Isis was the greatest, just as Ishtar was the greatest of all goddesses of sex. In her the idea of mother love was sublimated into an altruistic, civilizing force capable of leading men and women to a higher level of intelligent living. Springing from other earlier mother-spirits of the preliterate age, she was more widely worshiped in Egypt by both women and men than any other goddess there. She survived until the sixth century A.D., spreading her influence in Greece and Rome. An old Greek inscription shows the reverence accorded her in magnificent terms:

I am Isis, mistress of every land; I laid down laws for mankind and ordained things that no one may change; I am she who governs Sirius the Dog-Star; I am she who is called divine among women; I divided the earth from the heaven; I made manifest the paths of the stars; I prescribed the course of the sun and the moon; I found out the labours of the sea; I made justice mighty. I burdened woman with the newborn babe in the tenth month; I ordained that parents should be believed by their children; I put an end to cannibalism; I overthrew the sovereignty of tyrants; I compelled women to be believed by men; I made justice more mighty than gold or silver; I made virtue and vice to be distinguished by instinct. [3]

4.

The woman as mate evolves into the woman as mother. The woman as mother is a worker for her family, and as such she evolves into the presiding spirit of community work and welfare. There were many women spirits in all parts of the ancient world who reflected women's work and activities as extensions of the functions of motherhood. There was Ishtar, the potter; Neït, the weaver; the spinning and singing Fates; Athene, worker in the art and crafts of civilized life. Innanna, the great Sumerian mother and goddess came to the aid of women in childbirth with the words: "Maiden of the place of begetting am I; in the home where the mother gives birth, a protecting shadow am I!" [4] Many goddesses had the power of healing and carried the magic wand entwined with serpents later held by Aesculapius. Egyptian Taweret, called The Great One, presided over family affairs and symbolized ancient woman's authority in the home—the focal point for bringing life and for making music.

The most remarkable example of the way the ancients were thinking out the relation between private home and community was to be found in the impersonation and functions of the goddess Hestia in Greece and of Vesta in Rome. Since primitive women today are generally the keepers of a perpetual fire, these goddesses probably symbolized a very old association of woman with authority over the hearth. Hestia and Vesta were the guardians of the hearth in its twofold aspect, as symbol of the internal unity of the family and of hospitality to the stranger. As impersonations of hospitality, they were hostesses of suppliants and fugitives who might invoke the sacredness of the family hearth where they had taken refuge and so be protected. Hestia's home was in the prytaneum, where a fire, representing the common hearth for the whole city, was kept ever going. Colonists traveling from the city to settle elsewhere received a coal from the fire, as symbol of the continuity of life in their new home with that in their old. Similarly the Roman Vesta, a very ancient goddess, became an important state deity whose vestal virgins guarded the sacred fire and the Sybilline books with their treasured secrets of the way to live.

The Greeks expressed their sense of the communal importance of woman's work and authority by adopting a specific goddess as the guardian of a city. Of these personifications of woman as worker and manager, the most complete and authoritative is that of Athene, guardian of Athens. In this noble figure was concentrated the highest qualities of the feminine personality as shown in work and public leadership. She was the goddess of the pure ether, the dawn and the twilight, and goddess, in her moments of righteous wrath, of the thunder cloud and the lightening bolt. She was the guardian of women's arts and industries, protector of family and community life. As guardian of peaceful industry, Athene was goddess of peace. But to ensure peace she would go to war, resolutely and thoughtfully. In war she was goddess of counsel and prudent strategy as opposed to her reckless brother Ares, who represented brute courage and violence. The heroes like Odysseus whom she led and protected were "wise." They used their heads. They exercised forethought, they strove to overcome brawn and violence with intelligence and management.

In the many statues of Athene power and benign authority seem to be guiding the hand of the artist in the molding of the noblest kind of feminine face, with its broad, open brow, candid, thoughtful eyes (which in the Greek statues were carefully painted in), and firm, kind, resolute mouth. She stands with helmet on her head, shield and lance in her hand, the leader of states, the supreme authority in civilized life, the sure, unruffled, unflinching guardian of all that is under her care.

Such authority as Athene wielded might even be conceived of as extending beyond private hearth and city hearth to the whole world and to the universe itself. As a mother weaves her children's clothes, Neït in Egypt wove the warp and woof of the world's fabric. The Fates (the Teutonic Norns) occupied their time in spinning. The threads they span and cut were the threads not of garments, but of life.

5.

As mate, mother, provider for the household through industry, and guardian of home and community hearths, the woman sang at the altar to invoke the universal life for the protection of lives under her care. So she was, by necessity of her motherhood, a musician. In every country of the ancient world, divine symbols represented women in their role as dancers, instrumental players, and especially as singers.

The dance had many feminine and few masculine impersonations. All nymphs, fairies, and forest mothers danced. In India the Apsaras were in perpetual motion. In Greece the Horae danced to mark the march of time. The Charites, the Horae, and the Graces—symbols of the bloom of youth—moved with measured steps under their own leader, Thalia. The Greeks portrayed religious dance as a matron.

In Crete the great Mother Rhea "invented" the steps that made the Cretan youth famous for centuries. In Egypt, Hat-hor was goddess of the moon and goddess of the dance.

Musical instruments were often the property of spirits and goddesses. A certain type of drum was sacred only to Sarasvati, giver of speech and music to humanity, but various types of drums, tambourines, and cymbals belonged to the company of deified musicians. The Bacchae always carried them, and Cybele, the All-Begetting Mother, beat a drum to mark the rhythm of life. Flutes were also played by the Bacchae and by many others. A legend tells that Athene invented the instrument that blew the breath of life. To Isis was attributed the invention of the sistrum, a glorified type of rattle. Lyres and harps of different types were associated with supernatural musicians, especially Artemis. In Persia the spirit of the harp was personified by Azada, whose music echoed the harmony of the spheres. (See Plate 46.)

Singing was the genius of goddesses. Each separate step in the making of magic song became deified. The wail, the cry of joy, the imitation of natural sounds all had feminine impersonation. Every type of song—incantation, epic, lament—had a special feminine spirit.

As a result of its constant use upon occasions of birth and rebirth, the wail received impersonation. Little figures of clay or marble, representing women as wailers and weepers, have been found in the graves and on the sarcophagi of many peoples. When her son Ruadan was born, the Celtic goddess Anu gave the first wail ever heard in Ireland. Ishtar wailed "like a woman in travail" in her effort to bring about the return of creative energy to the sleeping earth. Isis invented the wail and taught it to the women of her country as a magical device to bring about birth. The Great Wailer herself, accompanied by Nephthys, her sister, the Less Wailer; Neget, a goddess known as the crier; Nëït and Nūt, two of the Great Mothers; Selket, protectress of the dead; and two lesser deities, Ibwet and Tayet, stood in the temple of Hat-hor at Denderah in the room consecrated to lamentations, ready to wail the image of Osiris back to life.

Wail songs, or laments, were composed by many supernatural women. All nymphs, forest mothers, and other semidivine creatures sang laments. The sirens, as playmates of Persephone, goddess of death, personified death lamentations—incantations to bring about rebirth. But whenever sirens appeared upon tombstones, they were depicted as both lamenting and rejoicing. In the earliest times they assumed the form of bird-women, and as such may be relatives of Sírin and Alkonóst, the two Russian bird-women from whom came all laments and songs of joy. (See Plate 47.)

A link between fantastical bird-women and real women singers is the common myth of women turning into birds. In Greece there were two such legends. In one, Aedon killed her son by mistake and prayed to be turned into a bird. "Daughter of Pandareus, the brown bright nightingale," wrote the poet, "pours forth her full-voiced music, bewailing her child." [5] In the other myth, two sisters are turned into birds and bemoan their sorrows. Philomela became a swallow and Procne a nightingale. (Ovid twisted the names—probably on purpose, as Philomela is the prettier sound.) Both bird-sisters lament. Pausanias, always interested in the origin of myths, explained: "The tradition of the change into the nightingale and swallow is, I think, because these birds have a melancholy song like a lament." [6] The significance of Pausanias' interpretation is that neither he nor anyone else, apparently, thought it odd for a woman to be identified with a songbird when in reality only male birds sing.

The same association is found in Lithuania, where the verb "to cuckoo" signifies "to lament" and where the cuckoo is nearly always compared to a woman. The reason this identification did not seem incongruous is undoubtedly because the association of women with the singing of laments was so strong that the sex of the bird dwindled into unimportance. All mother-goddesses, too, sang the laments and the songs of rejoicing. In Egypt, Isis and her sister Nephthys composed the laments that became the models for both informal and formal dirges. In other countries the name of the mother is mentioned in the lament as the one who is mourning and rejoicing.

Other types of incantations—those for achieving any purpose—often assumed human guise. The singing Sirens, for example, could influence the behavior of people, animals, and even natural phenomena. They could inspire some men to great and noble deeds; they could lure others from their chosen pursuits and chain them fast. Only the Great Mothers surpassed them in the art of making incantations. Nearly every one had a subtitle such as "Lady of Incantations."

In the mythology of ancient Rome, the Carmentes were pesonifications of the fortune or luck of the mother in childbirth, but they were also projections of the incantations made by midwives, whose chief means of assistance at childbirth was music. The Carmentes got their name from the word *carmen,* meaning a charm, and incantation or song. *Carmen* is derived from the name of a real person, Carmenta or Nicostrata, an ancient poetess of Latium, who is said to have introduced religion, poetry, and agriculture. She seems to have been a prophetess, bard, and cult heroine. To us the translation of *carmen* is more familiar as "song" than as "magic formula for aid in childbirth." The shift from the original specific meaning to the more generic one must have resulted from the innumerable incantations or songs made through the ages by women for aid in childbirth.

Not only each separate department of music had a special goddess, but the art itself was generally given a feminine impersonation. As we have already seen, some of the very ancient goddesses combined music with their other life-giving functions. Hat-hor, Bastet, Sarasvati, Bhāratī, Innanna, Artemis, and the Muses were all identified with singing and dancing and the playing of certain instruments.

The Muses, at first only three in number, had names that indicated their business. One was called Invention, or She Who Invents the Words and Musical Phrases. Another was known simply as Song, or The One Who Sings. The third Muse answered to Memory, or She Who Remembers, an important quality in an age when song and story were passed orally from singer to singer. This one inherited her name, her faculty, and her function from her mother, Mnemosyne. One very old set of their names was Nete, Mese, and Hypate. These also signify the low, middle, and high tones in the Greek system of scales. Such designations would not have been associated with feminine spirits if an identity with music had not been intended. In the oldest depictions of the Muses, they stand with a woman leader, sometimes Mnemosyne, sometimes Athene, sometimes an unknown figure—possibly Artemis. Throughout their long history the Muses, from whose very name the word music is derived, kept their musical authority. Around Zeus's altar they alone chanted the epic of the world's origin. Thamyris, the bard, was struck blind for daring to challenge them in song. Even after Apollo had acquired the title "God of Music," he rarely dared appear without their encircling support.

Taking the music deities from many ancient countries as a whole, we can thus reconstruct a complete hierarchy of women whose prestige and authority survives to the present day in painting and in literature. Chief among them were the Great Mothers. They were surrounded by specialized deities of lesser rank. Then came groups like the Bacchae—the mothers who brought Dionysos to birth—various grades of Forest Mothers, Heroines, Nymphs, Seasons, Hours, Nereids, Graces, Apsaras, Gift-bringers of Plenty such as the Charites, Fates, Sirens, other bird-women, even witches. These creatures were eternally dancing, playing instruments, and singing. When male spirits are found in their ranks, they come as consorts. The Gandharvas, a group of Indian spirits, were husbands of the beautiful dancing Apsaras.

When and where the first of these spirits of women's music was projected is a mystery. Many of them appear as fully developed and powerful musicians in the earliest strata of literature. In India, there were Sarasvati and Bhāratī; in Egypt, Bastet and Hat-hor; in Sumer, Innanna. In Greece, the Muses belong to the oldest company—Artemis, too, has been traced to the most ancient times. With various attributes, she was widely worshiped long before her so-called brother Apollo entered the scene and usurped her authority in music. (See Plate 49.)

In the beginning, these oldest goddesses undoubtedly reflected the musical activities of real women. In later times, when primitive naïveté gave way to sophistication and to what is called learning, they often became glorified into abstractions. The Muses, their number augmented to three times three, came to represent wisdom and knowledge. Terpsichore, She who Loves to Dance, became the abstract choral dance. Calliope, the One who Loves to Sing, became abstract epic poetry; Euterpe became lyric poetry; Melpomene, tragedy; Erate, erotic poetry; Klio, the storyteller became history; and Urania, from She who Dwells in the Heavens, meaning the moon and the stars, became astronomy. From images of the waxing, full, and waning moon, Artemis, with Selene, Hekate, and the dancing nymphs became the symbols of harmony and order in the universe. Anahita, Aphrodite, and Venus, from being personifications of sexual love became symbols of life—and symbols of music.

From the historical point of view, the music goddesses as abstractions, although very grand and noble figures, have tended to obscure rather than to fortify the former association of women with music. It requires a mental effort to accept an image such as Urania, muse of astronomy. In our culture, women astronomers are too rare to warrant their idealization. But Urania as She who Dwells in the Heavens is readily comprehensible to anyone. It is less difficult to accept the Great Mother, creatrix and ruler, because in everyone's experience, there is somewhere a mother giving birth and managing a baby. But if we can recognize a real woman in a divine Mother, why can we not recognize a real musician in a divine Music-Maker? Only because, in our culture, women have not so distinguished themselves. Without being oversublimated, Calliope, the One who Loves to Sing, and Klio, the One who Tells Stories, are obvious enough as reflections of reality. To them and others of their kind we must turn for an understanding of the woman-musician's past. Divested of vague and visionary attributes, the goddess-musicians are historical evidence, revealing real musicians of high creative intelligence and power.

6.

A woman, by reason of her sex, is mate and mother, and in performing her functions as such evolves naturally into worker, community manager, and musician. But even so, she must remain a human soul, free, unenthralled to sex, an individual self, which is a single expression of humanity. This idea of the freedom of the self in womanhood was very precious to women of ancient times, over-burdened, as they tended to be, by work and maternity. The determination to keep some freedom is expressed in the secret societies, among women everywhere, for whose rites women escape from children and household to the hills.

The supreme example among goddesses of this ideal of free selfhood is Artemis. She represents at once the creative individual who meets life with a proud, positive attitude and the creative freedom of collective womanhood. Artemis, the Maid, had no mate; she was not a mother, and remained forever "virgin," that is, herself, reflecting the value placed by the ancients on womanhood as an independent spiritual power. Coming from societies in which women predominated in religious and musical life, and in which men musicians admitted their debt to women by wearing feminine costumes, Artemis carried the lyre, an old moon-cult female symbol. Until late in Greek history, Artemis Hegemonia (leader) or Artemis Hymnia accompanied the lyre-playing Apollo, who dressed and wore his hair like his mother, Leto, or his great sister. (See Plate 50.)

Artemis as the protector of all young things and guardian of wild life was the protector also of women against the too insistent demands of Aphrodite—of sex and childbearing. She was woman, free, fleet of foot, strong of limb, serene of soul, woman as a creature of nature, forever untamed, able to slip out of the grasp of any man and take herself on her swift feet to the hills. Nothing could bind her. In many Greek representations of her she stands with her robe girt up and her hair bound for swift movement, with a hind, symbol of all fleet-footed wild life, at her side, and bow and arrows in her hand, ready to shoot a dart at anyone who would stop her.

Today Artemis is often misrepresented as the goddess of chastity —a sterile title indeed for the great moon spirit. When Sappho sang about herself, "I am forever virgin," [7] she knew that Artemis was integrity, the self; the part of the individual soul that must preserve its independence or perish. And as such she received the sacrifices of many women of Sappho's age. Among the most inspiring of these votive offerings is the small ivory figurine of the triple moon goddess holding the torch of life for the lovely dancing Daughters of the Moon. (See frontispiece.)

7.

Mate, mother, worker, communal guardian, musician, and free soul—such was woman's picture of herself in the thousands of years in which she worked out her own idealizations of her own functions and sang freely at altars of her own building to the great goddesses and their hosts of spirit attendants. Mirrors of woman in her different natures, avatars of the strength that can alter—as the moon alters— and yet preserve the feminine core,[8] they also symbolized life in its many manifestations. What the natural woman was, what she did, became the highest object of religious devotion, and so idealized and universalized, became an ever revered inspiration to effort and invention.

Before these spirits, the holy hymn of an ancient faith was chanted. Worshiping nature's rhythmic laws and striving to keep in touch with the life force, which is beyond human comprehension, men and women set a spiritual value on woman's natural way. Men and women both lived according to the principle that woman is creative in body and spirit. In the independence and originality of the spirit of collective womanhood, which was and remains the glory of primitive religion, a woman may have faith and courage —and the heart—to sing. When Artemis strikes her lyre, she sings no man's composition, and lifts her eyes to no man's heaven. She sings for herself, out of the deepest truths she knows as a woman, in the reassuring and lovely splendor of the moon at its full.

THE DARK OF THE MOON

CHAPTER IX

THE TWILIGHT OF THE GODDESS

1.

ABOUT 500 B.C. there fell on these hopeful civilizations of our earth a kind of creeping blight. It did not come all at once, but slowly in a change here and a change there that may have seemed at first a great improvement in the organization of life or a correction of a local abuse. Indeed, the Chinese, who went further than any other people in carrying out the new ideas, say flatly that real civilization began at the moment when men determined to know who their own children were and to assume responsibility for their care and education. This was, indeed, a change for the better—or might have been for the better if more intelligence had been shown in carrying it out.

But the men, in taking over, did it crudely. Their idea of making sure that their children were their own was to shut the women up from the moment they could bear a child, out of sight and hearing and contact with any man but a predestined father. In China they achieved this in the end by so crippling the women that they could not move beyond their own homes and courtyards unless they were carried. The long slow process of foot-binding began in childhood and continued through years and years of torture. At puberty, shame and fear descended on the girl, for now she was really a menace to society. She must be watched with all eyes and barred with all bars.

How different from the customs of the mothers, even among very primitive tribes, with their incantations to the moon, their holy baths, torch races, songs, dances, and flowers! Primitive mothers sometimes put the girls through very trying ordeals. But behind these ordeals is the grand sense of destiny, the taking up of the women's burden with pride and congratulation, the initiation into the sense of oneness with all birth and being.

The new attitudes were formulated in the hard, clean-cut maxims of Confucius, which became the official religion of China and the foundation of its education. Confucius was a wise man. But he was also the world's worst prude. He thought it immoral for a man's coat and a woman's dress to hang side by side on pegs on a wall. No wonder that Mme Sun Yat-sen, the great wife of the great leader of modern China, says that if China is to live, Confucianism must go. Yet even in China there are indications of an earlier and better day, astonishing to one who knows the pruderies of Chinese life even now wherever it is not yet touched by the spirit of such women as Mme Sun Yat-sen.

What life in China was like just before Confucius became its law-giver one may guess from the lays of Che-king, which Confucius edited. These lays represent the ancient customs of country people. As among primitive people today, the men and women were like two separate tribes and had each their own functions and collective activities. The men were farmers, the women weavers, having learned the art of raising silk worms from the wife of Huang-ti. This separation is indicated in a Chinese legend in which two stellar deities represent the female weaver and the male ox driver. Between them spreads the milky way, the Celestial River.

But according to the legend, this Celestial River could be crossed once a year. So, also, the peasant girls and boys had a spring festival to relieve the hard, monotonous toil of daily life and to awaken in them the joy of living. In the province of Honan they used to have a celebration that was very different from anything allowed well-brought-up Chinese girls after Confucius reformed China for the benefit of men.

This great seasonal celebration was the time for social intercourse and the sanctioned hour for the young people to meet and mate. At the spring rites the girls first bathed in the life-giving river, then exchanged flowers with the boys and played games that suggested the flight of birds as they pursue each other seeking a mate. The boys and the girls challenged each other in song, the girls drawing from their own experience as they gave the invitation. Since they were accustomed to weave both plain and flowered material, they sang:

"In a flowered skirt, in a plain skirt—
In a flowered robe, in a plain robe—

"Come, sirs! Come sirs!
Take me in the chariot to your home!" [1]

The boys prepared their own mind for courtship by suggesting that spring was in the air:

"Withered leaves, withered leaves,
The wind comes to blow upon you."

The girls expressed their longing:

"Until I have seen my lord—
My restless heart, ah, how it beats—
But as soon as I am united to him,
Then my heart will be at peace." [2]

The two groups danced and sang in antiphonal choruses, each group having its own leader and each group bringing to the festival its own musical contribution.

In this primitive festival, the origin of the symbolic sacred marriage of so many ancient societies is suggested. What was at first in the childhood of humanity a natural way to sanction sex intercourse became dignified in many ancient societies into a formal religious ceremony performed as a symbolic act by kings and queens to bring health and wealth to their people.

2.

While China was thus "civilizing" itself, by repressing women's rites and music, a great change had already come over India. As we have seen, the early Aryan people there had worshiped a trinity of great goddesses—Sarasvati, Bhāratī, and Ilā—who symbolized women's participation in both the religious rite and in music. At first the Aryan conquerors had held women in high esteem, and women had performed the sacrifices at the altars and had sung their hymns. It may be that the tendency to lock women up was intensified by the rabid color prejudices of the Aryans, who were determined not to mingle their blood with the darker native race, a prejudice that also created the great evils of the caste system. However this may be, Indian women fell under the blight of a peculiarly fanatical male fear of their sex.

Even before the spirit of Confucius froze down upon the early naturalness and joy of China, an old pedant named Manu in India had decided to put the singing women in their place and let man take over and perform the sacrifices, including those that women had invented out of their own intimate and unique faith as child-bearers and life bearers. Manu's regulations said, among other things: "No act is to be done according to her own will by a young girl, a young woman, or even by an old woman, though in their own houses. In her childhood, a girl should be under the will her father; in her youth, of her husband; her husband being dead, of her sons; a woman should never enjoy her own will. . . . Though of bad conduct or debauched, or even devoid of good qualities, a husband must always be worshiped like a god by a good wife." [3] This attempt to silence women was followed by a resolve to curse her very nature. Manu insisted upon woman's intrinsic wickedness. She was spiritually inferior to man—identified with the Sudra, the lowest order of life, akin to brute beasts. She must not participate in religious ceremonies, she must not study the sacred books, she must not even hear them read. Manu announced: "No religious ceremony for women should be accompanied by mantras (except marriage)—with these words the rule of right is fixed; for women being weak creatures and having no share in the mantras, are falsehood itself. So stands the law." [4]

Among the Brahmans, then, women ceased to function as a beneficent power. Although some of the goddesses survived in Hindu theology, woman as a living creature became associated with insignificance and even with evil. She existed merely to serve her husband and to bear the son who alone could open for the father the door of eternal life. Her marriage meant not a fulfillment of her individuality, but a sacrifice of herself even to the point of ending her own life when her lord died. This absorption of her personality into another's was reflected in a famous epic sung by women while grinding corn at the hand mill. Innumerable verses describe how Basti Singh's wife was wooed by a dishonorable brother-in-law who had murdered her husband; how the wife pretended to submit in order to ensure a proper burial for her husband; how, when she saw his corpse, her purity ignited the funeral pyre and burned not only the dead body but herself as well.

Manu's law for women resulted in the erection of a barrier between women and music entirely different from the taboos existing in the primitive tribes. There the barriers consist of local taboos upon special activities and almost never a denial of ability. Manu's barrier was different, too, from the limitations placed upon women by the Egyptians. In Egypt, woman and her goddess were always regarded as a dynamic and a beneficent influence, indispensable to the common weal. But the Brahmans established a theory that woman was not merely insignificant in the scheme of life but was actually a malignant force. Here was the sinister threat to self-reverence, to dignity, and to integrity of spirit. Here was a body blow to the principle that feminine urges are a dynamic power for advancing civilization. This took away from women the expectation that they would collectively develop their confidence in their powers and in their importance as a beneficent influence on humanity, backed by a sincere and universal respect by men for them as such. No one with such a handicap can become a creative musician.

3.

The threat to women musicians gathered tremendous momentum in the religious ideas of the Jews. Their history, as it concerns the relation of women to the life of the spirit, is strikingly similar to that of the Brahmans.

The Jews of the Biblical age had inherited some of their beliefs from the ancient Sumerians, who were worshipers of moon deities and especially of Ishtar and her son Tammuz. Other ideas and customs came to the Jews from the Hittites, also a goddess-worshiping people who identified Ishtar with the sun. Still other traditions came from the nomad tribes who wandered with their flocks and herds around the Arabian desert, slowly drifting into Palestine. In the very early days of this migration—about 3000 B.C.—the god of the Hebrews was Yahveh. Like so many other deities of that period, Yahveh was man-woman together. In some tribes he was male with a wife called Anat.

The women of these tribes displayed a strength that corresponded to the woman power represented in the male-female deity. In the oldest part of the Bible, women appear as chieftains, judges, and magicians. Deborah was a prophetess and a judge in Israel. She also possessed magic powers, as Barak well knew. When Deborah commanded the warrior to go against Sisera, the Canaanite, Barak refused to go unless she went with him and lent him the authority of her presence. The oldest existing fragment of Hebrew literature tells of the murder of the enemy of Jael and finally of Deborah's song of triumph.

> "Hear, O ye kings; give ear, O ye princes;
> I, even I, will sing unto the Lord:
> I will sing praise to the Lord God of Israel." [5]

Although the whole hymn is clearly Deborah's, there are some verses that seem to have been chanted antiphonally. Possibly Deborah led her rejoicing women and Barak led his warriors:

> "Awake, awake, Deborah, awake, awake, utter a song!"

To which the reply is:

> "Arise, Barak, and lead thy captivity captive."

And one chorus sang:

> "At her feet he bowed, he fell, he lay down."

Answered by the other:

> "Where he bowed, there he fell down dead." [6]

The chorus was a medium through which the patriotism of the entire tribe could flow. As long as the Jews continued to be a nation of warriors, women were expected to rejoice over victories collectively with their own leaders. When Moses and Aaron led the Hebrews out of Egypt and when the hosts of Pharaoh were drowned in the Red Sea, their sister Miriam, as prophetess and leader of the women, "took a timbrel in her hand; and all the women went out after her with timbrels and with dances." [7] And Miriam sang in triumph antiphonal response to the chorus of Moses and his men. "Sing ye to the Lord, for he hath triumphed gloriously; the horse and his rider hath he thrown into the sea." [8]

Years after Miriam we find Judith, with courage and craft, seducing and slaying Holofernes, captain of the invading Assyrians. On her return, and after the defeat of the enemy, all the women of Israel, in gratitude and thanksgiving, ran together to see Judith "and bless her, and made a dance among them for her . . . and she went before all the people in the dance, leading all the women: and all the men of Israel followed in their armour with garlands, and with songs in their mouths. . . . Then Judith began to sing this thanksgiving in all Israel, and all the people sang after her this song of praise. And Judith said, Begin unto my God with timbrels, sing unto my Lord with cymbals: tune unto him a new psalm: exalt him and call upon his name." [9]

Women's and girls' choruses are mentioned all through the Old Testament. Girl choirs, organized for the antiphonal singing of Psalms—such as Psalm 9—performed at public festivals. In this connection, the three daughters of a certain Levite priest are mentioned as being excellent musicians. Under King Solomon, an enthusiastic lover of music, the girl choirs performed in his second temple and also in his court orchestra. "I gat me men singers and women singers, and the delights of the sons of men as musical instruments, and that of all sorts." [10]

Like all other women of ancient times, Jewish women participated, as a matter of course, in religious ceremonies and in formal secular music. They also carried on their ancient rituals common to women the world over. Wailing to bring the rebirth was expected of them. The prophet Jeremiah called for the mourning women that they might come with their cunning and their knowledge. Sometimes to make their wailing more effective, they sat on drums— symbols of the rhythm of life. Dancing and singing, these natural musicians were creating, as they still are today, beautiful songs for christenings and weddings, for work and for play.

But as it was with the Brahmans, so with the Jews. Men's superior physical strength, necessarily emphasized and developed for aggressive warfare, began to dominate in the life of the spirit. Women gradually lost their prestige and authority. As the years passed, barriers between women and the affirmation of womanhood became firmly established. The ark—always like a ship, a symbol of the womb—remained the holy of holies for the Israelites, but it was guarded by men only. Women, excluded from the priesthood, were forbidden to enter the inner temple. The girl choirs did not sing in the most sacred place. Eventually, women became associated with spiritual inferiority and even with a definitely evil influence. In men's invention of the story of creation, the female was represented as having done humanity a gross disservice. Theologians could not deny that Eve possessed the secret of life and that Adam learned it only by receiving the apple (or pomegranate)—symbol of life and knowledge—from her. But they satisfied their craving for superiority by ordaining that Eve, instead of being reverenced for her power, should be humiliated for her audacity. Jewish men, to this day, thank God in public prayer that they are not born women.

No feminine attributes were mirrored in Jehovah, the fierce warrior God, who guaranteed never to change the rhythm of life. The numerous passages in the Bible alluding to Jehovah's unchanging character refer to the difference between him and the mother-goddesses of the moon cults, whose energy waxed and waned like that of the moon. The ancient practice of lamenting yearly for Tammuz, son of Ishtar, was branded as heresy. No wailing, no rejoicing with the Great Mother was to be tolerated. Much of Old Testament history deals with the struggles of the grim followers of the male warrior god Yahweh to keep their people from straying off to the more attractive altars of the kindlier feminine deities. There is no god but Yahweh, they said. All other idealizations of life, all personifications of the life force, were to be barred. If one could not lift one's soul in faith and adoration to this harsh, unforgiving, unchanging male, the soul must die. "For I the Lord thy God am a jealous God"—so spoke God to man and man to woman.

When women's rites did survive in formal religious ceremonies, men directed them. A good example is the rite of reintegration into normal life after the great experience of childbirth. Instead of being celebrated by women alone, as it always was among primitive people, it passed into the hands of men. The mother required "purification" by a priest.

Exclusion from the intellectual life of their times, exclusion from the spiritual life of men, identification with the unwanted, the undesirable, and the inferior, all contributed to the establishment of a diametrically opposed relation of men to music and of women to music.

Men had, in the male god, a symbol of their own sex; they had officials to perform their rites. They had, furthermore, the sanction of the group to regard their own activities, rites, and modes of expression as the proper expression for all the community. Women's divine images were banished with fire and sword, and women's rites revised or distorted into worship of the male god as the only God.

So Jewish men became the group expected to create the national literature and music. Jewish women did not lose their inherent power to express emotions in the language of music; but they were gradually excluded from the group preferred to make the important music of their times. Women's songs of joy and songs of sorrow ceased to have value for the religious leaders, ceased to be inscribed in the national annals. These leaders even said that for a woman to be seen with her hair uncovered was a disgrace, for a woman to sing verged on unchastity, and that the very hearing of a woman's voice was indecent.

Beginning with Ezekiel (26:113), the prophets warned women: "And I will cause the noise of thy songs to cease; and the sound of thy harps shall be no more heard." [11] And for many centuries the rabbis held to this murderous attitude. "Music in a house must bring that house to destruction." [12] As a consequence of such ideas, the artist singer did not perform solo songs in public from about 300 B.C. until long after 100 A.D., nor did the association of the natural strength and beauty of women's voices with seduction and lust lose force for many more centuries.

The fact that Jewish women had reached this low estate at the time of the birth of Christian culture has a direct bearing upon the relation of women to the music of our times. St. Paul, the first great doctrinaire of the early Christians, saw through Jewish eyes the immediate solution to many of the social problems of his times. It was largely Paul who took the lead in transmitting the prejudices of the ancient Jews toward women to the Christian world then in the making.

4.

In Greece the revolution was slow. Up until about 200 B.C. some women were attending the old colleges for priestesses and some were even organizing new colleges for the study of philosophy and music. Nevertheless, by about 400 B.C. Greek women were feeling the strong impact of male aggression in the institution of the state. School, church, art center, amusement place, and forum became integrated under one control, wholly masculine. Men cultivated a sex solidarity and favored men teachers, men religious officials, men artists, men dramatists and actors.

As a part of this usurpation of authority, men attempted to take over the art of healing, which like magic and music had always been, and is still subconsciously, regarded as an evidence of supernatural power. An Athenian decree, for example, forbade women to function as midwives. Since it was the prerogative of upper-class obstetricians to sing the hymn of exorcism that banished evil spirits from the presence of the mother and the newborn child, the decree, as far as it was observed, erected a barrier between women and an age-old incentive for the composition of incantations. Men were successful, too, in dominating the formal religious ceremony. Priests often took the place of priestesses and led the thiasos or congregation of women. Men took over the women's religious rites, gradually belittled the power of the mother-goddess, and altered the character of the rites to suit their own needs. They took over the training of the girl choirs and the task of composing music for the choirs to sing. We can see this shift, this transition going on; men taking over women's rites at first dressed like women. For example, at the great Pyanepsia, a food festival or bean feast in which the participants ate a common meal out of a common pot, the men porters dressed as women.

With the taking over of religious festivals—always accompanied by the mimetic rite and music—men removed from women's control the activity that had been since time immemorial the principal incentive for the development of musical imagination. Although women continued to practice rites and to sing religious music in organized choirs, their spiritual activity had but little significance for the group then in control. Even priests had lost some prestige, having defaulted in favor of philosophers and the now rising dramatists.

The most remarkable result of this taking over of the women's rites was the development, out of the choral dances of women's bacchantes at the festival of Dionysos, of the great art form of the Greek tragedy. The Greek tragedy is a choral drama built on the singing and dancing choruses of women. The collective reaction of these choral participants, their philosophical interpretations of each stage of the drama, and their invocations to the deities from time to time make the drama. The actual story of a Greek tragedy is slight. The participants are few and the whole is, from the point of view of modern dramatic technique, rather static. A Greek drama represents what would be only the last act of a modern play. All the preliminary material, all the emotional build-up for the dramatic action, is provided by the choruses. The subject matter is traditional and religious, representing a sophisticated secularization of themes, moral and philosophical concepts and stories, some of which were of immemorial antiquity in the women's rites, many of which had long before been given a finished art form in the women's rituals of Crete.

When men took over the whole basic material of the women's festivals, they made some remarkable changes. In the first place, they transformed them from religious rituals into great popular shows, performed not in the sacred place but on a large stadium. In the second place, they took them entirely out of women's hands, even though to do this, numbers of men performers had to dress as women, to cultivate women's voices and women's ways, and to sacrifice their own virile attributes to a silly feminization of their personalities. Men impersonated the women characters; only men and boys sang in the dramatic choruses. Outside of Athens, in small country communities, women may have participated, but in Athens they possibly did not even attend the performance.

In the third place, the writing of plays and preparations of choruses was thrown open to competition, from which the social seclusion and educational limitations imposed on Athenian women naturally barred them. Hundreds of men playwrights, artists, performers competed in putting on plays. The best were selected by the state and given a great public performance. Here, in the public performance before huge masses of nonparticipating spectators and in the intense competition in technical performance, is the characteristic form of much of modern musical and artistic production. It is in every respect a contrast to the original women's rituals on which Greek tragedy is based, performed often in secret, by women, in the sincere religious outpouring of feeling.

The fourth change the men made when they turned women's choral dances into tragedy is the most remarkable. As has been so often said, it was characteristic of women's sense of pain and sorrow that, while they made the most of it artistically with weeping and wailing, there is also implicit in every woman's ceremony the idea of rebirth. This, from time immemorial, had been the faith of women, the essence of their own observation of other living creatures.

The men who took over the choruses and gave them grandeur,

substance, and a kind of solid dignity had no perception whatever of the woman's faith, because they did not have the unique experience on which it is founded—the monthly cycle, pregnancy, and the supreme agony and triumph of childbirth. They saw the emotional effect of the wail songs and wished to keep it. They devoted a great deal of sound masculine logic to explaining the psychological value of a bath in sorrow. It was, said Aristotle, a form of emotional purification, a purgation of the two great fundamental emotions of terror and pity—terror of one's own fate, pity for that of others. But these men, for all their able and earnest efforts, missed the vital point in the women's sorrow—the hope and the intention of invoking the rebirth. There is no rebirth in Greek tragedy. There is really very little faith. Substantial, solid, and somber, the story moves to its climax in death or destruction.

All that remains in the handling by Greek tragic poets of the material they borrowed from the women's rites is the nobility of the women's characters. Many heroines appear in the dramas. Women characters in the great Greek plays are as numerous, as noble, and as intelligent as the men. They reflect the former power of the principle that female energy is creative and the traditional respect accorded it by the men and women of earlier times. Women's spiritual influence was still recent enough to be a suitable topic for the state players, but women themselves were excluded from this development of their ancient rites.

Sensitive men, who saw what was happening, felt that the stilling of women's voices might be the end of the true life of Greece. And so it actually proved. For after the great age of drama and art, which was the first flowering of men's taking over of women's rites, there was but little more inspiration. Euripides thought the women should not allow this usurpation. He even protested against the physical enforcement of chastity. It is deadly, he said, "to hold maids pure perforce."

"In them it lies, in their own hearts; no bawdy throng can soil the soul of her who knows no wrong!" [13]

He implied in *The Bacchae* that they might rise in their might and take back what was their own. One of the leaders of his rebelling Bacchantes sings:

> "With fierce joy I rejoice,
>   Child of a savage shore;

For the chains of my prison are broken, amid the dread
　　where I cowered of yore!" [14]

And he represents the maidens as singing their lament and their protest for what men have done to the great inheritance of Greece. The
women who have broken the chains with which men are trying to
bind them sing as they fly ahead of pursuing men and hounds:

"Will they ever come to me, ever again,
　　The long long dances,
On through the dark till the dim stars wane?
Shall I feel the dew on my throat, and the stream
Of wind in my hair? Shall our white feet gleam
　　In the dim expanses?" [15]

5.

As exemplified by the Chinese, Hindus, Jews, and Greeks—four
widely separated peoples of the ancient world—women's authority
for music making waned at the same time that it weakened for emphasizing her special way of life.

The primitive belief that woman's power to bring life was at least
as strong as man's gave way to an illogical exaggeration of man's
authority. A new theory was persuasively expressed by Aristotle to
the effect that *only* men transmitted the spark of life and that
women were merely incubators carrying the male seed. "The Father
alone is Creator; the Mother is but the Nurse." [16] He even taught
that woman was man in arrested development—a deficit of nature.

But in biological truth, it is the male who is the deficit. In the dis-
tribution of the great gift of life and life-giving, nature discriminates
against man in denying to him the high sense of destiny, the heroic
struggle of flesh and blood, the triumphant wresting of the new life
out of pain, followed by the joy and harmonious happiness of holding
the baby at the breast. Nothing in man's life can touch the ennobling
experience of bearing a child. For man, sex remains but a casual
matter, unless he shares the woman's responsibility for the offspring.

Woman's fundamental assumption for symbolic thinking has always rested upon a faith in herself as a creative being, pre-eminently
potent in the making of both children of the flesh and those of the
imagination. Accordingly, if she could not create life and if she were

inferior to men in nature's scheme, she had no purpose in performing rites which would enable her to transmit the strength of her sex to the community. Women collectively must have lost their primeval faith in their power to bring life or they would not have abandoned so many of their own religious ceremonies.

No one can deny that it was a great advance in civilization when men began to challenge women's natural monopoly of the higher values of sex, of the child, and of the home. There is no substitute for the permanent marriage tie or for a father's leadership over children. But when men, in their laudable determination to establish paternity and to know who their own children were, started shaming girls and locking them up at puberty and when men undertook to manage women's secret rites for them, they trespassed on holy ground.

This sin by men is poignantly expressed in a Persian myth about the beautiful Azada, Spirit of the Harp. As the favorite singer of Prince Bahram Gur, she often accompanied him to the hunt. One day, she taunted him for his cruelty to animals. He, riding his camel —symbol of unbridled male energy—turned upon her. In the vanity of his superior physical strength he killed her, though he loved her and needed her.

In real life, men's unbridled energy wounded women to the quick. For the mother-musician, singing naturally in rituals of her own making, out of the fullness of her own vital experience, they substituted young boys, castrated males, and the courtesan.

The whole romantic love life of Athenian upper-class male society was transferred to boys, dressed in imitation of girls and idealized by the immature son of Aphrodite—the little Cupid. One does not have to go up any dark alleys and by-ways of historical research to discover this. The refined homosexuality of the Greeks, coincident with the taking over by men of women's rituals, choruses, music, and dancing, is written large in the Dialogues of Plato. There one can see exactly how it functioned to the last social detail. And in some of Plato's greatest passages on love and life, one can still feel it in all its decadence and utter ridiculousness.

The castrati, whose singing was later utilized for many centuries in the services of the Christian Church, carried to an equally morbid extreme the attempt to turn men into women for the purpose of singing religious music. As early as 1000 B.C. in Sumer, eunuchs known as "kali" substituted for priestesses. A result of this change in custom was that a god Lumha emerged as the patron musician of religious song and replaced the earlier goddess, "Singer of the magic ritual."

Wherever women as childbearers have been locked up at puberty and kept out of male social life, the musical and highly educated courtesan has flourished. In Japan she became the geisha. In China she is the singsong girl, hostess of the gaily decorated floating restaurants, the "flower boats" on the great Chinese rivers. In Greece she was the hetaera. In the great age of Greece, when the men were taking over the long tradition of women's musical rituals and stimulating them to their last magnificent flowering, Pericles' social establishment was managed by a famous hetaera, Aspasia. She entertained for him, made herself the center of musical, artistic, intellectual, and social life, and functioned socially as the wife of a statesman in America might do today.

In some respects the musical courtesan was the happiest survival of the free woman-musician of antiquity. She had a certain liberty, status, and inspiration to do well which women immured in homes completely lacked. As entertainers everywhere, and especially in the Orient, women retained and even developed a fine musical art of their own. But the courtesans were nevertheless artificial creatures. For motherhood in its full honor and glory was denied them. Children, if they had them, had no status. They were borne furtively, concealed if possible, and were at best a hindrance and inconvenience to women who were entertainers and musicians. Beautiful as the singing courtesan's music might be, intelligently as she might serve as the transmitter of the social and cultural traditions of her race, she could never bring music to the highest point of her culture because she was denied a normal relation to life.

It was only gradually that the serious consequences of women's altered value to civilization affected women musicians. Changes in religious and musical customs did not occur everywhere at the same time, nor did women suddenly lose their prestige in the religious ceremony. For a long time, also, even after the loss of their prestige, women continued to have a theoretical ritual function. With it went the right to participate actively in the sacrifices. This was because ritual generally hangs on long after the hierarchy which developed it has ceased to have influence. Women continued as priestesses in the temples but often under the leadership of men. Women continued to dance and to sing in groups and to play instruments but, more and more, men taught and led them. Women continued to hold hereditary offices but often were not trained sufficiently in current standards of musicianship to compete with men in creating new art forms. The lyric poetess appeared again in Rome, but the sources of her inspiration for creating new forms had by that time run dry. In both Greece and Rome, naturally talented girls who might have developed into creative artists settled down into being mere performers of men's music, mere instruments for men to play upon.

Finally, when the mother-musician became denuded of her musical heritage, wedding songs and laments—always women's greatest contribution to song—no longer appeared in the lists of new compositions. And it is an undeniable fact that the quality of music was vitiated for several centuries until men developed another idiom from an entirely different inspiration.

6.

Inevitably the question arises—why did so many people allow this spiritual mutilation of women to happen? As with all great religious and social upheavals, it was undoubtedly due to the converging influence of a large number of factors—many of them imponderable—no one of which could have been determinative by itself, but which in juxtaposition were irresistible.

One of the direct results of the revolution, and one which profoundly affected the relation of women to music, was the twilight of the goddess.

When the lyric poetess was silenced, Orpheus usurped the power of the Sirens. Apollo assumed the leadership of the Muses and took the lyre from Artemis. (See Plates 49 and 50.) Zeus became the lord over Hera—she who had had a longer past than he and had always been an independent deity. The Father of the Gods even took upon himself the functions of a mother and after having swallowed, or absorbed, a pregnant woman, gave birth to Athene from his forehead.

Not only did many of the powerful old goddesses become subservient to the gods, but more than a few suffered degradation of character. Hera, for example, appeared in story after story as a quarrelsome and jealous wife instead of in her noble aspect as the reflection of woman's life span with its marked rhythm. Aphrodite, heiress of other older goddesses of sexual love and its higher values, once proudly displayed her natural body. In the later stages of Greek art she is depicted in an attitude of embarrassment and shame, trying to cover her female form with her hands. In the metamorphosis of Pandora, feminine strength became diverted into a menacing weakness. Originally one of Greece's great earth deities, giver of plenty and beneficence, she changed to a woman consumed with curiosity. With a child's mentality, she opened a chest and let out trouble and evil.

The Jews disposed of goddesses by simply ignoring them. Ishtar, one of those very powerful Semitic deities, became merged with various male divinities of near Eastern mythology. Hymns, formerly addressed to the Great Mother, later invoked the gods first.

Still more significant for us is the change in the text of an old Sumerian legend. In recently discovered tablets, a certain goddess is called Nin-ti. This name has a double meaning, as *tee* in Sumer meant both "rib" and "to make live." Nin-ti had been created—made to live—by the great goddess-mother to cure a pain in her son Enki's side caused by eating forbidden fruit. When this ancient paradise story was taken over by the Jews, they chose the title "Lady of the rib." In Hebrew the words "rib" and "to make live" have nothing in common. The legend then became transformed into the familiar Bible story—the lady became Eve, created by a god-father out of Adam's rib.[17]

From the psychology of the Jews came the omnipotent Father-God of our own religion today, with no daughter, no mate, and even no mother.

CHAPTER X

MARY

1.

AFTER the age of Pericles—with its drama, its beautiful architecture, its noble and lifelike sculpture, and its philosophy which rationalized the old popular myths—the real vitality of Greece rapidly declined.

The Greek states became involved in the long and exhausting Peloponnesian War. Finally they were organized in the fourth century by Aristotle's bright young pupil Prince Alexander of Macedon. He started on a career of conquest, in which he took under his rule practically the whole civilized world eastward as far as China, including Egypt and India. Everywhere he went, he carried Greek custom, language, and art. And everywhere he liberated the deities of the ancient world—such as Cybele, Isis, and Mithra, the Persian god of light—from their localities. When he brought these deities back to Greece, people enthusiastically grasped at variations of the principles of divinity and organized many religious associations for the worship of foreign gods and goddesses.

In these religious groups men and women banded together, ignoring ties of national or social rank, emphasizing the relation of the individual rather than the relation of the state to religious observance. The members themselves paid the expenses of the cult practices and allowed office bearers to serve in rotation. Greek women were always eager votaries of the new deities, and by taking a vital interest in the new art of proselytizing, they prepared the way for the missionary work of the early Christians, soon to make their appearance.

Meanwhile a new and powerful state was rising in the Italian peninsula, where some Greeks had settled and mixed with the Aryan-speaking peoples already there. They in turn had spread outward and eventually took over Greece as well as a good part of Alexander's eastern empire, adopting the Hellenized forms of Eastern religion along with much that was purely Greek. So at the beginning of the Christian era the ancient world was being ruled from Rome. Everywhere Roman engineers had built roads connecting different parts of the empire; everywhere Roman soldiers and governors were stationed and local customs of many sorts were being integrated under a universal, remarkably intelligent Roman law and political government.

Of religion the Romans were generally tolerant. The Romans intended to keep public order. But so long as public order was kept, they did not think what people believed or worshiped was of much significance one way or the other. So under the Roman aegis all sorts of religions flourished and some of the old goddess religions began to get a new lease on life.

Cybele, as the Magna Mater, had thousands of worshipers in Rome and in the Near East, the place of her origin. When the Persian god Mithra, with his secret rites for men, became popular, the women of a family served Cybele, the earth goddess of Phrygia. Shrines have been discovered showing a kind of combination cult of Mithra and Cybele. Romans knew that daughters of noble Phrygians who worshiped Cybele carried torches and tympani and wore the miter later associated with Christian bishops. A great Roman mother-goddess, representing food and fertility, the Bona Dea, received homage in a temple at the Porta Carmentalis, said to have been built in ages past by women's own hands. Her rites were celebrated by women alone in secret ceremonies. Isis, as the goddess who lighted the way of souls to the spirit world and who symbolized divine mother love, had many followers. Her attendants symbolically roused the goddess at matins, laid her to rest at vespers, mourned with her at the annual death of her son, rejoiced with her at his rebirth.

Many noblewomen in Rome and in the Roman provinces served as priestesses. Roman women, indeed, never lost the sacerdotal prestige they had inherited from their feminine forebears of the goddess age. Until the passing of Roman grandeur, the vestal virgins remained hallowed as guardians of the Sibylline books and of the sacred fire. In the goddess cults, it was the custom, too, for rites to be celebrated in the home at private altars. Every woman could offer sacrifice, burn incense, pour the libation, play instruments, dance, and sing magic formulas for all the rites of the life cycle. She could play the flute, double flute, lyre, zither, horn, and trumpet, especially at weddings and funerals. Accompanied often by hired female mourners (*praeficae*), she could participate in the important ceremony of waking the dead, she could sing the dirges (*nenia*) and make the gesture (*planctus*) appropriate for calling out to the deceased (*conclamatio*). She could carry on the immemorially old customs of primitive faith. (See Plates 51, 52, 53, and 54.)

2.

While the goddess cults were thus reviving, something much more momentous happened. In a small province of the Roman Empire, in what had formerly been the kingdom of Israel and Judea, an obscure young woman bore a child and laid him in a manger. He was born in Bethlehem in Judea, but he grew up in his mother's home town of Nazareth—which was a very different place from the grim, semiarid land around Jerusalem, dominated by the equally grim and arid male intellectualism of Jewish teachers and leaders, who were called Pharisees. Jesus grew up in the sweet garden land of Nazareth, where spring comes with a sudden mantling of fresh green grass and a burst of flowers, not far from the port of Haifa on the Mediterranean. All the winds of Greek and Oriental thought blew across Nazareth. Life was much pleasanter here than in Jerusalem and semi-desert Judea. So Jesus grew up in his mother's house with a clear-minded, sunny indifference to the Pharisees and the extremes of male intellectualism and dogmatism they represented. When he set out to challenge the Pharisees, in the three intense years of his ministry, they finally killed him. But not before he had become the representative of a great new hope for the human race.

When Mary brought the savior of mankind into the world, the majority of people in the Roman Empire were still imbued with the primitive religious idea of keeping in touch with the flow of all life. To this idea Jesus gave a new meaning. Jesus believed in a life force of which everyone was a part. To him, this life force was God, the Creator of the universe and of every living thing. He taught, "Thou shalt love the Lord thy God with all thy heart, and with all thy soul, and with all thy mind." [1] This, he said, was the "first and great commandment." Having identified himself with God, the Creator and the life force, he, being the son of God, told his followers that they, too, were one with him, saying: "I am the vine, ye are the branches." [2] By using imagery to which the people of those times were accustomed, Jesus showed that he did not belittle the old beliefs or deny their validity. His criticisms were directed only against the Jewish scribes and Pharisees, "hypocrites," caring for the dead letter of the law and overemphasizing the dogmas of the priests.

The superlative contribution of Jesus was what he added to the old idea of keeping in touch with the life force—of "loving God." He introduced a new idea associated with that force. He taught that human beings—children of God—were also to keep in touch with each other. They were to cultivate a new and a more mature idea of what the ethics of human relations should be. "Thou shalt love thy neighbor as thyself." This, said Jesus, was the second great commandment—to have a dynamic sympathy for one's struggling fellow creatures. In this ideal is inherent a faith as dynamic and as enduring as the old ideal of unity with a higher power. The principle of keeping strong a bond of love among human beings of different races is as independent of dogmas and as widely applicable as the principle of keeping in touch with the flow of life. Each age, every people can use whatever symbols correspond to the thinking of its age and of its people. And so can each group shift to new application as events change. In the beginning, under the direct rays of Jesus' magnetic personality, the validity of that ideal must have been understood by his followers. Otherwise they would not have been believers and would not have gone out into the world as a great civilizing force.

Jesus' two commandments were both compatible with the life of women's spirit. Women had always been conspicuously active in the cults of the life cycle. Women had always been active in the cultivation of unselfish human relations. It has often been admitted that mother love is the basis of all altruism. And goddesses, symbolizing mother love, had been worshiped by both men and women aeons before Jesus called his Father the God of Love. Jesus' nature itself had none of the overmasculine characteristics, such as physical strength and aggressiveness. Rather it reflected qualities common to civilizing motives in both men and women. Jesus clearly intended his commandments to be accepted by both sexes. He never intimated in any way that he considered woman less able than man to understand his message. In the Gospels and in the other traditions, Mary Magdalene is represented as excelling all the disciples in her understanding of the life of the spirit.

Throughout the period of his life on earth, Jesus was surrounded by women. A mother bore and nurtured him. Women were his friends and disciples. Almost five hundred years later, Bishop Cyril of Alexandria wrote about seven Marys—Magdalene among them— who were the intimate companions of Jesus. Mary and Martha, the sisters of Gospel fame, have long been regarded as symbols of many women followers. Martha represents the woman who is interested in the practical details of fostering life. Mary reflects the ever present longing in women for spiritual development. In this symbolism the intense natural spirituality of women has been emphasized.

Women followed Jesus to Calvary, bewailing and lamenting in anticipation of their Lord's death. His mother watched him die, and according to the custom of her people, made her own lament:

> "My Lord, my son, where has the beauty
> of thy form sunk? How shall I endure
> to see thee suffering such things?
> For this I weep, my son, because thou
> sufferest unjustly, because the lawless
> Jews have delivered thee to a bitter
> death. Without thee, my son, what will
> become of me? How shall I live without
> thee? What sort of a life shall I spend?
> Where are thy disciples, who boasted
> that they would die with thee?
> Where are those healed by thee?
> How has no one been found to help thee?
> Bend down, O Cross, that I may embrace
> and kiss my son—
> Bend down, O Cross, I wish to throw
> my arms around my son.
> Bend down, O Cross, that I may bid farewell
> to my son like a mother." [3]

After Jesus' body had been placed in the sepulcher, Mary Magdalene, Mary the mother of Jesus, and Mary Salome went there to see whether the body had been properly cared for. Again the women acted according to custom and so were the first to see the risen Lord and to rejoice over his resurrection. At birth, in the intimate circle of friends, at death, and at the rebirth—at all of the rites of the life cycle—women were beside the Lord.

3.

Supreme among the women associated with Jesus was his mother, Mary. She was always held in great esteem by the first friends and disciples of Jesus. Women followed her all her life, saying: "We will not separate from thee, O Mary, blessed Mother, except through death." [4] The apostles revered her, too, and were at her bedside when she died, watching the women burn incense and listening to their laments. In this universal honor to Mary, the harsh and fearful barriers men had placed about her sex were quietly swept away. Joseph, as husband, became the woman's best friend, her shield against scandal, the first and most ardent believer in her divinely inspired mission. So the holy family, Joseph, Mary, and the child, emerged as a beautiful collective image, full of tenderness. It wanted only a daughter to make it complete.

The new religion of Jesus gathered into itself many of the beliefs of the old goddess cults. Although the first friends of Jesus—the first Christians—were of course Jews, worshipers of the great gods and goddesses of the countries visited by missionaries soon came to believe Jesus' message. Christians then became a larger group of people with very different religious backgrounds. Owing to the variations in race and in temperament, men and women could not avoid giving Jesus' parables different interpretation. Sects, or "heresies," as schools of thought were often called, developed in different localities, each one with its own idea of what Jesus had intended, each with its own version of a Christian religion.

In the days before Christ was born, one of the favorite attempts to represent the relative values of men and women was the personification of the life force as mother, with a young or male god, often but not always her son. The son-mother concept was the most appealing of these because it was the most readily understood by the human heart. It was natural that Mary, with her son, should step into the place prepared by these old popular beliefs. John of Damascus even spoke of Mary as "the soverign lady to whom the whole of creation has been made subject by her son."

Many early Christians saw in Mary another great goddess-mother. Among these were the Copts, who lived in Egypt and whose church was founded by St. Mark. A statue of a woman holding a child has been recovered from that region. It is so like the old Egyptian representations of Isis holding Horus that one can see in it the eternal theme of mother and child. In the Coptic spell known as the "Prayer of the Virgin," Mary sings her own holy dogma in the attitude of affirmation familiar to the great mothers of earlier times: "I am Mariham, I am Maria, I am the Mother of the Life of the whole world!" [5]

A variation of the new thinking about man and woman was that of the Gnostics, who carried reverence for the beneficent power of women over from the old world to the new. They professed a belief in the union of a world mind (masculine) with a world soul (feminine). Since each principle represented resources that they assumed not to be possessed by the other, they thought that contact should be made with both. This is similar to saying that, to a satisfactory theology, a goddess is as important as a god. These people worshiped Sophia, divine mother, and her two daughters, who, as the spirit of wisdom, were represented by a dove, exactly like the old dove-goddess of Crete. The Gnostics also kept to the ancient way of expecting women to have official positions in the priesthood. Women and girls invoked Sophia in choral hymns:

"Thou Mother of Compassion, come—
Come, thou revealer of the Mysteries concealed!
Come, thou who art more ancient far than the five holy Limbs—
Mind, Thought, Reflection, Thinking, Reasoning.

"Come, thou who givest joy to all who are at one with Thee;
Come and commune with us in this thanksgiving (eucharist)
Which we are making in Thy name in this love-feast (agape)
To which we have assembled at Thy call!" [6]

A sect called the Marianites (also called Priscillians, Kollyridians, or Montanists) agreed with the Gnostics in deifying female power. Two prophetesses from Phrygia, Priscilla and Maximilla, had been among the founders of this sect. They came from the east with a legend that Priscilla had met Jesus in a mystic embrace by which she had been inoculated with a superior wisdom. From the scanty records that remain about the Marianites, women's authority and activity stand out with more force than in any other early Christian group. They, too, had a hymn that they sang at death in anticipation of the rebirth:

Grace goes with the round-dance,
I wish that the double flute might continue!
Let us all dance with all our hearts—Amen.

Whenever one dances the mourning dance!
Beat your breasts—Amen.[7]

The significance of these verses, entirely aside from the evidence
that instruments and dancing accompanied the singing, lies in the
word "grace," which was interpreted as meaning "mother," "regeneration," or "alleluia"—the ancient cry of joy for the rebirth. Somewhere the alleluia received an impersonation as a symbol of feminine
potency and appeared during the Middle Ages as a tangible object.
At the alleluiatic offices for Saturday in Septuagesima, it was buried
in the earth while a verse closely resembling the Marianites' hymn
was sung:

"Alleluia, joyful Mother,
Alleluia, voice of rebirth,"

to which a response, similar to the hymns of longing for Ishtar, was
given:

"Alleluia, while she is present, they
entertain her, and they greatly long
for her when she withdraws herself." [8]

To this day, the alleluia is never sung in the Roman Catholic Church
during Lent, the time of mourning and waiting for the rebirth.

4.

In time the figure of Mary, who was replacing the old goddesses in
popular love, became the storm center of the battle between the
male intellectuals, who wanted to assert the dogma of exclusive
male supremacy in heaven, and the people, who wanted to feel that
they could open their hearts to a divine mother. The Jewish element
in Christianity was naturally opposed to a goddess-mother, since one
had been ignored by the Jews for centuries. So, also, was a certain
kind of Greek and Roman intellectual trained in the precepts of
Aristotle. Sermons delivered to the congregation were frequently
devoted to a discussion of Mary's status. According to fifth-century
custom, the people applauded or hissed as the preacher pleased or

displeased them. When Dorotheus shouted, "If anyone says that Mary is Theotocos [Mother of God] let him be anathema," [9] the congregation made a great uproar in protest and stampeded out of the church.

Finally the popular determination to have Mary as the divine mother with Christ caused Bishop Nestorius to be brought up before a council of the Church at Ephesus in 431 on charges of detracting from the glory and sacredness of Mary. No more dramatic setting for a trial on such a charge could have been chosen than the city of Ephesus. For in Ephesus the worship of Artemis, under her Roman name of Diana, had flourished from of old. Here in Ephesus, Mary herself had died, according to one legend, and had been carried to heaven by choirs of singing angels.

The council was opened by Cyril of Alexandria, who made what we would call the keynote address. In terms long sacred to Artemis, he described Mary as both "virgin," or free and independent in her selfhood, and "mother." Through her as virgin and mother, he said, "Heaven triumphs; the angels are made glad, devils driven forth, the tempter overcome, and the falling creature raised up even to heaven." [10]

While the Church Fathers were thus debating, the crowds surging outside cried, "Hail, Mary, Mother and Virgin," as crowds in Ephesus had once surged and sung, "Great is Diana of the Ephesians." And when the judges determined to excommunicate Nestorius for his heresy in denying the glory of Mary, the crowds with a great uproar picked up the judges and carried them through the streets with torchlights flaring, incense floating in fragrant clouds. The whole city sprang into light and music with illumination and the cries of alleluia.

Elsewhere the controversy settled itself by merging a pagan goddess with Mary, and henceforth devoting to Mary, as mother, many of the old rites of rebirth and the women's symbols of birth. The union of Artemis as guardian of the crops with Mary as the blessed one who protects the harvest took place in the celebration of Mary's assumption into heaven on August 15, the day formerly dedicated to Artemis in Syria. Among the Celts whom Christian missionaries were converting, the moon goddess Bridget was transformed into Mary. The Celtic woman's festival, which had to do symbolically with sacred fires and the torch of life, became the Christian festival of

Candlemas, and was merged with the celebration of Mary's ritual purification after childbirth.

5.

With Mary thus established as queen of heaven, in the glory of the old moon goddess, there was a precedent for keeping lesser feminine spirits. More than one specialized goddess became a Christian saint; many pagan shrines on a holy mountain or beside a sacred spring became the site of a church or monastery; many feminine symbols of creative power endowed Christian edifices with holiness. The water of life became the holy water, and its container, which primitive women thought of as the womb, became the baptismal font. The old flower symbol, which had seemed to women to represent her own organs and the seat of her power as mother, became the rose window. There were rivers of life and trees of life in the new Christian symbolism—new images that were also as old as woman's faith in birth and rebirth. Without these, Christian art would have lacked much of its beauty. Without the alleluia, triumphant cry of women's ancient rites, Christian music would have been deprived of its most gracious song.

Women gave the new religion their goddess. They also gave it their rites. From the beginning, the old rites of the rebirth were of the very essence of the Christian ritual. None of the sects broke completely with the past and all of them adapted old rituals and familiar forms of music to the new Christian ideals. Of all the ceremonies of the early church, the most sacred and the most characteristic was the partaking of bread and wine—symbols of the body and blood of Christ, the tokens of the rebirth. From time immemorial, human mothers had offered their bodies and their blood in actual childbirth. Goddess-mothers had done the same in symbolic births of the fruits of the earth, of the new moon, or of the life-bringing child. Epiphanius, one of the early bishops (second century), tells of a prayer about the bread of life used by the Kollyridians, a sect that took its name from a loaf of coarse bread. The prayer was taken from one of the cults of Cybele, the Magna Mater: "Bread of Life, the eating of which brings immortality." [11]

Probably no primitive rite has been more closely associated with women than the one connected with grain or bread. Women, as

wielders of agricultural magic, had a long tradition of symbolic representations of feminine food bringers and also of ritual in honor of
the various grain goddesses. In Spain, women of the Marianite sect
held secret rites at which the eating of sacrificial bread, dedicated to
Mary, was the principal feature. Baskets filled with loaves of bread
featured in the annual grape festival at Aquileia and were carried by
certain elderly Christian women who had an official position in the
hierarchy of that sect. Old Russian sermons describe ritual meals
served by women for *Rod* and *Rojánizi*, a pair of words meaning
birth or race or family. *Rojánizi* means women in labor. Sometimes
the same rite was performed in honor of the Virgin Mary, who had
inherited the attributes of the old goddesses of the family cult.
"White bread and cheese were served, the goblets were filled with
wine or drinking honey, and the troparion to the Holy Virgin was
sung. Passing to each other the bread and wine, the women drank
and ate, thinking that they were praising the Holy Virgin and the
birth of mankind." [12]

But in addition to the traditional ritual of eating and drinking
symbolic sustenance, early Christian women had a real association of
feasting with Jesus. Nothing in the gospels bears a greater stamp of
human reality than the reports of the moments when Jesus sat down
at the table to break bread with his friends. At the home of Lazarus,
Mary and Martha were with him. His mother, Mary, was at the marriage of Cana. Gnostic Christians included women in the list of the
faithful who gathered at the last supper. Catacomb pictures show a
woman seated at the Lord's table.[13]

Many of the other primitive and pagan devices to bring about the
rebirth survived—incense, the holy water for baptism, the torch of
life in the guise of candles, the dance, the cry of joy as the alleluia,
musical instruments, and song in the form of incantations or litanies.
According to variations in practice among the different Christian
sects, many are used today with the intent of bringing about resurrection and spiritual regeneration.

In the early days, women participated fully in the rites of the rebirth. All Christian men and women were baptized, confirmed, and
given extreme unction at death. All communicants partook of the
sacrament. Women continued to officiate at times when devices for
the rebirth were needed with their old symbols of incense, lights, and
flowers. Mary burned incense when she visited the sepulcher, and so
did her women followers use the censer at her deathbed. Many other

references can be found relating to the burning of incense by women, enough to give the impression that its use was quite customary. In one of their formal ceremonies the Marianite women carried candles or torches to symbolize the light of the world, and the idea of women guarding the light of the world persisted for many centuries. The Brigittine nuns of the Middle Ages in Ireland kept the sacred fire of Kildare burning and evidently were the successors of priestesses who had been officials in a cult of Bridget, the moon goddess of the Celts. It was a general custom for women to wear flowers and to wave green branches at the rites of birth, marriage, death. Is it not still usual in most Christian churches for women to have charge of arranging flowers on the altar?

Just as the old power of the mother-goddess was transferred to Mary, so women retained in many places the positions as priestesses, officials, and musicians they had held in earlier days. The Arabian Christians counted a symbolic disciple, Helena, or Selene the moon goddess, among the chosen of Christ. The Gnostics recognized the three Marys—the mother, Salome, and Magdalene—as members of Christ's inner circle. Extant fragments of Gnostic literature reveal that women participated in the religious ceremonies of that group as representatives of the divine mother, just as the priestesses did of old. Some of the groups made women bishops. Some allowed women to baptize converts—the rite of the rebirth. Many recognized the prophetess. The four daughters of Philip the Evangelist were lauded by historians long after the first century, the era of their high activity, and the mantle of their age-old power fell finally upon the shoulders of the deaconess. The Arabian Christians appointed women as readers and chanters of the holy word. More than one sect must have invested women as regular priestesses, and in some places women as priestesses must have continued to function for many centuries. Otherwise, Roman women holding office in the ninth century could not have been visited by Alcuin and urged on by him to greater activity in preaching.

6.

The old religious associations of women, against which men as fathers of families had battled so long, both by passing laws against them and spreading scandals about them, were revived in associations of Christian women pledged to further the new religion. All accounts of early Christian activities agree that women's wholehearted espousal of the cause was a determining factor in enabling the first Christians, a mere handful of people, to survive in a hostile, military-minded world. Rich women were donors of wealth, of their houses, and of their time. They supported and comforted traveling missionaries. They distributed alms and nursed the sick. Women and girls startled the civilized world by their steadfastness to Christian ideals and by their ready consent to martyrdom.

Among these first Christians, organizations of dedicated women developed more than a century before monasteries for men were started. This was a natural outcome of women's priestly and ritualistic function. For centuries there had been organizations of women in attendance on the temple and generally vowed to chastity, at least for the period of their service. Immemorially old in women's religious life was the idea of escape from men and children for certain periods. Such escape involved, naturally, a period of release from the demands of sex. This was very different, in essence, from the lifelong vow of chastity later taken by women, for that was founded on an idea of her biological functioning that degraded women. But their earlier assumption of, or assertion of, their right to freedom in the service of the goddess, at least for periods, was an assertion of spiritual dignity.

The earliest known Christian leader in organizing girls was Thecla, who traveled with Paul as a missionary. About 50 A.D. she settled with a large following of women in the caves of a mountain near Seleucia, Syria. From beginnings such as these the great monastic system eventually developed.

Women and girls who voluntarily chose to develop the life of the spirit enjoyed a prestige comparable to that of the priestess. St. John Chrysostom estimated them as high above other women as the angels are higher than mortals. The word "nun," as such a woman came to be called, is a translation of *nonna,* which means "a holy person" and also "mother." Curiously enough, the masculine term *nonnus* was never used by the men celibates. They were called monks (*monazontes*). A fourth-century writer, Basileus, in describing Thecla and her followers, said that he could not enumerate the holy women of the first century without making a book as large as that of Hesiod. Over and over again, until late in the Middle Ages, nuns were credited with miraculous powers of healing and with prophetic vision. Many of them attained the rank of saint.

Aside from the purely religious reason of wishing to save their

souls, women were undoubtedly attracted to the monastic ideal by
the reverence to their persons. They found in monasticism a counter-
action to the growing tendency to exclude them from the governing
group. By joining the ranks of the select, they remained in the sacred
circle. Christian women by becoming nuns raised themselves from
the status of Jewish women. Apparently they were approaching the
status of the pagan priestess. Still another reason for the Christian
woman's support of asceticism was the practical advantage offered
her. In those turbulent times, the convents provided not only social
security for the timid but a career outside of marriage for the bold.
Women found scope for energy and talent, opportunity to cultivate
intellectual, spiritual, and especially musical tastes. It was here in
the convents, where women and girls assembled in the name of the
Lord, that they participated in the evolution of the ritual and music
of the new culture.

For this they surrendered the right in which primitive woman had
founded her sense of spiritual dignity—the right to bear a child.
They did this more easily because they were under a delusion almost
universal among early Christians—the idea that Christ would come
back to them shortly, in all his heavenly might, and they would all
be caught up with him into glory, where there is no marrying or giving in marriage, but male and female are "as the angels in heaven."

So women transferred from physical birth to spiritual rebirth their
sense of their mission as women. It was a hopeful beginning of what
was to prove ultimately a devitalization of their power as women.
But women were not to realize this for many centuries.

7.

In these early Christian centuries, in many places, dance and ritual
remained much as they had been in the mother's ancient religion.
Most of the Christian sects retained the religious dance with its long
social and artistic history. The Therapeutae, the Kollyridians, the
Marianites (also called Priscillians or Montanists), and the Gnostics
were groups who danced at ceremonies that were identical with
primitive and pagan ceremonies. The reborn disciples of the Marianites, a sect in which women had great influence, were united to
Jesus by means of performing a sacred dance called the Hymn of
Jesus (incorporated with the Leucian Second-Century collection of
Acts of John). A surviving form of this choral dance was performed

by village boys and girls in Cornwall up to a hundred years ago. Dancing to stimulate fertility was usual at weddings, at spring festivals, and at funerals. The custom of dancing at funerals was kept up by the Christian Bogomiles until the fourteenth century. Sarcophagi have been discovered in the south Slavic region of Bosnia showing dances in which men and women holding hands and singing dirges stepped backward instead of forward. That women participated in the religious dances of the first Christians until the fourth century is certain from St. Chrysostom's question: "If neither girls nor married women may dance, who then will dance?" He answered himself with the words: "No one." [14]

To all Christians, dance and song had the same significance that it had to the ancients and that it has for the primitives to this day. None of the early Church Fathers doubted the divine origin of music or its magic power. They thought that music affected the mind and pushed the will into action. "Without music, no discipline can be perfect," [15] said Isidore of Seville. And Theodoret attributed to music the faculty of changing the mood of the soul and of inducing any desired emotion.

Christians authorized the use of music to enhance the affective power of their rites and their prayers. At death, especially, they believed that the purpose of music was to lead the departed spirit to the grave and that music had a necromantic influence on the souls of the dead. In the beginning they naturally lacked original Christian music for these vital needs. Just as the ritual and the liturgy had to be developed, so did the appropriate music.

In its learned and studied aspect, music met Christianity chiefly in the great pagan cities like Rome, Alexandria, Edessa, Antioch, and Byzantium. These centers were inhabited by thousands of prosperous people, many of whom belonged to the most noble families of the pagan world. Music was an integral part of social and religious life and women were expected to be musicians. The Roman historian Pliny said of his wife, Calpurnia: "She takes my verses, sets them to music and sings them to the harp." [16] Lucian of Samosata, second century, described the musical customs of his times. The musicians he mentions are almost exclusively women, both amateur and professional. In developing their music, the early Christians of pagan origin could hardly avoid the woman musician. As we shall see presently, the most renowned of the choirs in the first centuries consisted of girls.

Early Christian annals are filled with references to the participation of women in music. The leaders clearly wished to utilize this musical talent to further Christian ideals. With the idea of binding music to Christian texts, many of them composed litanies, work songs, and hymns for women and girls to sing. The mother Mary herself was held up to them as an example: "None was found before her . . . more elegant in singing!" [17] Young people were taught to greet their father upon his home-coming by singing alleluia. Widows were "to sit at home, sing, pray, read, watch, and fast, and speak to God continually in songs and hymns." [18] St. Chrysostom exhorted fathers to sing daily with their wives and children: "I tell you this: that you should not only sing praises yourselves, but that you should also teach your wives and children to sing canticles, such as these psalms and hymns, while they are weaving and doing their work, and especially while they sit at meals." [19]

In the early church services, when men and women often had to meet secretly in underground catacombs to avoid detection by the authorities, and when the co-operation of women signified life to the sect, congregational singing was a feature of worship. Even among people of Jewish affiliation, the women evidently took part. Philo, the Jew (first century), gives a vivid description of the vigils of the Therapeutae, Jewish people who had become converted to Christianity.

The vigil is conducted on this wise. They all stand up in a crowd, and in the midst of the symposium first of all two choirs are formed, one of men, and one of women, and for each, one most honoured and skilled in song is chosen as a leader and director. Then they sing hymns composed to the praise of God, in many metres, and to various melodies, in one singing together in unison, and in another antiphonal harmonies, moving their hands in time and dancing; and being transported with divine enthusiasm, they perform one while lyric measures, and at another tragic plainsong, strophes and anti-strophes, as need requires. Then when each chorus, the men separately, and the women separately, had partaken of food by itself, as in the feasts of Bacchus, and quaffed the pure God-loving wine, they mingle together and become one choir out of two—the mimetic representation of that of yore standing on the shore of the Red Sea on account of the miracles wrought there. To this (the singing of the Son of Moses) the chorus of the male and female *Therapeutae* afforded a most perfect resemblance with its variant and concordant melodies; and the sharp searching tone of the women together with the baritone sound of the men effected a harmony both symphonious and altogether musical. Perfectly beautiful are their motions, perfectly beautiful their discourse; grave and solemn are these carollers; and the final aim of their motions, their discourse, and their choral dances is piety.[20]

During the fourth and fifth centuries many of the Church Fathers spoke of the congregational singing and of women's part in it. St. Jerome, St. Augustine, St. Zenobi, and St. Gregory of Naziana all praise the beautiful choral singing of women. St. Ambrose of Milan said: "The women sing the psalm well." [21] He was one of those bishops who exhorted the faithful to let antiphonal singing delight them, being particularly interested in the artistic effect that could be procured by using to musical advantage the different timbre of male and female voices—the men having a choir with their own leader and the women having a choir with a woman conductor. Singing at funerals was also often performed in the antiphonal manner, psalms having been substituted for pagan songs and instrumental music. Among the Marianites, men and women had separate choruses. In behalf of the departed soul, the women sang, "Lord, have mercy!" and the men responded, "Christ, have mercy!" Another favorite mode of group singing was the custom of having people give a response to the celebrant. In the Mozarabic rite, used principally in Spain, the Lord's Prayer was given in this way: "Our Father who art in Heaven"; the congregation would respond, "Amen," to this verse and to the three succeeding verses. After "Give us this day our daily bread," they chanted, "Which is God." To the celebrant's "And lead us not into temptation," the people voiced their appeal, "But deliver us from evil!" [22] Upon occasions when special invocations for mercy seem to be required, the amen to special prayers was repeated three hundred times, then two hundred, and finally one hundred. Evidently, there was no objection to the mixed group of singers, and women were eagerly solicited to enhance the affectiveness of congregational singing with their rich voices. In many Christian communities, men and women together chanted the Kyrie Eleison—the worshipers' own plea for mercy—and the Alleluia—their own hymn of praise.

From the middle of the second century, some of the church leaders sponsored the singing of women and girls in liturgical choirs. So proficient an instrument for furthering Christian ideals was at first highly valued, always, of course, with the understanding that Christian words and melodies be provided. Clement of Alexandria was one of the first leaders interested in establishing an official status for girl singers. He explained clearly how he intended to transform the old women's rituals into a Christian ceremony. "This is the mountain beloved of God . . . consecrated to dramas of the truth. . . . And there revel on it, not the Maenads, the sisters of Semele, the thunderstruck, but the daughters of God, the fair lambs who celebrate the holy rites of the word, raising a sober choral chant." [23]

The "sober choral chant" was raised as early as the year 150 by the girls of the Arian sect. Bardasanes and Harmonius made their church famous by the lovely singing of the young women, and drew thereby many converts. One of the most renowned of the girl choirs sang in the parish of Bishop Paul of Samosata. Leader of the sect known as Marcion, he had his headquarters at Antioch. The Marcions gave women a high status and allowed them to have positions of responsibility. During the second century, Antioch belonged to the kingdom of Zenobia, one of the masterful Arabian queens. Women there evidently enjoyed a liberty and independence similar to that of their queen. Elected to the office of prefect and president of the games that occurred there annually, they took an active part in social life. Antioch was a rich community, the home of some of the noblest people of pagan society. It was also filled with women musicians, both amateur and professional. Obviously, in order to satisfy the requirements of a musically cultured society the church choirs must have been the finest. They were formed of girls, both because women musicians abounded in Antioch and because the Marcion Christians sanctioned the woman musician.

Girl choirs are mentioned by Aetheria, a Galician lady who made a pilgrimage to the Church of the Holy Sepulchre in Jerusalem in 392. "Every day before cockcrow all the doors of the Church of the Resurrection are opened, and all the monks and virgins, as they call them here, go thither, and not they alone, but lay people also, both men and women, who desire to begin their vigil early. And from that hour to daybreak, hymns are said and psalms are sung responsively, and antiphons in like manner. . . ." [24] The practice of training women and girls to sing psalms is also referred to in other early documents.

By the fourth century a girl choir had become a well-established institution. Any group that did not have one fell behind in popularity.

The good Bishop Ephraem of Edessa in Syria frankly organized his "Daughters of the Convent" as a counterattraction to the Arian choirs that had been functioning successfully for three hundred years. An anonymous Syrian biographer described Ephraem's ardor in training his girls and mentioned the fact that he "arranged for them different kinds of songs." Besides singing odes and responses every morning, the "Daughters" often journeyed to the dwelling of a dead woman, even far away into the mountains. According to the Syrian custom of the times, they acted there as professional mourners.

In the Jewish Christian portion of that population today, women are still singing dirges and often go as trained groups—the *lattâmât* —to the house of the deceased. Sometimes there is a special solo singer, and after each verse of the *kauwâla's* dirge, the chorus utters its lamentation. In the country districts the trained choir of women is often absent, and the chorus is then made up of all the women, who form a ring around the tent. They are called the *reddâdât* or *neddâbât*—the sorrowing women who sing the response to the soloist.[25] The dirge sung by Ephraem's nuns was probably an adaptation of the Syrian poetess-musicians':

"Tears are in the eyes, in the ears are sounds of woes,
In the mouth is wailing, and sadness in the heart:
Comfort me, Oh Lord!
This day separates a woman from her house.
Her soul hath gone away, as Thy command hath decreed!
Behold, she hath become dust, as Thy command hath decreed!
Lord, make her live anew!" [26]

8.

In the early centuries of Christianity, when Mary was becoming established as queen of heaven, there is every indication that women participated more fully in the ritual and in the music of the various groups than they did in the period following the fourth century. In the beginning, they accompanied Jesus in close intimacy. Nor were their natural ways ever condemned by him. Consequently, women were welcomed by men as co-operators in establishing the struggling faith. Some groups gave women positions of authority. Women frequently celebrated secret rites in a manner similar to goddess worshipers. Evidence is not lacking that they were initiating their own rites, recasting their own music, and preparing in their own way for a renaissance.

In music, mothers joined in congregational singing. For about four hundred years nuns functioned as liturgical choirs in important churches, notably those in Edessa, Antioch, Jerusalem, and Alexandria. These choirs have been traced back to the second century and were regarded by many Christians as fitting instruments for the performance of sacred music.

The teachings of Jesus appeared to have arrested the threat of universal male dominance. Women were released by this touching new faith, which kept the best of their original religious practices while regenerating them and making them more simply and appealingly human. The idea of mother love, of women as the bearers of life and invokers of rebirth, could be insensibly transformed into Christ's definition of divine and human love and spiritual rebirth into life everlasting.

There was everything inherent in the ideals and practices of Jesus' immediate followers for the institution of a way of life patterned on the two great commandments. There was the Saviour, incorporating in his sublime person the noblest and most lovable characteristics of both men and women, symbolizing the rebirth from childhood into maturity, showing the way, the truth, and the life. There were the men and women believers, led by the mother, symbol as always of love and the good life. An organized theology, hierarchy, and system of rites with both male and female symbols and with men and women representatives of the divine symbols should have been the natural result of Christ's teaching and example, the normal way to interpret the new commandment of love and the new ideal for the rebirth of the spirit. And although the very first Christians were Jews, the worship of the Father-God of the Jews was from the beginning combined with the worship of the beloved son and his holy mother.

Above all, in the early days of Christianity the benign woman spirit began to live anew in the beautiful personality of Mary. The people of those times perceived that the ultimate life of the world is not exclusively or even predominantly male. No father, even a Father in heaven, can give all the heart craves. But Mary was not an old goddess revived. She was a unique spirit, with a place peculiarly her own in the love and memory of the earliest Christians. Independently of any attributes inherited from the goddesses of ancient times, Mary rose by virtue of her own power to be the symbol of the Christian virtues love and mercy. In medieval times she was regarded by men as the spirit that drew them irresistibly heavenward, by women as their special guardian, and by all as the chief mediator between sinners and divine mercy. Mary received the prayers of those who craved tolerance and love, the very qualities Jesus had sponsored and the very essence of the Christian ideal. Her authority rested on the human appreciation that these attributes are qualities native to women and that a feminine image of them is essential to a Christian way of life.

Theological edicts can settle a theoretical dispute but not a psychological reality. No theologians could destroy Mary. They could, however, and they did prevent Mary from securing for her women followers their normal function of representing her as priestesses and singers. For side by side with this promise of the resurrection of women's spirit and song there was, in early Christianity, another power working to imprison and degrade women. So the story must move on to the fateful end, in the so-called Dark Ages of Europe, when Artemis was at last completely gagged and bound.

CHAPTER XI

ARTEMIS BOUND

1.

"DAUGHTERS of Jerusalem, weep not for me, but weep for yourselves, and for your children. . . . For if they do these things in a green tree, what shall be done in the dry?" [1]

On his death march, Jesus turned to the wailing women with these pregnant words. Was he not presaging the tragedy that was to befall the Christian way? He had shown the people the way to rebirth—"death unto sin, rebirth unto righteousness." He had explained that the primitive child must mature into the civilized adult, into a new state of humanity in which tolerance and love for others were to be the controlling force. Far in advance of his time he had forecast the unity of male and female, pointing out that in the realm of the spirit, in "heaven," there would be no distinction of sex and implying an equality on earth in human ability to cultivate the life of the spirit. But already, as the heaviness of his mood indicates, he had sensed failure in drawing disciples into a unit sufficiently strong for the realization of his ideals.

From the beginning there had been dissensions in the ranks of Christians. Questions of doctrine having nothing to do with the principle of "death unto sin, rebirth unto righteousness," had interfered with the practical application of Jesus' ideals.

The most important of these barriers against the full flowering of Jesus' ideals arose from a misunderstanding of certain of Jesus' sayings. Men and women were firmly convinced that the end of the world was coming immediately. Judgment Day, with its system of rewards and punishments, they thought was close at hand. This belief led them to regard the material world as of no importance and to think of the spirit as separate from the body. On the ground that procreation was useless in view of the approaching end of the world and also that sex intercourse bound the body to the earth, they condemned both and set up an ideal of chastity and continence. Marriage between men and women was tolerated only of necessity for those who were less pure in heart. A real union with Christ was deemed possibly only by the chaste. The ideal was for the individual perfected soul, and for the whole church, to become the bride of Christ. Generally, people began to believe that no one could be truly holy without forsaking the natural urges to love and to reproduce life.

And so the ascetic ideal took root and quickly grew to fantastic proportions. Some devotees, in fanatical enthusiasm for mortifying the flesh, retired to caves in the mountains, ate only the minimum amount to sustain life, and denied themselves all human intercourse. A little later, others established communities and organized their lives for the rites, prayers, and music that were to save their souls. In the beginning, these enthusiasts were not interested in or moved by our ideas of Christian charity, which we have derived from Christ's second great commandment. They were concerned solely with a technique for gaining life everlasting.

Thus there was a split in the ranks of Christians. Only some took the vows of obedience to the antinatural way. The majority of men and women kept on mating and having children, but even they accepted as more holy the idea of the negation of life.

This morbid idea was woven into the warp and woof of early Christian thinking. Instead of birth being a holy thing, a symbol of the human being's share in the creative power of the universal life force and of humanity's link with all living things, it became a symbol of man's "fall from grace." Children henceforth were to be born "in sin," and "redeemed" only by the Church. Mothers, after this fall, must be "purified." One version of this idea is the foundation of the first great formulation of Christian thinking by an old bachelor of genius who, by his own account, had some chronic malady of the flesh, possibly epilepsy—the apostle Paul. Paul believed—as a rhymed version of this doctrine later put it—that "in Adam's fall, we sinned all." Adam had fallen because Eve gave him an apple (symbol of life and knowledge). Because of this "sin" of Adam's, all human beings are condemned and can be redeemed only by the grace of God through Christ. Out of this concept evolved the belief that the spirit could be enriched only by denying the flesh. Thence came the tendency to identify the female with the flesh and to call it low and ignoble. This sequence of ideas represents the spiritual catastrophe whose repercussions still influence our thinking and feeling about women.

The identification of women with the flesh was based, of course, on the obvious fact that women bear children. In their natural ways, women embody and symbolize the idea of a human tie with earth and nature. Always recognized by men of pre-Christian times as being the stronger manifestation of the life force, women were still recognized as such. But now the strength inherent in women was distorted into a weakness—worse than a weakness, a menace. Instead of opening the door to life, women, because of their association with physical birth, closed the door forever.

"Woman, thou art the gate of Hell—thou ought always to be dressed in mourning and in rags—thine eyes filled with tears of repentance to make men forget that thou art the destroyer of the race." [2] Tertullian's estimate of women forcibly illustrates a point of view held by certain second-century groups. The giver of mortal life became the withholder of the spiritual life, instead of the symbol for both, as in times past.

Woman's integrity and honor quivered in Clement of Alexandria's devastating blast: "Every woman ought to be filled with shame at the thought that she is a woman." [3] This was the inevitable result of the distorted idea that the living world is evil. And it proved to be the doom of the goddess. Sex was no longer a fateful and august force, to be exercised or not, in accordance with a woman's natural rhythm, as symbolized by the great goddess Ishtar. Motherhood was no longer a holy participation in the mystery of creation, allying all mothers with the creative power of the universe as represented by Isis. Virginity meant no longer the service of the inviolate personal self as represented by Artemis, free, courageous, and creative. Woman no longer had a self in this sense. Her inmost being as a woman was "evil."

2.

Theoretically, the period of early Christianity ended in 325, when the emperor Constantine recognized the faith of Jesus as the hope of the world. Practically, of course, the period of indecision and experimentation ended at an earlier date in some localities than in others. But eventually, the goddess and the principle that women are creative lost authority.

When Constantine, in 325, recognized Christianity as the official religion of the Roman Empire, the heresies were forced to combine and to declare a common creed. At that time the strongest group was dominated by antinatural views on life. To that group of leaders, who had always shown enmity to the interest of women, Christian affairs were entrusted. If at first one or two abbesses sat in their councils to determine the form and content of the organized church, women soon ceased to be represented in the governing body and allowed the new hierarchy to be formed without a recognition of their highest values.

The arbitrary laws of the theologians and not Jesus' love established the godhead. Contrary to the timeless female-male combinations, God became idealized in a trinity of male power—Father, Son, and Holy Ghost.

The word "god," which in Gothic and old Teutonic had been neuter, now became purely masculine with masculine pronouns. The Holy Ghost had a similar metamorphosis. Derived directly from the dove-goddess of antiquity, it had formerly signified a spiritual possession of women by the śakti, their own female life force. Although some of the very early Church Fathers taught that the Holy Ghost was the feminine principle in God, the later theologians neglected to emphasize the natural man-woman concept of a creative power. Eventually the Holy Ghost came to signify the spirit of love passing between the Father and the Son—the spirit that led to the incarnation. In pictures of the Anunciation the Dove is usually seen hovering over Mary's head, but it came to be associated, of course, with the male element in generation, and so the Holy Trinity materialized without a divine woman spirit.

The beautiful figure of Mary that was drawing into itself and regenerating the old popular faith in the goddess became in the teachings of the theologians something of an anomaly. In the conception of Mary as both mother and virgin, there was an opportunity to crystallize an idea that had run through much of the thinking of the creators of religious imagery in the pre-Christian era. This was the idea that a woman as "mother" might be "virgin"—that is, she need not be the helpless slave of sex in herself or in the male. She could accept motherhood as a holy responsibility, ally herself with universal mother power, and still retain a proud freedom of the spirit. "I am forever virgin" meant something much deeper and more universal than physical abstinence from sex intercourse.

This idea, after which Christian thinking has constantly groped through the centuries, might have been represented by Mary. It may be that it could have been formulated if women themselves had taken the initiative in a matter of which they should know something! But the thinking about Mary was checked and somewhat distorted by the conflicting idea that women were evil and motherhood a disgrace, and by the determination also to assert that a male God must be the one and only divine image to which humanity might look. The result, so far as the divinity of Mary was concerned, was a series of compromises.

The mother Mary was never a goddess in the same sense that God is a god, or in the same sense that the old mother-goddesses were superhuman. She was not a creator of life in her own right. Only God the Father was supposed to have created the Holy Child. The term "only begotten son" does not mean "this *one,* or *only* son." It means "alone-begotten," that is, begotten by the Father without any mate—a reversal of the emphasis upon the goddess-mother of an earlier age who, as "whole," "complete," *alone* created life. Mary was not even the counterpart of God, the role of the Great Mothers when they lost their original supremacy. She no longer possessed even half of the responsibility or honor for bringing to birth the Saviour, the deliverer of humanity. Mary the mother lost her active and primary part in creation. Although in picture after picture she wears the sky cape of azure blue bequeathed her by Cybele and Artemis, she sits beneath it as if it were the cover of the sky god. Humble and passive, as Christian women are supposed to be, she sings her new song: "Behold the handmaid of the Lord." [4]

Mary, as projected by the theologians, lacked the independent power of Cybele, Ishtar, Isis, and the other Great Mothers of the pagan faiths. On the other hand, she rose from the anonymity accorded women by the exaggerated Jewish patriarchy, in which the creating Father-God triumphed. A compromise was effected by recognizing her presence in the holy family. But in the family circle she was shorn not only of creative power but of the essential female attributes that made the old goddesses symbolize the normal woman. Her virginity, instead of meaning independent creative power—such as Artemis idealized—came to mean chastity and continence from sexual intercourse. Even the value of her motherhood was belittled. Bishop Epiphanius (second century) went so far as to maintain that the glorification of mothers was a morbid feminine sentiment—"silly and devoid of reason." [5] And St. Chrysostom (fourth century) also scorned motherhood as an ideal for women. He called only the chaste nuns "imitators of Mary." [6] The woman spirit of the Christians made no claim to represent the natural woman.

With no symbol for an active, creative womanhood, there was no need for a hierarchy of women. The oracles, seers, and prophetesses officially vanished. Of that group, the deaconess alone remained, with only a suggestion of mantic power surviving in her prayer of dedication. The priestess was demoted to nun. In 367, the forty-fourth canon of the Council of Laodicea contained the first formal limitation of the priestess' age-old sacerdotal functions:

"It is not fitting for women to draw near the altar nor to touch things which have been classed as the duty of men. . . ."

Measures to restrict women from exercising priestly power were extended to include the celebration of formal rites at home. In 392 the laity (men and women both) gave up the custom of sacrificing at private altars and performing other ritual acts that had, of course, preceded any organized church service by many centuries, and that had been the inspiration for so much of women's music. After the establishment of the orthodox church in 325, the formal funeral "wake" was transferred from home to church. The rulings affected women far more adversely than men, since women now could not become priestesses, whereas any man who wished could enter the priesthood.

By excluding women from the priesthood, the Church Fathers separated women from men. They allowed only men to be sponsors for the life of the spirit. They denied women a similar prerogative. Woman never received from organized Christianity her authorization to re-create the spirit according to her own feminine conception of Jesus' teaching. Christianity theoretically dedicated itself to a cultivation of the incorporeal quality of existence. It denied woman an official status of equal rank or value with man's in the quest for this spiritual existence. It thus closed the door to the state from which artistic imagination had formerly evolved.

The prohibition preventing women from entering fully into the life of the spirit was not merely a deterrant to activity. It went fur-

ther than a negation of power. It took a positive direction toward the
identification of women with the undesirable and the unwanted.
Without the slightest foundation of evidence in the Gospels, Mary
Magdalene—once regarded as the most spiritual of all the disciples,
the most sympathetic with Christ—came to be the personification
of carnality, the state despised by the Christians. She symbolized
sexual desire. And sexual desire itself, a re-creative power, was given
an evil, destructive significance.

In primitive religion, women had symbols signifying all of the
creative attributes of normal womanhood. Ishtar, for instance, reflected creative energy—that driving female urge to bring to birth.
She was the re-creating mate and the creating mother, giving both
physical and spiritual life. In the Christian religion, Mary the mother
and Mary Magdalene the spiritual friend were reduced to models of
the passive and the corporeal with no possibility of ever regaining
the active, noble, and spiritual forms of the great goddesses.

Not content with fixing the spiritual status of women for the future,
the Church Fathers turned to the past in order to obliterate every
trace of woman's soul at work. Churchmen displayed particular
animosity against women's poetry and music. As they tossed Sappho's musical poems into the flames, they manufactured the in-
famous reputation of the Lesbians. All priestesses, led by Bacchae—
the Mothers—became lewd and obscene. All free musicians became
branded as sirens of seduction.

Sections of written accounts of Christ's contacts with women were
methodically expurgated to suit the ideas of the ecclesiastical authorities. On the ground of inauthenticity, Mary's lament did not appear
in the New Testament. Even in the manuscripts omitted from the
Bible, falsifications in translation invariably tend to belittle the tremendous influence exerted by women in the early days of Christianity. Thekla's activity in the first century as a Christian teacher,
preacher, and baptizer of converts has vanished from the extant copy
of the *Acti Pauli et Theklae.* The account of the "Greek women of
honorable estate" in Macedonia who flocked to Christian standards
has been changed to read "men and women in considerable numbers." So flagrant and so numerous are these misrepresentations of
the truth that a modern historian has summarized them in accusing
words: "Christian writers, from Eusebius Bishop of Caesarea down-
wards began to enter into the domain of falsehood . . . And the
19th century has witnessed . . . the most senseless and shameless

attempts to re-establish ancient and modern fraud, falsehood, and nonsense, and pass it off as orthodoxy." [7]

Backed by the authority of the Emperor, the orthodox group undertook to disband the other sects and to destroy their records. Heretics were portrayed as immoral and undisciplined, outside the pale of sanctity. While undoubtedly Roman society had degenerated and while the aristocracy had fallen from their high estate of setting the fashion for noble conduct, still there were many groups of people who led normally good lives. The Marianites of Bordeaux in the early centuries of the Christian development were austere and dignified, very much like the Puritans of colonial America. They respected women and sanctioned the participation of women in the larger life of the community. Several women are recorded as doctors and as scholars. It was within this sect that Christian women conducted secret rites and took official part in the regular ceremonies. And yet no heresy has been censured more strongly by the orthodox Church Fathers than the Marianites. Because they—and many others —did not conform to the ideas of the orthodox group and especially because they admitted the creative power of women, they were condemned to annihilation.

While the integration of the Christian sects was progressing, the formal rites of the new church quickly adapted themselves to the ideals of the dominant group. The story of the Christian year unfolds like the mighty drama of life and death and rebirth so dear to the nature worshiper's mind, but this is a drama in which women play an inert instead of a dynamic role. There was every reason in tradition and history, every social and psychological reason, too, for giving women a part equal to that of men in the Christian story as developed in the seasonal rituals of the Church. But the power of a group of fanatical leaders was such that to this day women's symbolic participation consists almost wholly in their being adjuncts to men—now the possessors of the superior "mana."

By mimetic rite, by verbal description, by symbols, Christ's life on earth is rendered vivid to the worshipers. During the period of the shortest days of the year, his advent is longed for. With the first sign of the sun's renewed activity, Christ, as the light of the world, appears on Christmas Day. Then comes Epiphany, the manifestation of Christ, when the Wise Men bring their gifts. Later in the Church year is Lent, the period of repentence and mourning when Christ retreats to the wilderness. Then the entrance into Jerusalem and the last supper, the vigil at Gethsemane, the trial and condemnation. Good Friday is the day of death, the Crucifixion. The time between the death of Christ and his resurrection on Easter Day is three days and corresponds exactly to the time that the moon is invisible. As the moon god and goddess always resurrected themselves, so did the new light of the world rise on the third day from the dead. Easter signifies the rebirth. Ascension Day marks the miraculous translation of Christ into heaven, and Whitsuntide signifies the descent of the Holy Spirit as a comfort to mankind. Through the summer months, until Advent comes again, the Trinity is worshiped.

Although Mary has festivals given in her honor, the only one in which she has complete independence is the feast of her assumption into heaven. Otherwise, she is not the principal figure. In the rite of Christ's birth, celebrated as Christmas for the first time in 395, the focus of interest centers upon the Child of the Divine Father of Love, rather than upon the collective mothers whose self-sacrifice and effort had brought the longed-for Saviour into the world. In the rite of the Resurrection, interest revolves around the Son's transfiguration rather than upon the collective mothers who had made the rebirth possible and who had themselves experienced transfiguration in the process. In the rite of Pentecost—the descent of the Holy Ghost— the Holy Spirit becomes a symbol of the love between Father and Son. Mother love, or woman as a beneficent power, had representation only in the antinatural symbol of Mary. Even in the rite of the last supper women were forgotten, and according to the interpretation of Christian artists, only men received the symbol of rebirth from Christ's own hand. When even a nun went to receive Holy Communion—symbol of the initiation into the life of the spirit— she was not allowed to receive the sacrament in her bare hands as men did, on account of her inherent impurity (Council of Auxerre, 578).

3.

Women's own rites of the life cycle, which they had invented themselves to affirm the natural way peculiar to their sex, became altered to suit the Christian idea of life negation for the natural woman.

In the mothers' religions, puberty rites signified a crossing of the threshold to maturity. Girls prepared themselves physically and spiritually for mating and for motherhood. In the Christian religion, on the other hand, emphasis was placed upon a denial of natural functions, upon *chastity*. From the days of early Christianity until the sixteenth century, the state of marriage was theoretically despised and the state of continence dignified. Innumerable treatises, sermons, and letters upon the topic were addressed to girls. Voicing the long existing sentiment, the author of "Holy Maidenhood" in the thirteenth century called a wife the slave of the flesh, contrasting her with the free nun, who in his eyes was alone able to follow the spiritual way. But since the large majority of girls married, the precepts could not be followed and merely served the purpose of creating an irreconcilable emotional conflict in a normal girl's mind.

But however men may try to banish women and the image of the natural relation of woman to man from the human mind, it cannot be done. All that can be done is to offer an unnatural substitute. Just as homosexual love for young boys had been developed when the romantic love of young girls had been banished among the Greeks, just as castrated males or boys in women's dresses had to be substituted when women were banished from religious choirs, so when natural marriage was condemned or degraded to the position of an ignoble necessity, an unnatural marriage was substituted. The woman keeping herself from physical sex intercourse is dedicated to a rapturous union with Christ. In the Christian description of this marriage the most sensuous details are borrowed from the songs of earthly love and sex. Not so did Artemis assert, "I am forever virgin!"

An example of the transformation of women's wedding rites into Christian poetry was the hymn written by Methodius, bishop of Lycia, in 303, for the members of his flock. It was entitled "The Banquet of the Ten Virgins" or "Concerning Chastity." The style imitated the partheniads—songs for maidens—written by Alkman and Megolostrata for Spartan girls. Its theme was borrowed from women's wedding rites still used in Adrianople today, where it is the custom for a Jewish bride and her women companions to sit for hours in their wedding garments while waiting for the bridegroom. At last the cry is raised: "Behold, the bridegroom cometh!"

This hymn was written by Methodius to be sung by girls—an early example of the now prevalent custom for men to formulate what women think and feel about their most intimate personal lives, and women, parrot-like, to repeat the words in song.

So in singing this hymn, according to the statement in *Prolegom-*

ena de Poetis Christianis Graecis, girls impersonated Thekla, the
first virgin martyr, and others of the noble band. "We give the name
'Parthenion' [song of Virgins] to the hymn of Methodius because it
was sung by virgins. . . . The ten virgins are introduced after a
cheerful and modest repast, during which they discussed the merits
of inviolate virginity. Afterward, they all rose as though inspired
by a divine spirit and dedicated their lives to Christ as though to the
noblest spouse." [8] Thekla, named by Arete (Virtue) as the chief of
the virgins, sang the versicles of the virgins' song. The other virgins,
standing in a circle around her under the willow tree—symbol of
chastity—entoned the response. The hymn has twenty-four stanzas,
of which we give two:

Stanza

> The Bridegroom cometh! overhead
> The shout descending wakes the dead!
>   Go forth to meet the King,
>   The gates just entering!
>
> Virgins, white-robed, with lamps haste
>   eastward forth to meet him,
> Haste ye, O haste to greet him!

Response

> With holy feet, the lamps bright burning,
> I go to meet my Lord returning.

Stanza

> My home and country for Thy sake,
> And maiden dance, I did forsake,
>   And mother; pride and race,
>   And thoughts of rank and place;
> For Thou, O Christ the Word, are all in all to me;
>   I long for naught save Thee!

Response

> With holy feet, the lamps bright burning,
> I go to meet my Lord returning.[9]

When the ideal of marriage to the heavenly bridegroom was dramatized for nuns, something was offered them—morbid, silly, but a

kind of substitute for normal living. The greatest crime consisted in modeling the religious instructions for girls of marriageable age, who would normally become wives and mothers, upon the ideas of marriage to the heavenly bridegroom. Music as well as sermons impressed upon young minds the value of an unnatural mode of life. So was a Christian girl forced to repress her natural instincts or to accept the guilt of sin.

Marriage rites for goddess worshipers emphasized the holiness of sex relations and reproduction. Women played the major role, symbolically passing on the torch of life to their daughters and also impersonating a goddess in the rites of the sacred marriage. But in the Christian religion, the holiest thing in the world for women was not regarded as such. Marriage was not even made a sacrament by the Church until 1550. For fifteen hundred years, married women were held to the monastic ideal, being told that sexual intercourse was sinful. In one of the first-century documents, our Lord is made to assume the disguise of Judas Thomas and advises a young couple on their wedding night with these words: "Know that as soon as ye preserve yourself from this filthy intercourse, ye become pure temples, and are saved from afflictions manifest and hidden, and from the heavy care of children, the end of whom is bitter sorrow." [10]

Rites for a mother after childbirth have a particularly arresting history. As practiced in primitive tribes, they are ceremonies for reintegration into normal life conducted by women themselves. Among the Jews, these rites were conducted for women by priests—women being excluded from the priesthood—but the idea remained identical. The so-called "purification" was a ritual detachment of the mother from her close contact with the life force. No blame on the part of the women was suggested, rather a superholiness. Among the Christians, the rite of the "churching" of women, as well as that of presenting her newborn child to God, became completely distorted. A Christian mother was told that her child was born "in sin," that she herself had erred, that she required absolution. She was made to kneel outside the church and be "purified" before she could again share in common worship. Thus she was given a sense of guilt rather than a sense of fulfillment.

No rites were ever instituted in which fathers were required to apologize for their natural ways.

The godhead, the priesthood, the rites, and the liturgy as established by the Church Fathers during the fourth, fifth, and sixth centuries had the primary purpose of saving the souls of the cult members for life everlasting. The idea of salvation and resurrection was carried over from primitive and pagan religions. Although the Christians pretended to despise birth and the earth, they kept most of the primitive magic devices for bringing about birth and rebirth. Music especially was regarded as the same important magic it had always been.

In the performance of the formal rites, and even in the privacy of their homes, women were forbidden to touch the symbols that they themselves had invented. They could not burn incense or light the sacred fire symbolizing the light of the world. They could not watch the torch being plunged into the baptismal font—symbolic act of sex union. They could not even baptize their own babies with the holy water, symbol of the life-giving fluid surrounding the child in their own bodies. Pope Zacharias (741 A.D.) in interdicting the celebration of mass by an abbess, made a classic statement: "We were indignant to hear that a series of holy ceremonies were degraded by suffering women to read the Mass." [11] So the very touch of women, which had always been regarded as life-giving, became transformed into a contamination.

Let Mary stand at the bar of heaven and ask if any symbol of the rebirth could be degraded by a mother's touch!

From a disinterested point of view, the whole theory of woman's spiritual incapacity as depending upon her motherhood seems to have been a mass neurosis. The enormity of the accusation that a woman's touch could contaminate any symbol of birth or rebirth has been belittled by time and habit. To the modern mind, such men as Pope Zacharias appear as almost mythical characters who can be blown away like a phantom. But in the eighth century—indeed, until the eighteenth century—they were powerful realities and loomed like giants in establishing customs that denied women leadership in the Church and so in Christian music. And the effect of what they did survives in our culture today to a degree that should shock both men and women.

The participation of either men or women in the musical life of the newly forming Christian culture depended primarily, as it must in any age and among any people, upon the ideas of the group concerning the utility of music. Christians believed in the power of music. They sanctioned its use with the religious ceremony in order to enhance the affective quality of the rites and prayers. Music was held, however, within certain bounds prescribed by the ecclesiastical authorities.

The dance was absolutely forbidden and has never been reinstated in Christian worship. Dancing is too much associated with the body to permit its transformation into a purely incorporeal state. For several centuries the wail laments disappeared from choral literature intended for Church use. Laments were too actively associated with women to be divorced suddenly from their begetters. Instruments were probably allowed, but did not play an important part until later. Singing was the method employed to affect the deity. In melody to accompany the liturgical texts, Christian musical art developed.

There was a fierce struggle to suppress all singing outside of church and monastery. Religious canticles could be sung at home, but only those with Christian texts. Choral spring and love songs, wedding songs, and especially songs based upon the wail assumed a sinful character. When the bishops issued prohibitions against the choruses of men and women who were carrying on age-old customs of song and dance at the seasonal festivals, they alluded invariably to the character of the songs and dances as being "erotic," "obscene," "scurrilous," or "the Devil's songs." Bishop Caesarius of Arles (Sermo XIII) made the complaint in 542: "How many peasants and how many women know by heart and recite out loud the Devil's songs, erotic and obscene." [12]

Except for religious canticles in the home, song—Christian music —existed only in the churches and monasteries. At that time, no other institutions functioned. Because a woman could not enter religious institutions in honor without trailing with her the fancied dishonor attached to human birth, her performance of instrumental and vocal music fell into the same category of evil that she herself assumed.

Because prostitutes played instruments of music, Christian girls were never to play them. The great teacher Jerome wrote in his letter *Ad Laetam,* concerning the education of girls: "Let the maid of God be, as it were, deaf toward instruments. Let her not know why the flute, the lyre, and the zither have been made." [13] Basileus said that it was a pitiful sight for pious eyes to see a woman singing to the lyre instead of weaving. This attitude is taken by Arnobius, Commodian, Basil of Caesarea, and others. That the notion persisted is evinced by numerous medieval representations of the wise and foolish virgins in which the foolish ones hold musical instruments in their hands as an indication of their levity. Nothing was said about boys not playing instruments. It was not that girls were incapable of playing the cittern and the flute and the lyre; it was not that they played less skillfully or with less musicianship than boys; it was simply that the risk that their music might distract men—the chosen leaders for developing the life of the spirit—could not be taken. (See Plate 52.)

The liturgical choirs of girls, who had preceded the boy choirs, eventually became cloistered in their own monasteries and no longer served in the public churches.

Choirs of laywomen and girls, as well as of professional musicians, were absolutely forbidden. Congregational singing by women was also forbidden, even when they were in church with their families. The converted Jew St. Paul, imbued from childhood with a distrust of women, commanded them to be silent in church. A little later, Cyrillus of Jerusalem, also a bitter enemy of women, taught that they were to read and pray softly with the lips, without sound: "For I do not allow a woman to speak in church." [14] In the Didascalis of 318 the singing of women in church was forbidden; in the Council of Laodicea (367), congregational singing was abandoned and the musical portions of the service were placed in the hands of a trained choir of men and boys; in the Synod of Antioch (379), women were forbidden to join with men in chanting the Psalms. Mothers could not give their own thanksgiving for motherhood in imitation of Mary. Mothers could only listen to little boys or nuns singing the song of rejoicing for the birth of the Saviour. As already shown, such customs had at first only local authority, but they gradually came to be accepted as proper by the whole Christian body.

Professional women musicians submitted to regulations that practically prevented them from pursuing a musical career and remaining respected members of the Church. St. Chrysostom (fourth century) despised the professional mourners. "Anyone who hires these wretched women shall be excluded from the Church for a long time, like an idolater." [15] Bishop Hippolytus (fifth century) had the same feeling: "A woman who attracts people with her beautiful but deluding sweetness of voice (which is full of seduction to sin) must give up her trade and wait forty days if she is to receive communion. Then only may she receive the mysteries." [16]

Finally, the authority of several sects began to disapprove of the girl choirs unless the girls had taken the vow of chastity and had become nuns. Women and girls were expected to sing their religious canticles in humble tones or with a sexless quality like that of immature boys. The natural, rich, low-pitched voice of the mature woman was absolutely tabooed, and was not introduced as a vocal instrument for many centuries. The musical terms used now to designate vocal parts that are higher than the normal range of men's voices developed from men's usage, not women's. Soprano means *superius,* or the highest, no matter what the pitch. Its feminine form—never used —would be soprana. Alto means *altus,* or high—high for men. The form "alta" would be meaningless and never appeared. Neither term, soprano or alto, had originally anything whatever to do with women, and there is still no word for the woman's natural voice.

The training of little boys to sing the high vocal parts of Christian music was the beginning of a practice that has persisted to this day in the Church, and that perpetuated the morbid idea of the Greeks at the beginning of their decadence—that the innocence of young boys could be made a healthy substitute for the natural purity of girlhood. The whole conception symbolizes the movement to degrade the natural woman and to limit her opportunities to be a musician merely because she was a woman.

The Church Fathers themselves made an explanation and an excuse for their attitude. The charm of women, the appeal of their voices, and their whole emotional life as expressed in music had unfortunately been associated with a kind of ritual that in the fourth century had fallen from its former high estate. At various times it had been necessary to regulate the extremes of orgiastic worship associated with the old goddesses and with primitive religion. Exaggerated demonstrations of grief at funerals had fallen into this category. Early in the history of Athens, one of Solon's laws had forbidden citizens to hire more than ten professional mourners and flutists to perform music at funerals. And in 185 A.D. the Romans, usually tolerant of any religion, suppressed the order of the Bacchantes after women had held a three-day secret celebration that seems to have caused public protest. There had long been denunciations on the part of all decent people against the sexual orgies and other vulgar exhibitions of some of the aristocratic Romans. Music by women had always accompanied and stimulated the obscenities. A reaction to such excesses was both inevitable and healthy, to be regretted only because Christian leaders allowed the incurable human failing of immoderation to becloud the issue.

Despite their belief in the power of music as practiced by *men* to enoble character, the Church Fathers apparently never made any provisions for *women* (except as nuns) to integrate music with formal religious devotion or for women to take the lead in finding spiritual sustenance through Christian music. After about the fifth century, laywomen dropped out of the organized musical life of Christianity. The singing and dancing of peasants and of the noblewomen in their castles continued, as we shall see, in spite of and in successful revolt against the plans of the priesthood for the use of music. Whether women made any formal protest against the rulings that fixed their relation to music for a thousand years to come and more, whether they realized at the time the full extent of the repression, is unfortunately not recorded.

This movement reached its height as the whole civilized world was falling into decay. Just as the brief brilliant triumph of classical Greece in taking over women's rituals and music and in suppressing women's part in them was followed by the long slow decay of Greek creative talent, so now the triumph of the Church leaders in eliminating women from all authoritative participation in ritual and music coincided with the beginning of general social darkness in Europe. The Roman Empire fell. The old civilized life of the Mediterranean cities was overrun by barbarians, or decayed of itself. It was to be several centuries before the fresh energies of the still primitive and pagan north of Europe could become effective in reviving Western culture. Under such circumstances it was hard for women to unite and make a stand. Isolated as individuals and groups, amidst general social chaos, they had to make the best of things as they were.

The unfortunate thing is not that all this happened long ago. The unfortunate thing is that, fundamentally, it has not yet been undone.

When men departed from Jesus' way of love and tolerance, they broke with women and created a situation that has never ceased to be death-dealing to woman's imaginative faculty. The Church, which should have enabled the noblest men and the noblest women to seek spiritual regeneration for all humanity, became primarily an institution for men's point of view, men's imagery. From the fourth century to the twentieth, Church leaders have given no serious thought to the needs of women for ritual and music created by women themselves—ritual and music both being capable of nourishing that part of the spirit known as the imagination. Although men would not be satisfied without their own symbols, rites, leaders, and their own spiritual sustenance, they have expected women for nearly two thousand years to feed their imaginations on crumbs from the men's table.

Women lost their symbols, their rites to emphasize their own strength, their leaders. They lost more than that—self-confidence in their own powers to be a dynamic, beneficent influence on humanity backed by the reverence of men for them as such. It was because women were regarded as a menace to the life of the spirit and as interfering with the quest of their men for salvation that they were forbidden to be priestesses and choristers. As recently as 1928, bishops of the Church of England gave the reason identical with that of the early Church Fathers for refusing the petition of women for ordination. Men might be emotionally disturbed, they said, by women's presence near the symbol of spiritual regeneration.

Barriers between women and music did not arise from any lack of natural musical talent, skill, intellect, or imaginative faculty on the part of women. Merely because nature had fashioned her body for the purpose of carrying a child, a human being was deprived of the use of the mimetic rite and music—two of the basic means of expression and communication. The inevitable result has been slow spiritual starvation.

Instead of entering the Christian way in the pride of womanhood, in affirmation of her "Artemis value," woman approached it in negation. Instead of glorifying her existence, she started apologizing for it and so killed the spirit in which imagery gestates. "Daughters of Jerusalem," said Jesus to his followers, "weep for yourselves and for your children."

Weep for yourselves, O Daughters of the Moon!

NEW MOON

CHAPTER XII

THE NUN

1.

*I*N THE darkness that had fallen on women at the end of the fourth century A.D., in many parts of the Christian world, even in its highest councils, and in the silence that had been laid on their music, there began to gleam again a faint, thin crescent of light. Like the moon in her nights of darkness, the music of women had not really vanished. It was only obscured. And to this day it is still only a crescent, with the full moon still a long way off. Nevertheless, the waxing had begun.

This new moon rose over rude collections of huts and clumsy farm buildings surrounded by walls, in which some rough, stormy princess of the north gathered the more rebellious and self-assertive women of her circle and defied men to marry them against their will or keep them married, by putting themselves under the protection of the Church. For as the Roman rule over the forests and farmlands of France and Germany crumbled, the missionaries of the Roman Christian Church took over and began to organize the turbulent north.

The first to see the many advantages these polished, cultured, and subtle persons from the old civilized world had to offer were often the wives or women relatives of the so-called "kings" and "nobles" of the northern tribes. One of these, the high-spirited Chrotield, adopted Christianity, and was then, with some adroit persuasion on the part of the Christian bishops, married to the leading German barbarian, King Clovis. She forthwith required him to become a Christian and all his people with him. Thus was Christianity established among the Franks. In the next three centuries this Germanic tribe took over the rule of all Europe and produced a great emperor,

185

Charlemagne, who was crowned in Rome in 800 A.D. as emperor of New Roman Empire—the Holy Roman Empire. Chrotield, in order to assert her independence of any man, even the King, established a religious house for women near Rouen, but she was no model of Christian meekness.

The example of Chrotield was followed by "princess" after "princess" among the conquering Teutonic tribes. No man of the royal Frankish house entered a monastery. But the women formed religious establishments everywhere. In so doing they were able to reassert the ancient power and independence that women had held among the uncultured Aryan-speaking tribes of Europe from time immemorial. Big, blunt women, strong of limb, downright of speech, resolute of will, most often flaxen-haired or red-haired and blue-eyed, splendid in fur mantles and heavy gold ornaments, these princesses were still of the race of the old mother-chieftainesses and priestesses. They did not intend to be broken by men if they could help it. So, one after another, the noblewomen, with the help and connivance of the Roman bishops, set up their own religious establishments, often on lands they themselves owned and flatly refused to transfer to a husband.

In the centuries to come, succeeding generations of "nuns" were slowly broken to the rule of the Church. But meanwhile they were given at least a limited opportunity to develop their talents in literature and music.

One of the early religious houses for women was founded at Poitiers by Radegund, the high-tempered wife of King Cloathcar, who ruled all of France, Burgundy, and Thuringia, and some lands in Italy and Spain. But he could never rule Radegund. When he objected to her failure to have his meals on time and her neglect of his company for that of any scholarly man who came to her court, she appealed to the bishop to consecrate her a deaconess and let her set up her own monastery for women. And thereupon she offered up her embroidered clothes, her girdle heavy with gold, and all her gems in the oratory of St. Jumer, and went forth clad only in thick flowing robes of a brownish, undyed wool. When King Cloathcar appealed to the Church to send her back, she said she would die rather than return to him. Since Cloathcar had seven recognized wives, of whom she was the fifth, she may have thought he could find feminine company for himself.

As head of her own religious establishment, Radegund led a vivid public life in touch with bishops and various turbulent kings. She left an equally vivid literary record of herself, including three poems in the form of elegies. One of them told the tragic story of her young friend Galeswith, who was murdered shortly after her marriage to King Chilperic. The lament in this poem is intoned by several women in turn. "The cry which sounds through these lines is the cry of a woman—the expression of tender and fiery passion . . . a suggestion of the strength of a woman of all countries and for all time." [1] When Radegund died in the year 587, the women who had left homes and families to follow her crowded around her bier, wailing after the immemorial pattern of the women's dirge, "To whom, Mother, hast thou left us orphans? To whom shall we turn in our distress? . . . The earth is now darkened to us . . . Woe unto us who are left by our holy mother." [2]

Radegund could not only read and write but was as well educated as any man of her day. For it was one of the great attractions of these monasteries that in them women could acquire the mysteries of reading and writing and learn the spiritually beautiful music of the Church. Women set themselves to learn the church music with much eager experiment over pitch and tone and with hours of devoted practice.

In the time of Radegund this music was reaching its climax in the marvelous art of Gregorian plain song. From Italy the churchmen who were converting and organizing the barbarians were bringing it to the north.

2.

To understand the relation of women in convents to this church music, it is necessary to review what had happened to music in the Church. As has been said, dance music, wedding music, laments, and many types of social and ritual music formerly composed by women, as well as men, had been forbidden. This was a barrier to the creative musical power of men composers as well as women. Since the religious dance was forbidden, men gave up composing dance music. For centuries, musicians avoided the laments that had been so rigorously prohibited by the Church. They did not compose music for weddings, since the marriage rite was not, at first, a part of the religious service. It is possible that men suffered no great deprivation by abandoning the dance, the wedding songs, and the laments. These forms of expression had always been associated with women and were never used as freely and consistently by men. This fact may explain why the prohibitions against pagan music were largely directed against women.

However, despite the many prohibitions against women's music and their exclusion from priestly offices, women in convents in the more civilized south and east had cultivated Christian music. This is evident from what Bishop Gregory of Nyssa wrote of his mother, St. Emily of Cappadocia, and his sister Macrina.

St. Emily of Cappadocia and her daughter Macrina are striking examples of leading Christian women. These two fourth-century saints were hereditary Christians of noble family. Macrina was both beautiful and brilliant. When she was still a child she knew all the Psalms by heart. Later she instructed her brother Basil in philosophy. She would not marry, but settled near her mother and gathered young women around her, teaching them to pray and sing in the Christian manner. Macrina was regarded by the whole countryside as a holy person, possessing supernatural powers. She miraculously cured a distinguished soldier's daughter of blindness and caused corn to grow in her own fields in time of famine. Upon the occasion of her last illness, her great brother Bishop Gregory of Nyssa hurried to her, and afterward wrote an account of her death and burial. In his book *Life of St. Macrina,* Gregory mentions first of all, in enthusiastic terms, the spiritual qualities of his mother and sister. "Such was the manner of their life, so great the height of their philosophy, and so holy their conduct, day and night, as to make verbal description inadequate. . . . These women, Emily and Macrina, fell short of the angelic and immaterial nature only in so far as they appeared in bodily form." [3]

All through the account, Gregory alludes to the singing of the nuns. "The voice of the choir was summoning us to the evening service . . . Macrina wished to repeat the thanksgiving sung at the lighting of the lamps." [4] Gregory describes the mourning rites: "Virgins' voices singing psalms mingled with the lamentations were filling the place; somehow the news had quickly spread throughout the whole neighborhood, and all the people that lived near were streaming towards the place, so that the entrance hall could no longer hold the concourse." [5] When they were all assembled Gregory ordered the psalms to be sung by both sexes in the rhythmical and harmonious fashion of choral singing.

The most significant part of the account is the description of the all-night vigil preceding the funeral, when the nuns, alone with their abbess' body and their own grief, cried and bewailed in the manner customary at Christian wakes:

> "The light of our eyes has gone out,
> The light that guided our souls has been taken away.
> The safety of our life is destroyed,
> The seal of immortality is removed,
> The bond of restraint has been taken away,
> The support of the weak has been broken,
> The healing of the sick removed.
> In thy presence the night became to us as day,
> Illumined with pure life,
> But now even our day will be turned to gloom." [6]

These Cappadocian nuns were only one community out of hundreds established in Christendom. In many monasteries the holy women were adapting old pagan rites into Christian ways and were contributing their own expressions to the stream of song that was to be liturgical music. The lament of Macrina's followers is merely a link in the chain of dirges that extends from Mary's own song of mourning to Queen Abbess Radegund's magnificent epic six hundred years later.

Men did not begin to create music for the religious ceremony until after Christianity had been established as the official religion of the Empire, until the persecutions had stopped, until a hierarchy had been organized, and until the circumstances gave them an objective upon which to focus their musical ideas. Then singing was authorized as the direct extension of the functions of religious officials. Musically minded churchmen directed their imaginations toward creating the liturgical song known as plain song.

Plain song had no utility except as an integral part of the religious rites and the liturgical texts. The melodies followed exactly the rhythm and intention of the words, just as much as any primitive song ever did. Only these persons who celebrated the rites and who repeated the prayers had the proper qualifications to be authoritative musicians. Christian music makers were the members of the hierarchy—pope, cardinals, bishops, priests, clerics, monks—and nuns.

For many centuries the composition of music was limited to liturgical song. The laity, although undoubtedly as talented as their brothers and sisters in the hierarchy, were not expected to compose the liturgical music. If one did not belong to the class chosen to make the music, one had no opportunity or incentive or training to do so. In the early days this barrier applied to men as well as to women. The names of robber barons do not appear among the composers of church music. Only later did the work of professional men musicians—trained, of course, by monks, the only educators—begin to be acceptable to the ecclesiastical authorities. But although the class of chosen musicians was later enlarged to include the professional who was not a member of the hierarchy, all churchmen at first submitted to barriers against a free use of music.

The limitation on the composition of any music except liturgical music by churchmen was increased by the social disorder that prevailed everywhere except in a few religious retreats. Until about 800 A.D., Christian Europe struggled against the inroads of the barbarians from the north and the Saracen invasions from Spain. Only gradually did the medieval castles and their walled towns become permanent centers for civilization. Universities, theaters, and other public forums were as yet unorganized. Learning and music lived only in church and monastery. Christian music was religious music, created and performed under the authority of the Church.

3.

Plain song was introduced into the convents for women, and became an earnest expression of their own spiritual life. In the early days some abbots and abbesses observed perpetual adoration, keeping shifts of singers on duty day and night. In later times certain orders prescribed only the recitation and not the singing of prayers and psalms. Between these two extremes, customs varied. From the fifth century until about the thirteenth, when many other orders arose, the rule of St. Benedict and St. Scholastica attracted the majority of the noblemen and -women who entered monasteries. Benedict and his sister advocated the use of music. Monks and nuns of the numerous Benedictine monasteries often spent from five to eight hours daily in the practice and performance of liturgical song.

The life of the monastery revolved around the performance of the prayer service and the celebration of mass. The rites were conducted and the liturgy recited at regular intervals during the day and night. Mass was celebrated once, and often more than once, every day. Its choral portions are the Introit, Kyrie eleison, Gloria, Gradual, Alleluia or Tract, Sequence, Credo, Offertory, Sanctus, Agnus Dei, and Communion. The prayer service consisted of matins, at about two A.M.; lauds, at about four-thirty A.M.; prime, tierce, sext, and nones during the day; vespers at twilight; and compline before retiring for the night. The whole set of devotions was known as the *horae,* canonical hours, or the offices.

The singing of nuns was a serious religious matter, sanctioned chiefly for the purpose of enhancing the value of prayers to the Almighty. Provisions were made for the singers to be properly trained. Each convent had its own nun-teacher. She was called *cantrix, cantorissa, Sängerin,* or *Singmeisterin* according to the language of her country. At Syon (England) the chantress had to be "cunning and perfect in reading and singing." [7] Women conducted the services at the canonical hours by themselves, under their own leadership, but a priest always intruded upon their privacy for the purpose of celebrating mass, thus limiting the opportunity for them to make innovations in the service as the monks did.

With a few strokes of the pen, one can describe the number of hours spent by medieval nuns in the pursuit of music, or depict a group of them in action. But a whole volume could scarcely do justice to musical life in the convents. To begin with, it is no insignificant achievement to assemble a group, large or small, eight or nine times a day for the purpose of singing to God. With no thought of an earthly reward, for almost two thousand years, in the dead of night, in cold, unheated chapels, these dedicated women have been earnestly striving to save their souls and those of humanity. Throughout the centuries the excellence of nuns' singing has been commented upon by their contemporaries. The beautiful, clear voices rising and falling to the incomparable melodies of Gregorian plain chant seem to have given musical satisfaction to all who heard them. The nuns functioned in a narrow groove, but they deepened it by genuine devotion.

4.

Plain song reached its greatest beauty in the sixth and seventh centuries, and again in the ninth when it first began to be written down. During these years the skill and inspiration that flowed into it were anonymous. So we have no way of knowing how much of it can be credited to the women in the early religious houses. If their music was as fresh and real as some of their writing, their contribution was considerable.

Nevertheless, despite the scope given to women's talents in the convents, it must be recognized that they were under severe repressions, which did not affect men, in the development of their talents. It is true that on the practical and material side, all Christians respected the abbess, who, as leader of women under monasticism, inherited many of the prerogatives of the primitive queen and priestess. St. Macrina exemplifies the high status of many abbess-saints whose advice was sought in the early synods and councils. Throughout feudal times these aristocratic women had the power of a bishop within the limits of their monastic precincts and carried the crozier as a sign of their rank. Again and again they demonstrated themselves to be the intellectual and spiritual peers of their relatives the popes and bishops, emperors and kings.

But ecclesiastical ideals in the Middle Ages, firmly established by men and acquiesced in by the majority of women, stood uncompromisingly against the emancipation of women from the stigma of spiritual inferiority. For all her proven ability and her acknowledged beneficent influence, any abbess stood *potentially* lower on the rungs of the hierarchal ladder than the most obscure little boy. She could never be a Christian priestess. Even for her own nuns, whose spiritual mistress she was, she could never celebrate mass. The rich abbess of Las Huelgas, supreme over twelve monasteries of noblewomen in thirteenth-century Spain, was deprived of her revenues and finally excommunicated for defying this inexorable law. Church annals are filled with such edicts.

Between all nuns and monks lay a great gulf. The monks belonged potentially to the upper ranks of the hierarchy; a monk could become a priest, a bishop, even pope. The nuns were ranked in the lower bracket only. And instead of being liberated from the distorted ideals of the early Church Fathers (as well as of their women followers), the sisterhood became tainted through and through with the devaluation of women's collective potentiality for good. Singing had been authorized as a direct extension of the functions of the religious officials. But music in the churches was performed by men and boys —not women. Nuns, therefore, lost the prerogative of being the liturgical choir in public as they had been in early Christian times. Nuns became more and more cloistered in their own precincts. Even there, they sang out of sight, behind a grille or curtain.

Women in the hierarchy were both outnumbered and outranked by men, being excluded from the enormous company of Church officials, from pope down to humble clerk. Until the thirteenth century, the clergy could be married men and so had the advantage of being able to lead normal lives. Nuns had the same status as monks, but were not nearly so numerous. The majority of women married and from them no music was expected. The total number of women from whom music might come was far less than the number of potential men musicians.

Particularly pertinent to the development of creative imagination is the fact that a monk was always in the position where he could exchange ideas with his fellow men, some of whom were leaders of the Christian group. A nun, on the other hand, was rarely admitted to the inner circle of authority. The convent was not the highest forum for discussion and women did not freely enter the men's forums. A nun, therefore, was given no broad chance to test experiments in symbolic thinking, or to match artistic effort, or to prove the validity of such effort by trial before auditors who were at the same time sympathetic, skilled, and also of the highest authority. Before original work could be accepted by the whole society, it was subject to the approval of men, who openly announced their scorn of everything feminine. In a handbook of canon law, the principle of women's subjection is clearly stated: "The very nature of religious life demands from the sisters submission to the ecclesiastical hierarchy." [8]

There was a further difficulty, and one that strikes at the very root of the matter. This was the ideal of virginity, as elaborated by men and preached into the ears of women in their tender and impressionable years. Since for men sex begins and ends in a swift impulsive release with no further effects or consequences, save as a man assumes them vicariously, the Christian preacher tended to think of sex as the sex act only. And having determined, in pursuit of peace and self-discipline, to deny or limit this in their own lives, they feared and distrusted the attraction of women. Women were to be suppressed because men's own impulses toward women were to be suppressed.

But for women, sex is only the beginning of instinctive movements of mind and feelings which, so far as the deepest unconscious life is concerned, they have entirely to themselves. The true soul of woman, her unique psyche, distinct from that of the male, is that of the woman who grows a child in her own body, bears it in sweat and blood and tears, and nourishes it with milk from her own breast. The total experience is so tremendous that it dwarfs all others of the physical and emotional life. It involves the depths of pain, the heights of triumph. However woman may try to put the subconscious awareness of this from her she never can, because month by month she is relentlessly reminded of it.

When men talked of sexual abstinence or of the glories of virginity in terms of their own biology—which in comparison with women's is a deficit of nature—they completely ignored the psychological necessity for women to respect these great life facts. They further injured women's psyche by taking over the imagery of women's lives and elaborating it into allegory and theology. Christ, God, or the bishop nourishes something or other "as a mother." Something or other flows as "milk from the divine breasts." There is no end to this ingenious pretense. To this distortion of their own woman's experience, and to a man's terror lest he should be turned from his way of salvation, women, as virgins dedicated to God, were subjected.

Sometimes the effort to tell women how they might sublimate their own impulses, instead of permitting them to find the far nobler and grander way to which nature had pointed them, approached downright indecency. Imagine some lone male priest, of the sex that alone was allowed to officiate at the altar, coming into a convent of women, some of them very young, and exhorting them in these words: "After the kiss of peace in the mass, when the priest consecrates, forget there all the world, and there be entirely out of the body; there in glowing love embrace your spouse, Christ, who is come down from heaven into the bower of your breast, and hold him fast until he has granted you all you wish." [9]

Between the suppression of woman's every normal impulse, the identification of her sacred power of giving birth with the evil and undesirable, and the feverish tendency to interpret religion to women in terms of their own repressed male impulses, the dominance of men in the higher offices of the Church kept women's real soul in a position in which it could not really function. What a woman was offered and what she accepted in the nunnery was an artificial and inferior and crudely imitative substitute for her own real spiritual life.

Yet the temptation to accept this was very great. In the Europe of that day the opportunities for lifelong monogamous marriage with dignified and free motherhood were very few. The monastery was freedom from the rude dominance of some unloved man. It was freedom, too, from very crude physical toil. "And now I ask," ran one apology for the life of nuns, "how does the wife stand when she comes in, hears her child scream, sees the cat at the flitch, and the hound at the hide? Her cake is burning on the stone hearth, her calf is sucking up the milk, the earthen pot is overflowing into the fire, and the churl [or servant] is scolding. Though it be an odious tale, it ought, maiden, to deter thee more strongly from marriage, for it does not seem easy to her who has tried it. Thou, happy maiden, who has fully removed thy self out of the servitude as a free daughter of God." [10]

The way in which the tendency of men both to suppress women's musical artistic expression and to take over and perform themselves what women had thought out is shown in the case of two inventions that are natural expressions of women's life, but not nearly so natural for the men who appropriated them. One was the liturgical play, which turned upon the experiences of such women as Mary, the mother of Jesus, and the other Marys who were his friends. The other was the ceremonies associated with the death of their own women friends and leaders in the monastery. Over and over again, nuns were forbidden to act in the liturgical plays. Women could not even reproduce the scene in which the three Marys visited the holy sepulcher on Easter morning. In all Europe and England, the Easter drama has so far been found in only six monasteries for women, whereas in the monasteries for men the play was never suppressed. Monks elaborated the idea, imitated it for other feasts, such as Christmas, Epiphany, Palm Sunday, and Pentecost. They took it from monastery to church and finally to the public market place. Freedom to develop the events of Christ's and Mary's lives in forms of the mimetic rite according to their own interpretation was consistently withheld from women.

Yet there is evidence that women participated in the forerunners of the medieval liturgical play. The very character of the people— accustomed to display feelings of joy or grief in church, drilled for centuries in the mimetic rite—implies that action was often integrated with worship. The *History of the Blessed Virgin Mary* records that Mary and her women followers used to talk about Jesus all day long and that they mourned for him at regular intervals. *Feminae Sanctores* of the Marcion sect, marching in a procession into the hall where the congregation sat, carried lamps and gave laments for the sins of the world. Bishop Methodius' girls impersonated the characters in his play *Concerning Virtue*. A first-century fragment of a story about Seilah, Jephtha's daughter, suggests that some early writer had planned another play for girls. Men and women worshiping in the church at Gethsemane during the fourth century acted out the events of the day of Crucifixion—probably the original form of the Stations of the Cross. The few surviving traditions about the powerful Marianite women of Spain and Bordeaux (France) indicate that they imitated, at their secret ceremonies, the grief and joy of Mary and her disciples. In at least six medieval monasteries nuns performed the Easter rite of the visit of the three Marys to the sepulcher. In the version presented at Origny St. Benoîte, one verse of Mary's lament is unique; in the Barking text, there is a special verse for the lament and another for the cry of joy that appear nowhere else.

It is surprising to find that the dramas developed by monks in medieval times were so frequently scenes in which women characters dominated. The visit to the sepulcher was the oldest and the most frequently performed by men. Monks acted also the visit of the pregnant Mary to the pregnant Elizabeth, the lament of Rachel for her children slain by Herod, the episode of the wise and foolish virgins (*Sponsus*), and the Christmas story. How very odd that they so rarely dramatized events in which men had had the foremost place, such as the last supper! One might reasonably infer that the first Christian women had been inventing their own rites for two or three hundred years and that men had been impressed through these centuries with women's interpretation and selection of material for use in the religious ceremony. Some abbots did perceive that it really was not suitable for men to take the women's parts in these plays. It was degrading, they said, to pose as women. Others objected to the falsetto voice—it reminded one of the evil inherent in women's voices. But it was not suggested that women be allowed to take the women's parts in representing episodes in a woman's intimate life, which, badly played in a crude, secondhand way by men, were still the most moving episodes in the religious drama.

The refusal to accord women their immemorial privilege of officiating in the rites of death was another example of the appropriation by monks of women's rituals and women's musical inspiration. As early as the third century, when the first convents were being established in Egypt, St. Schenute of Atripe and St. Pachomius ordered that funerals of nuns were to be conducted by monks only. The sisters could merely listen to the praying and singing. Pachomius moderated the rule by allowing six nuns to follow the cortège at a suitable distance.[11] In the double monasteries housing both monks and nuns, such a direction from the abbot in charge was indeed a cruel deprivation to the women and is a striking example of the unwillingness of men in authority to give qualified women responsibility for correcting abuses in their own affairs. To cut them off arbitrarily from participation in the rite that had been since time immemorial the chief incentive to women's most notable musical achievements meant the erection of a high barrier between the second-century nuns and the composition of music. That the custom of having monks take the lead at nuns' funerals persisted can be seen in the account of Abbess Hathumoda's funeral in ninth-century Saxony. In the great, rich abbey of Gandersheim, where the famous Hrosthwitha wrote her plays and her music, the nuns had to send for the monk Wichbert to compose the funeral chants and merely give the response themselves to his verses. That such limitations upon the freedom of nuns to create existed in some, even if not in all monasteries, lowered materially the possible number of nun composers at the same time that it raised the possible number of monk musicians.

Unfamiliarity with this aspect of Christian Church history is largely responsible for the general failure to understand the relation of women to music in the convents. On the surface, monastic life appears to have provided the necessary incentives to all musically minded nuns. Certainly many women in the convents were able to ignore the prohibitions and went their own way. Hundreds of edicts repeated again and again through the centuries prove the active resistance of women to their prescribed status. Undoubtedly, many individual churchmen were Christlike in their attitude toward women and had no deliberate intention of denying them the right to think in terms of music. But on the whole, organized Christianity—Church and priestcraft—effected a repression of the natural woman. Even those men who appreciated the value of womanhood to Christianity failed to take a militant stand against the profaners of women. If some few did favor giving women recognition as officials in the Church, they were greatly in the minority. On the whole, men imbued with the Christian spirit believed in being kind and merciful to individual women but not in allowing women to be self-assertive or independent *collectively*. "The head of the woman is the man," said St. Paul, and in this principle most people concurred. How limited were the opportunities of nuns to succeed as musicians!

5.

But as time went on the women's monasteries acquired such wealth and power, such a tradition of skill and learning, that in a few rich and favored houses, from the ninth century on, women began to assert considerable artistic independence. In the ninth century, the Byzantine nun Kassía composed a canon and a sticheron that were incorporated with the liturgy of the Greek Orthodox Church for Holy Week. In the tenth century the nun Hrosthwitha displayed remarkable talent in writing poetry and drama. Into her various works she inserted dissertations on mathematics and music, demonstrating her familiarity with these subjects.

Hrosthwitha got the materials for her dramas and legends in the well-stocked library of Gandersheim, which included every kind of classical and medieval literature, copied and decorated by generations of nun-scribes. It is thought that the reading of one of her legends, retold in her fresh and novel way, was a regular feature that preceded the convent meal in the refectory and that the reading closed with a grace of eight lines, probably intoned. This shows the great stimulus that regular institutional support can give the artist and musician. Hrosthwitha had a regular incentive, a participating audience, a critical and sensitive group who wanted her work and whom she tried to serve.

The women in great rich monasteries such as Gandersheim, Barking, or Origny St. Benoîte often had not much in common with an ascetic, detached life and the dark garb of the traditional nun. This is shown by the recurring efforts to get them to dress more soberly. The greatest work of art produced in the women's houses—Herrad's *Garden of Delight*—shows women in gowns of different colors, with brilliantly colored red and purple veils. Herrad was a scholar, artist, and poetess whose large and varied talents blossomed at Hohenburg, a monastery on top of a high spur of the Vosges mountain, overlooking the Rhine. In the words she wrote for the nuns to celebrate their espousal to Christ there is something of the spirit of the old epithalamium or wedding song of Greece. It is a very different spirit indeed

from the sickening sexiness of some masculine treatments of this idea
of the sacred marriage.

Hail, cohort of Hohenburg virgins,
White as the lily and loving the Song of God,
Herrad, your most devoted, your most faithful,
Mother and handmaiden sings you this song.
She greets you times countless and daily she prays
That in glad victory you may triumph over things that pass . . . .

Delights await you, riches are destined for you,
The court of Heaven proffers you countless joys.
Put around you noble circlets, and make your faces to shine
Fair, freed from mental strife.
Christ hates spot or stain, he abhors time-worn lines . . . .

With a dove-like faith call upon your Bridegroom,
That your beauty may become an unbroken glory . . .
Mary's Son's heavenly castle with its beauteous halls
Be your home when the term of life is past . . .
The shining Star of the Sea, the one virgin Mother
Will join you to her Son in bond eternal . . .
May you not leave the way before you have attained. Amen.[12]

Beside the great work associated with her name, Herrad wrote an
encyclopedia and much verse. The fragment of a two-part song and
two lines of a liturgical play remain to prove that the Abbess of Hohenburg cultivated music.

Another nun of great attainments was Mechthild of the literary
convent of Helfta, in Germany. Mechthild's visionary poems and
writings are thought to have been one of the inspirations of Dante's
Divine Comedy and to have been acknowledged by him in the
lovely episode where he meets Matilda in the earthly paradise. As
cantrix for thirty years in the Cistercian Convent at Helfta, Mechthild existed in music and for music. Whether she was in the work-
room or in the chapel, she poured out song from the bottom of her
heart. One large group of her compositions consisted of the so-called
"spiritual love song"—the love song to Christ. This whole category
had developed directly out of the prohibitions issued by Charlemagne and other authorities against women singing "winileodi"
(love or sex poems) as they worked at their daily domestic tasks.
Not being allowed to express love for a man, or even for the spring-

tide, the nuns transformed the words into passion for Christ. Lamprecht von Regensburg in 1218 recognized that women had invented the spiritual love song: "This art has originated with the women of our day in Brabant and in Bavaria. Good God, what kind of an art is it, that an old woman knows better than a witty man?" [13] Mechthild made many "winileodi," but her best work was centered in her musical settings for conventional ritual texts. When she was about to die, she asked the attending nuns to sing her own requiem.

One of the most typical of these nuns of the Middle Ages, in her association with music, her encyclopedic knowledge, her fresh approach to much that the male intellect was fumbling with, and her inevitable limitations, was the Abbess Hildegarde of Bingen on the Rhine. Her *Play of the Virtues* (*Ordo Virtutem*) is unique in the history of medieval music. There is no other liturgical drama of her era, or before, that treats spiritual material an as allegory. Its whole conception is original. In its thought and text, it contains the principles developed by Cavalieri four hundred years later in the well-known *Rappresentazione di Anime di Corpo*. The play, however, was only one of seventy musical compositions—antiphons, responsoriums, sequences, and hymns—that Hildegarde composed for the nuns and novices in her monastery at Bingen on the Rhine. The great abbess' favorite hymn, "*O virga diadema*," is still sung in the village church at Bingen and in other convents. An edition of some of her works was made in 1895 by Dom Pothier of Solèsmes Abbey.

Hildegarde was also steeped in the life of the spirit. When very young, she had visions and made prophecies that brought her public recognition. In maturity she was credited with superhuman intelligence. Kings and bishops not only sought her advice but abode by her decisions. According to the way of all sibyls, she claimed that she had received her knowledge of musical modulation and harmony direct from God and called herself the zither (or harp) of the Holy Spirit, the strings of which were plucked by the spirit of the Lord. The abbess was equally famed for her practical contacts with the poor and sick of her community. She had an intimate knowledge of the medical lore of her day and a reputation for almost miraculous healing. Her book *Materia Medica* is still consulted for information about medieval medicine. As saint, prophetess, abbess, healer, musician, this remarkable woman seems like a primitive priestess, combining in one person all the ancient magics. She would have been a power in her time even if she had never composed a note of music.

6.

The histories and the musical achievements of these extraordinary nuns are significant for the relation of women to music in two ways. First, the fact that they composed music deemed important by their contemporaries goes far to explode the theory that women are inherently incapable of thinking in terms of music. Second, in the case of each of them, their place in history depends primarily on matters having nothing to do with music. The musical reputations of Kassía, Mechthild, and Hildegarde were by-products of their achievements in activities other than music. Kassía was the beloved of an emperor who pursued her until their affair became notorious. In the thirteenth century the popularity of mysticism brought several women into prominence, and nun-musicians became known because they were also mystics. Mechtilde, who lived in the Cistercian convent at Helfta with the celebrated St. Gertrude, was one of these visionaries. Having secured the attention of their contemporaries, whether intentionally or not, these nuns became recognized also as musicians and found a place in later histories of music and musicians. May there not have been scores of other nuns who were equally good composers, conducting their choirs, arranging and adapting the chant to suit the particular needs of their groups? Certainly in the early days this must have been the custom, since before the eleventh century and in some centers long after, music was not notated but was transmitted orally from teacher to teacher, from leader to choir. Such a practice naturally gave opportunity for local variations in the chants. For centuries, therefore, all nun-musicians worked in an environment that encouraged originality on the part of the choral conductor—provided, of course, the women were allowed to function freely. Even a Hildegarde could not rise out of a vacuum. Like Sappho, she had behind her and all around her other musically talented nuns. If they had been monks or clerics they would have been in the class from which the composition of music was demanded. On account of the stigma of inferiority cast upon women *collectively,* only those few nuns who were outstanding in some other way won a recognition that was accorded to many men of no greater ability. (See Plate 55.)

CHAPTER XIII

THE LADY

1.

THE abbess Hildegarde was the sibyl, the mystical oracle of a movement in Europe that was to have great consequences for the relation of women to music. In the late Middle Ages some abbesses enjoyed considerable intellectual companionship with churchmen, in a position of something like personal equality. Between high-minded and gifted men and women, these relations might be frank and quietly devoted, in a way not really possible in the case of men and women in any other walk of life. Such was Hildegarde's relation in her ripe middle years to a simple, earnest, rather narrow-minded monk named Bernard of Clairveaux.

Bernard deplored the selfish fighting amidst the princes of Europe. In conversations with Hildegarde and others, he developed the idea that all these warlike princes and knights could be made to live like brothers and their energies turned to a noble purpose if they could be inspired with a single social aim requiring the pooling of all their resources. Some knights and lords from northern France had already discovered such an aim—they had gone on a crusade to rescue the Holy Land from the Saracens. Bernard thought this idea of a crusade should be preached to all the people. He started on a preaching tour that soon had all Europe seething with excitement.

Meanwhile Hildegarde had a series of visions, of which she wrote in vague and burning words and which Bernard was convinced came straight from God. He presented these to the pope, saying that God had provided the world in this crisis with a prophet. The pope and the high councils of the Church, perceiving the great inspirational value of Hildegarde's writings at this moment, put the seal of the highest authority on them and granted that she was indeed in-

202

spired and ordained by God to guide them all in the great enterprise
of recovering the Holy Land.

Thereafter kings and nobles who thought of taking the sign of the
cross, and churchmen of all ranks, wrote to Hildegarde for advice or
came to see her. Her writings, earnest, beautiful, though vague, were
everywhere circulated among the few people who could read, and
passages from them were repeated, intoned, trumpeted abroad.

Bernard entreated her not to slacken in her efforts to inspire the
Crusade. "They tell us that you understand the secrets of heaven and
grasp that which is above human ken, through the help of the Holy
Spirit," wrote Bernard. "Therefore we beg and entreat you to remember us before God and also those who are joined to us in holy union.
For the spirit in you joining itself unto God we believe that you can,
in great measure, help and sustain us." [1]

Since Hildegarde was widely recognized as a musician, it is interesting to speculate how much of her music was included in the inspiration, the exhortations, and the prophecies she poured forth as
the divinely appointed and officially recognized prophetess of the
Crusades.

In any case, between her prophecies and Bernard's preaching, all
Europe was seething. From every side bands of knights, trailing yeo-
men, peasants, and runaway serfs, were converging on the routes
that led to Mediterranean ports, beating footpaths into roads with
the ceaseless tramp of their feet and the clatter of their hoofs.
Though there had been no congregational singing in churches, the
great assemblages sang, fervently and religiously, finding their own
tunes and words. "Fairest Lord Jesus, Ruler of All Nations" is one of
the hymns of the Crusades we still sing in our churches.

Women and men, high and low, everybody wanted to join the
Crusades. At all the gathering places and along the main routes,
tradespeople set up shop. Entertainers staged shows with acrobatic
stunts, tricks of magic, acting, and singing. Many of the entertainers
were women—gypsy-like creatures traveling with their men and telling fortunes. The crusaders were often accompanied by their wives,
who rode along beside them and joined boldly in all public services.
Some highborn ladies even went without their husbands, volunteer-
ing to nurse or to set up hostels for pilgrims. The wife of the knight
Hausten von der Niederburg bei Uelmer traveled eastward to find
her lost husband. After a long search she discovered him bound to a
plow, slaving for a harsh unbeliever. By means of her harp and her

lovely voice, she charmed the owner of the fields to free the knight.[2]

Thus all the wild, free spirits of Europe were brought together and their disturbing energies turned on the infidel. And never again was Europe to be the same. In this great movement all bonds were strained or broken. The serf ceased to be tied to the land. He could run away, set up a shop on one of the crusaders' routes, and get rich. The knight ceased to be tied to his lord. He could carve out a piece of land for himself with his sword in one of the wildernesses of eastern Europe and became a lord himself. The people ceased to be tied to the Church. Great outdoor masses of people, even when they feel religious, cannot be bound and shackled to liturgy and doctrine. The moving masses of the Crusades were full of heresy, conscious and unconscious. And so in all this stir both women and music began to be released.

The Crusades, thus started, continued at intervals for three hundred years and were associated with profound changes in European life. The feudal system gradually disintegrated, and since feudalism was the mainstay of clerical dominance, the fortunes of the Church followed the fortunes of feudalism. Both were being undermined by an aggressive individualism and by a revolt from asceticism. There was, consequently, the beginning of a new development in the social aspects of music, a development that had its roots in changed ideas about women and in a changed utility for music. It is true that, throughout the Middle Ages, no lady could escape the ideal for her conduct set by the Church. Monasticism, far from declining in popularity, flared up with renewed vigor in the thirteenth century. Many new orders were established, some of them for women of the lower classes. In Russia, until the time of Peter the Great, it was the fashion for noblewomen in their castles to pray and fast at regular intervals exactly like nuns. Even those with no religious inclinations lived under the influence of the ecclesiastical interpretation of life. A European girl received her tutelage in books from a monk brought to the castle, or in a convent school where she was taught as if she were going to become a nun. But there was, at the same time, a partial return to the value of natural living. The "progressive nun" of those times threw off the veil of her dedication to chastity and appeared boldly as her natural self. Instead of becoming the bride of Christ in retreat, St. Elizabeth of Hungary remained true to her earthly lord and traveled over the countryside on errands of mercy. Although she identified herself with the real world, the Church recognized her as a saint and so sanctified the new ideal of at least a suggestion of conformity to the natural way.

2.

Up to this time the Church had been more or less successful in limiting the composition and performance of music. If the way of the autocratic theologians had been consistently followed, only a few Christian men and women to this day would have had the opportunity to compose or perform music. Since dancing was forbidden altogether, one of the greatest incentives for the creation of music fell into disuse. Instrumental playing was at first frowned upon by the Church for men and forbidden entirely to women. Singing was strictly limited to liturgical uses. Even at home, Christians were expected to set music only to psalms or religious canticles. Such restricted use would have changed the social aspects of music in our own culture completely.

The Church's all-inclusive ideal for music was challenged, however, from the beginning. Many people were reluctant to give up an art that had for ages past provided pleasure, spiritual recreation, and also a magic weapon. There was never a wholehearted, complete acceptance of the restrictive rulings. If there had been, the continuous repetition of prohibitions would not have been necessary. If there had been, the ritual music and art song of the former pagan epoch—rites and music that we now call folklore and folk song— would have disappeared; whereas the fact is that many of the ancient rites are still being practiced and are often accompanied by music that itself shows traces of an ancient origin.

Throughout the period known as the Dark Ages and throughout the Middle Ages, the majority of people continued to sing and dance and play upon instruments of music with the intention of influencing their environment. Peasants, townspeople, and nobles all believed that music had a supernatural power. The people of fourteenth-century France believed that music could influence the passions when they allowed a girl from Armentières in 1380 to be fined and arrested for making charms over a young man upon whom she had matrimonial designs. Artists even depicted a girl surrounded by a veil, a spiral, a heart, drops of blood, flowers, and birds practicing magic to attract her lover. Today, in Oberpfalz (Germany), an incantation for the same purpose is sung during the time of the waning moon:

"God thee greet, dear star of Eve, whom now and ever I love to view;
May the moon shine in the nook where my dear love now lies in bed;
Give him no rest, leave him no peace, until to me he needs must come." (See Plate 56.)

As late as 1517, Francesco Gonzago of Mantua ordered a *frottola*, composed by one Marchel de Cara, for soprano, violin, viola, and cello, to be played for the express purpose of curing his syphilis. The Duchess of Orleans employed musicians to play instrumental music for her at every confinement. She believed in the power of music to alleviate her suffering during childbirth. King Henry of Navarre implored his beloved daughter, Jeanne d'Albret, to bow before an image of the Virgin Mary at the foot of a certain bridge and sing:

"Help me, Mother divine,
Deliver me safely of a son!" [3]

This conception of the magic properties of music prevailed among both people and priests throughout the whole of Christendom. The challenge to the Church's authority came, therefore, not from a disagreement about the nature of music, but from a dispute as to who should wield its power.

The rebellion of Christian women against these restrictions upon their musical activities was strengthened by contact with new pagan blood. As the Church spread out through Europe, it converted Celts, Teutons, Slavs, and other northern races to Christianity. In contrast to the effete Orientals and the luxurious Romans, the barbarians were strong, sturdy, and freedom-loving. Women had their own deities, priestesses, rites, and music. Morrigu, one of the famous Irish queens, led men to war and taught them stirring battle hymns. Bridget, goddess and priestess in Ireland, played her harp even as a Christian saint. Slavic women were endowed with magic powers of intuition, especially with the power of making music. Wild and untutored these northerners were, compared to the sophisticated Greeks and Romans. Lascivious and obscene they certainly were not.

Against the might of their nobility and against the wealth of their musical expression the Church struggled in vain, and was eventually forced to compromise.

About the thirteenth century, one compromise was the introduction of congregational singing into the Roman Catholic Church. Religious words and familiar tunes that had never been silenced out-of-doors became formalized into hymns sung at the high festivals of Christmas and Easter. These had come from outbursts of religious emotion among the singing multitudes on the Crusades. Another compromise was to dedicate a pagan festival to a Christian saint. Upon such occasions, women and girls continued to sing and dance in the traditional manner. In the little village at Vigo, Spain, the girls even now dance up the church aisle. In the Vosges Mountains today, during Whitsuntide, girls march in little groups to the abbey. They wear wreaths of flowers and sing certain songs called *kyrioles,* associated in that district with the girls' flower festival.

*Kyriole*s are popular religious songs that had their origin as far back as the ninth century, in the response of Kyrie eleison (Lord, have mercy), given over and over again in church by the people to the priest. Those of the Vosges Mountain girls are only a sample of a very large number. In Russia, especially, there is a whole category of women's songs known as "spirituals." The Church's early sanction of the singing of religious canticles in the home bore fruit in many lands—the one opportunity open to women was, like the talent of the faithful servant, increased tenfold.

There is no doubt that Christian priests have been the implacable foes of women and women's music. Even today, women's musical activities are much greater in regions where the whole population remained pagan until a comparatively recent date. Europe became converted to Christianity only gradually. Germany and Scandinavia came into the fold during the eighth and ninth centuries, Russia even later—at the beginning of the eleventh century. Lithuania, Latvia, and Estonia were the last strongholds of paganism. In their deep forests, the *pagani,* or backwoodsmen, of these remote regions held aloof until about 1400. Russia, Estonia, and Lithuania are the very places where, until the great world wars, peasants had the richest folklore, dance, and music. They are the countries in which the creative peasant-woman-musician had the highest standing.

How many Christians of the aristocratic class conformed to the ascetic musical ideals of the Church is not definitely known. Many undoubtedly did, just as some people today still object to dancing and just as Quakers, until very recently, denied themselves music in any form. Customs varied in time and place. But the very condition of women's life in the medieval castle made it difficult to enforce restrictions against music upon them. Medieval noblewomen lived in feudal households and spent a large part of their time with one another, separated from the men. They attended to childbirth themselves, occupied their time in sewing tapestries, and whiled away their long hours of leisure by singing. In Russia, especially, the ladies were segregated in the *térem,* that section of the medieval castle set apart for women. There they indulged in gaiety, in dances, games, and songs upon occasions of birthdays, baptisms, weddings, or at Christmastime. There the women held feasts separately from the men and sang special toasts to one another, songs for good health, called *zazdrávnizi.* They hung up swings and sang old songs to the rhythm of the swing. Many of these songs were brought into the medieval castle by the laundresses, the peasant nurses, and especially by the embroideresses—the "hall girls," as they were called, because they slept in the castle hallways.

At weddings, especially, enthusiasm for song and dance ran high. According to legend, Queen Guinevere and the Knights of Round Table (*c.* 500 A.D.) rejoiced when two of their company were married.

> The women sang . . .
> The men shouted. . . .[4]

Guinevere herself composed the songs. And according to history, it was during the seventh century in Rome, in Greece, in Byzantium, that many respectable upper-class Christians engaged formal choirs of girls to sing during the wedding feast.

In Scotland about 1050 Queen Margaret was famous for the ballads she composed and sang with her ladies in waiting. The French queens and duchesses, with their maids of honor, sang long historical romances. One, looking up from her needlepoint, would give the verse, and the others would answer with the refrain:

> "The Queen sings softly,
> Her voice blends with the harp;
> Her hands are lovely, her songs good,
> Sweet the voice and gentle the tones."[5]

Her theme often dealt with the equality of love between man and woman—an unrealized ideal for those days but one always popular with women.

3.

The forces that were making for a new secular music and poetry in defiance of the Church were all represented by Eleanor of Aquitaine, who was married to Louis VII of France, divorced by him, it is said, because she bore him only daughters, and then married to Henry II of England. Eleanor was a brilliant, strong-willed, high-spirited woman, who accompanied Louis VII on the Second Crusade and left a trail of legend in the Holy Land. Upon her divorce from him— a divorce she seems to have desired—she married the heir to the English throne, who was much younger than herself. She then carried to England the arts and stories she had picked up in the East and the arts of her homeland. Meanwhile she also discovered the charm of the Celtic singers, the "Breton minstrels," as they were called, and made the court a center for them.

The indications of what must have been, under Eleanor's direction and encouragement, a very considerable enterprise in collecting, adapting, and making socially available the folk music and folklore of Europe are to be found in the lays of Marie de France. These are generally recognized as the most finished storytelling in any European vernacular up to that time. The lays purport to tell stories picked up from minstrels and folk singers. "Folk tell it to the harp, and to the rote and the music of it is sweet to hear," [6] wrote Marie. "The lays usually please the ladies. They hear them joyfully and eagerly, for they are much to their liking," [7] wrote Denis Pyramus.

Whether Marie adapted folk tunes as she adapted folk tales is not known, but literature and music were at that time so much a single artistic impulse and a single art that it is quite likely. Since Eleanor's own son John, when he later signed the Magna Carta, used a seal because he could not write his name, we cannot assume any habit of reading at his mother's court. The lays must have been made known by being sung or rendered in a sort of recitative to the twanging of a harp. The melody of the recitative was the music of singers whose song Marie purports to translate. The purported taking of the music from somewhere may, however, be only an artistic device. Marie may have formed the melody of the recitative out of strains she had heard as neatly and artistically as she formed her stories.

These stories are written in clear, clean, musical, octosyllabic verse. With sure and graceful literary art, Marie frees the folk stories and legends from the monstrous accumulations and contortions of medieval invention and tells a clear, intelligent tale with quiet beauty and good sense. Out of Oriental tales, European folk tales, and King Arthur stories, which were just beginning to be retold and circulated in a literary form by court entertainers, she forms a kind of manual of the manners and ethics of courtesy from the point of view of a civilized woman. The civilized and almost modern tone of these works, admittedly inspired by women and representing their point of view on men's doings and women's personal lives, is sharply contrasted with the style of some *chansons de geste* composed at that time by men. Who Marie de France was is not definitely known. She is thought by some to have been Mary, Abbess of Shaftsbury, natural sister of Eleanor's husband Henry II and daughter of Geoffrey Plantagenet, Count of Anjou. She appears to have been a sort of mistress of court entertainment, at least in the women's circles. As such she may have directed or worked with a number of minstrels, encouraging the development of songs in a civilized and polished form of the vernacular, with music of an equally civilized quality.

4.

Provençe, the sunny southeastern corner of France, whose principal city, Marseilles, had originally been a Greek colony, had been overrun in the tenth century by Saracens. Saracen women, as courtesans and entertainers of men, were creative musicians, fashioning both words and melody in a sort of social and artistic ritual to the glory of love between men and women. It was a kind of love that had nothing to do with marriage and mating. It was a celebration of the free spirit and its defiant right to love according to its own laws. Ultimately the Provençals expelled the Arabs. But they did not restore the control of the Church over their hearts and music. Instead, they organized a heresy, a kind of religion of the "gentle heart," as they called it, in which a knight, as troubadour, worshiped a high and noble lady in song. Thus began the art of the troubadour, a kind of musical wooing of the lady of the castles. This lady, married without her consent to a husband she did not love, might, with proper musical incantations, be brought to love the troubadour.

At the turn of the twelfth century the aristocratic music makers grew bolder in defying the Church's rules concerning the use of music. They dared to set their spring songs and love songs to the rhythmic patterns and melodic lines of the liturgical plain chant. Considering the Church's point of view about the sinfulness of sex, the adaptation of religious chant to frankly sensuous poems was a radical move in the direction of musical freedom. It began, indeed, the new school of secular music, which was eventually to broaden into the operatic and symphonic art of our time.

Thus began four great social changes that were to direct the whole orientation of women to music. One was a kind of woman worship, artificial, without roots in any real function or value of women and without much effect at the time on their actual status. The second was the establishment of wooing as a complicated art, to be humbly performed by men, with the women in a passive position on a pedestal. The third was the limitation of the woman to the position of being the object of men's music, instead of the creator of music of her own. The fourth was the exaltation of the woman as the inspirer and sponsor of men's music.

But it is pleasant to record that the Provençal ladies, despite long discipline by the Church, by severely patriarchal husbands, and by the almost Oriental seclusion of their lives, still had spirit enough to make a little poetry and music of their own. Thirteen of the Provençal ladies have left songs. Others are reported to have composed songs of which no record remains. A typical lady was Beatriz de Dia, who has left five songs, one with music. A dark-eyed, olive-skinned young woman, in a society that prized golden hair and blue eyes, Beatriz found her whole soul and body lighted with beauty when she knew that she was loved. "On gladness and young-heartedness I feast," she sang. "May they ever be my meat. For my friend is the gayest of all. And so I, too, am gay and attractive." [8]

When she tried to hold off the advances of her lover, she cried desolately, "Now I see that I am abandoned because I have not given all my love." But the day came when she sang in exultation, "My heart have I made his, and my love, my every sense, my eyes, and my life." In the end her lover forsook her and she sang, "I now must sing of that I fain would not. So dark and sad my friend had made my lot." [9]

These few simple words, spoken out of the real heart of a real woman, illumine the psychological reality behind this new outburst of song—the radiance, the release of the young woman, married without love, when she is loved by her troubadour, and the inevitable heartbreak for a real woman in such an artificial situation. The wonder is not that troubadour lady artists were not as numerous as the lords, in a formal and rather learned pattern of verse and music set by men. The wonder is that, withal, these caged birds could still sing.

CHAPTER XIV

PRIESTESS OF BEAUTY

1.

*F*ROM the fourteenth century on, there was a wonderful revival of the old Mediterranean culture, and with it a new value for women's voices. This Renaissance, as it was called, centered in Italy, where many cities had grown rich on the business of outfitting and transporting the crusaders and keeping them supplied. A flourishing trade between East and West had developed. From the lands opened to trade by the crusaders came rich rugs to cover the stone floors of castles, rich hangings to decorate the bare walls, silk brought from far-off China, and strains of different kinds of music. The old pagan world revived. People began to read Plato instead of the Church Fathers. Venus was rediscovered as a great goddess and representations of her appeared everywhere, with Venus shown in all her glowing nudity. The Mother and Child, a strong, natural deep-bosomed mother, a lusty and not always angelic child, appeared in a thousand reincarnations in church and chapel. They called her Mary and the child Jesus. But she was the natural mother coming to life and taking her place even in the holy of holies. In the relations of upper-class men and women there was a new and exciting freedom. Women began to take a natural part in the conversation of men, to sing and dance when men were present. (See Plate 57.)

The most wonderful release was the release of the woman's natural voice. Up to 1400 the Church had persistently refused to countenance anything but the high, clear singing of the Gregorian chants by the nuns. The rich, natural voice of the mature woman was considered to be outside the pale of decency. The peasant women were constantly forbidden to sing their myth-laden popular songs. But by 1400 the natural woman was beginning to come into her own, de-

213

spite the priests. The Church was forced to yield to the popular will and tacitly condone the performance of pagan music under Christian titles, in the form of popular hymns and carols, even by women singing in the warm, rich tones of mothers not ashamed of their sex. This change of policy re-established freedom for music in the home—the focus of woman's activity. It would be difficult to overestimate the importance to women of permission to sing what they wished and in a natural voice. Everywhere the people were singing new folk songs, popular ditties, Christmas carols, and spirituals—many of them composed by women and girls. The names of these women composers have been remembered by later generations and have also been inscribed in old editions of songbooks.

> The one who had composed this
> and has prepared it anew,
> is a delicate maiden,
> she will make us many more of them
> in honor of a youth
> whom she knows well. [1592] [1]

Christmas carols as well as love songs often had their origin in rites that women and girls had long regarded as their own. One of the prerogatives of the ancient priestesses everywhere was the right to bless the home. All through the Middle Ages the "sorceresses" or "witches" whom the Church relentlessly persecuted had carried on the old practices of the priestesses. With charms and fortunetelling they had traveled around the country, knocking at the doors of those whom they might bless. By 1400 even these determined survivors of the pagan hierarchy were drawn into the movement that allowed the old charms and chants if they were duly Christianized. The familiar carol:

> God bless the master of this house,
> And bless the mistress too,
> And all the little children
> That round the table go. . . . [2]

was customarily sung in Yorkshire during the Christmas season by an old woman who came begging to the doors of the villagers' houses. She carried a box with dolls impersonating the Virgin and the Holy

Child, which she held out as a blessing while she sang her ditty. She was the spiritual descendant of those priestesses of the good goddess Hat-hor in Egypt who went to the people's houses shaking their emblems to bring prosperity.

In the general release of women and song, music began to be liberated from the restrictions that bound it to a single melodic line accompanying the liturgy. Experiments in polyphony were at first forbidden by the popes. Eventually, however, the authorities admitted that the new harmonic arrangements enriched plain chant. Creative musical imagination was thereby stimulated to proceed along the modern line of harmony and counterpoint—an apparently limitless field for artistic development.

2.

The change toward a sensuous enjoyment of music initiated in the rather grim castles of the troubadours was carried to a climax in the open, gaily frescoed, gorgeously decorated palaces of the princes of Italy whose families the Crusades had made very rich. Thence it was carried throughout the civilized world in aristocratic homes, first of the nobility, then of the rising bourgeoisie. Not the priestess, as in former times, not the nun, not the mother in her peasant home setting, but the queens of small courts in small states established new ideals and new customs involving a new relation of women to music.

A typical example of such a court was that of Ferrara. At the height of its glory, when two of the greatest ladies of the Renaissance, Beatrice and Isabella d'Este, grew up there, there were only a hundred thousand people living in Ferrara, but its ruling family was allied by marriage to ruling families of other states in Italy.

Among them they controlled a great deal of the money the crusaders had left in Italy. This money they poured into their daily living. Goldsmiths and silversmiths were busy all day long making chalices, goblets, and dishes. Tapestry weavers were weaving all ancient history, Greek history, Bible history, Roman history into hangings for walls. Fresco painters were painting the history of the family on other walls. Jewelers, sculptors, engineers converged on these ducal towns, bringing their finest work or most ambitious plans. And meanwhile there was a whole corps of musicians, poets, and entertainers to devise masques, dances, processions. In such a milieu, under the sunny smile of the reigning princess and often with the direct co-operation of her well-trained singing voice, music began to be elaborated into the art forms we know today.

For the most important asset of these rich families was frequently the baby princess. By bringing her up carefully and trading her off in marriage shrewdly, a family could do much to consolidate and expand its power. A girl was carefully educated to this end under the immediate direction of her mother, with the intention of making her a walking compendium of everything she ought to know by the time she reached the marriageable age of twelve. All day long the masters and mistresses were busy with her. One hears of girls who learned Greek, Latin, Hebrew, philosophy, theology, and medicine; girls who read the works of Plato through in the original by the time they were fifteen. They learned Greek mythology and Bible history and were equally acquainted with goddesses, nymphs, and the more interesting saints. They learned to make tapestry and to play the harp. Above all, they learned to make verse and to sing and compose in the new contrapuntal style.

The little princess was usually married between the ages of twelve and fourteen. Artistic talent and money combined to make her marriage a great day in Italian history. Family vied with family. She was received by her new relatives with celebrations that would make what her own family could do for her shrink to nothing. When King Alfonso of Aragon was married, fountains ran with wine and tables for thirty thousand were set up beside the sea at Naples. When the Duke of Urbino returned with his bride, the ladies and children of the city were ranged on the hillsides, carrying branches. Just as the people caught their first sight of the young couple, they all burst into a song composed especially for the event. The Goddess of Mirth descended to welcome them. Nymphs in Grecian robes and singers on horseback surrounded the Duchess and triumphantly escorted her in. At Milan, Leonardo da Vinci devised for the young wife of Giovanni Galeazzo a sort of firmament with planets circling and singing her praises. Sometimes the solemn and sedate little bride was carried by throngs of singing attendants bearing torches to her bridal chamber. There she was divested of layers of stiff brocade and her jewels and gilded headdress and put to bed behind the crimson curtains of the great carved nuptial couch with her husband, while all night the sound of singing and merriment rocked the palace.

So Beatrice d'Este went from Ferrara at fourteen to her young

From J. Quasten, Musik und Gesang, etc.

51. A bas-relief from the Villa Albani shows Roman women of the early Christian age shaking incense, beating a drum, and playing the double flute at a domestic altar. (See page 146.)

Musée de Louvre

52. Carved on a sarcophagus of the early Christian age are two Roman girls, typical of those young musicians condemned by St. Jerome as corrupters of men's morals. (See page 146.)

53. In an old Roman painting, the bridegroom watched women prepare the bride for marriage. Priestess-musicians burned incense and played the lyre at the home altar. (See page 146.)

54. Carved in stone, a Roman lady of early Christian times lies on her death-bed. Two women mourners and a woman flutist officiate. (See page 146.)

From O. Ursprung, Katholische Kirchenmusik

55. An illuminated initial in a religious book shows nuns singing in antiphonal chorus. (See pages 185 and 201.)

Courtesy of C. V. Mosby Co.

56. A fifteenth-century girl practicing magic to attract her lover. (See page 205.)

Vatican Library, Chigi CVIII, 234

57. The return of women to a natural participation in music came by way of social diversion. Men and women are depicted on a miniature of early Renaissance times, playing and singing together. (See page 213.)

Photograph by Anderson, Rome

58. Francesco di Cossa, sixteenth century, painted a group of young women musicians such as might have performed at any Italian court. (See page 221.)

husband, the Duke of Milan; she was his ambassador to the court of Venice at sixteen. And when she died in childbirth at twenty-two, she was already known as a great patroness of music and art, and is so remembered to this day. For during her brief youth as a lovely young wife, much of the talent of Italy—poets, artists, and musicians —had converged on her court and had been encouraged by her eager interest in them.

So her sister Isabella went to her husband, the Duke of Mantua. But Isabella lived to the ripe age of sixty-five. She devoted herself so earnestly to the encouragement of every kind of art and beauty that she is usually considered the perfect type of these ladies of the Renaissance. In her status as mistress, she had the opportunity to patronize artists and musicians. Besides being a skilled performer herself, she was a critic. Since she had the authority to command her employee—the professional musician—and since she also usually possessed an intimate knowledge of good music, the lady as patroness was able to exert a real influence over new trends in artistic endeavor. As more literary and musical manuscripts from the period are being discovered, it becomes apparent that many great ladies played a part in directing the development of secular song away from popular vulgarity. From their consistent choice of aristocratic poems to be set to music, a definite change in musical taste resulted. As it was still the custom to enhance the emotional content of the text by means of music, the quality of secular song was heightened and refined.

At her best, in the courts of the Italian Renaissance, the lady was earnest, high-minded, and well trained. When the young bride took her place in one of these courts, which were lavishly competitive with each other in music and art, it was as if she had entered a university for the rest of her life, for she was henceforth in daily association with scholars, artists, and musicians of the highest caliber, and called on to exercise her judgment with respect to what they did. So, in time, some of these ladies, such as Vittoria Colonna, became very wise persons in their own right.

The solemnity with which these women regarded their functions is shown in a letter of Vittoria Colonna to Margaret of France.

In our day, the long and difficult journey of life compels us to have a guide; it seems to me that everyone may find in her own sex the most appropriate models. . . . I turned towards the illustrious ladies

of Italy to find examples for imitation, and though I saw many
virtuous among them . . . yet one woman alone, and she not in
Italy, seemed to me to unite the perfections of the will with those of
the intellect; but she was so high placed and so far away that my
heart was filled with the gloom and fear of the Hebrews when they
perceived the fire and glory of God on the mountain-top, and durst
not draw near because of their imperfection.[3]

So, in Italy, and in all other courts where the new influence prevailed, as in those of England and France, the lady of the castle
flowered into the priestess of beauty. As the patroness of social music
and the object of song, she established a social and artistic norm for
the literary and musical language of the emerging modern world.
She fixed the code of social manners that prevails to this day and
whose pattern determines the social functions of music. Through her
mind and talk the revived culture of the classical age, in combination with a portion of the Christian culture of the Middle Ages, was
filtered and passed on to us today.

3.

The education of the princess and the ladies attendant on her included all the essentials of music, because much of their waking
hours would be spent on entertainments involving music. Historians
and biographers of the Renaissance have written in glowing terms of
the hundreds of musically talented ladies who spent a great part of
their time singing and playing—"abandoning themselves in ecstasy
to the composition of poetry and music." [4] They were encouraged to
play the viol, lute, flute, and harpsichord, and especially to sing. A
girl's training consisted in learning to read at sight, to harmonize
melodies, and to express herself in the language of both poetry and
music. It was the custom for composers to render their own music;
and even when they wrote down notes for others to play and sing,
they left a great deal to the musical imagination and discretion of the
performer. A person would not have been worthy of the title "musician" without ability to embellish a melody with newly invented
phrases or to improvise an accompaniment on lute or harpsichord.
The two branches of musical art—performance and composition—
went together as they had since time immemorial. Women appeared
as performer or composer and frequently as composer-performer.
    One of the highborn women musicians was Lucrezia Tuorna-

buoni, mother of Lorenzo the Magnificent. She composed Christmas carols and sang them with her children. Margaret of Austria (wife of Philip of Savoy) was another; she made beautiful love songs. Anne Boleyn was a third; she learned her music in Paris, where she had gone with Queen Mary, wife of Louis XII. Her accomplishments were many; she could dance and sing, she could play the lute and other instruments. One of her sad songs—"Death; O rocke me on slepe"—has been preserved. Still another song maker was Louise of Savoy. A skilled instrumental player herself, she often played for hours and presided over her women companions with their harps, flutes, and organs.

The lavish scale of social entertainments involving music demanded large numbers of trained voices. Most of the courts maintained *castrati*, whose soprano voices had been preserved by an operation performed before puberty. The *castrati* had been introduced into western Europe by the ecclesiastical authorities to sing soprano and alto parts in the church service. Having banished women from the liturgical choirs, they had to have a substitute for them, which they obtained by mutilating men. These strange creatures, spoiled, bedizened, spuriously feminine in appearance and personality, often had voices of unsurpassed strength, endurance, and brilliance.

After the fourteenth century, many kings, queens, and nobles had private chapels attached to their courts. They employed a choir, orchestra, and conductor to make music for both chapel and court. Queen Elizabeth, for instance, maintained four sets of singing boys. One set, called Children of the Revels, performed theatrical shows for the diversion of the courtiers and ladies in waiting. The Duke of Bavaria kept a group of about fifty men, boys, and castrati to sing in his chapel and also to perform at banquets and other secular occasions where music was desired. At one time his court musician was the famous Orlando di Lasso.

Since women were trained in music and since polyphony required many voices, there developed a need for the participation of women in addition to the castrati. But, despite the many references to the singing by women of *frottoli*, madrigals, and part songs, it is impossible to specify which of the songs were written for women. For when the polyphonic music was written down, the composer inscribed the music in any clef he preferred with no intention of indicating the pitch to be taken. *Cantus* meant the top part, *bassus* the lowest, no matter what the pitch. Any music of that period may, therefore, have been performed by women.

4.

In any case, the taste for women's singing at the courts soon developed to the point where it could not be satisfied by amateurs alone, no matter how well trained they were. There began to be a demand at the courts for professional women singers. During the year 1553 Donna Giovanna d'Arragona gave a musicale at her palace in Naples. Two castrati and two women singers performed. The women received the congratulations of the discerning guests for their perfect singing. About 1600 Vittoria Archilei and Francesca Caccini sang so beautifully that they turned the tide of the castrati's popularity in favor of the women singers.

As early as 1378 the professional woman singer had appeared. She traveled around from court to court seeking employment. Chantresses were paid by Philip at Cambrai. As the taste for women's singing developed, the courts began to compete for the finest talent and voices. At the court of Mantua, where Isabella d'Este had gone as a bride, one woman after another won fame as a singer, among them the famous "La Ariana." To display the singer's voice, musicians inserted more and more difficult coloratura passages into the madrigals. More and more attention was paid to a sensuous quality of voice. More and more interest was taken in showmanship. The most famous of these court singers were the trio at the Este court at Ferrara, Tarquinia Molza, Laura Peperara, and Lucrezia Benedidi. They performed with the many talented amateurs of the court in "concerts," which were not performances for an invited audience, but regular features of the social life at the palace. Under the leadership of Tarquinia Molza, Laura Peperara, and Lucrezia Benedidi, "the concerts of these ladies were for some time the greatest marvel of the Este court. . . . His Highness required the ladies to practice together every day, so that in those days in Italy and perhaps out of Italy, were no concerts of ladies better than these. Every day in summer they sang from 7 to 8. The organist sat at the harpsichord. Signor Firono, master of the chapel, played on the big lute. Signora Livia played the viola, Signora Guarina played the lute, and Signora Laura the harp." [5]

An orchestra of ladies, led by the brilliant Tarquinia Molza under the patronage of the Duchess Margarita, was a feature at Ferrara. An account in Otto Kindeldy's book on Italian music gives a vivid description of the women in action.

The orchestra consisted of ladies. On the days of the concerts they prepared in the hall a long table, at one end of which a large clavicembalo stood. The instrumentalists (women) stepped silently in one after another, took their places with their instruments at the table and waited in silence. Then the directress stepped out and sat herself at the other end of the table opposite the cembalo. She took a long flexible polished stick which lay ready for her and threw her glance over the orchestra, gave the signal and the orchestra played with a wonderful ensemble.[6]

When the Duke and Duchess of Ferrara visited other courts, they took the three ladies with them along with their men musicians and their most musical ladies in waiting. There was one particularly famous performance before Rudolph of Austria, whom Duke Alfonso had gone to meet at Brescello in 1571. In this concert sixty ladies and gentlemen took part. "And they make one of the concerts of about sixty voices and instruments: and behind a clavichord played by Luzzascho Luzzaschi sang the Signora Lucrezia and the Signora Isabelle Bendido, both together so well that I never heard better." [7]

Of the famous trio Tarquinia Molza stands out with a brilliance that makes one regret that the record of her so far discovered is so incomplete. One would like to have copies of the music she composed for lute, viol, and harp, as well as for the voice. It was performed by the ladies of the court orchestra conducted by her. It was also sung. (See Plate 58.) The extravagant praise of her concerts was apparently for the music as well as its performance. But none of it remains. Her brilliant career was cut short when Duchess Margarita dismissed her from the court as the result of her unhappy love affair with Jacques de Wert. She retired to her mother's country estate, and in her disgrace her music was perhaps banished with her. Since she had no longer an opportunity to present her works, her talent was stifled—at least so far as the known record goes. Such was the penalty for the woman who incurred the displeasure of the reigning priestess of beauty.

Tarquinia Molza was typical of the versatility of the woman musician. When she sang with Laura Peperara and Lucrezia Benedidi, composers from all over Europe flocked to hear the marvelous trio.

Luzzaschi, the concertmaster at the court of the Duke and Duchess of Ferrara, wrote a series of madrigals especially for these ladies. Few singers today could perform them. But she was almost equally admired as a conductor, and she was a composer.

So it was with most of the professional women musicians at the courts. Their unique assets were their singing voices. But they were all-around creative musicians. Many of the brilliant singers at the courts and *accademie* brought their own songs. Laura Peperara had her own style of reciting verses to the harp. Barbara Strozzi always performed at her father's musicales and often wrote her own songs. She published a set of madrigals for four voices. Laura Bovia, calling herself player and composer for the court of Mantua, published a volume of five-part madrigals. Francesca Caccini, one of the best of the sixteenth-century women composers, wrote madrigals, *ballate,* and dramatic works that were extremely popular wherever she took them. In France, Clementine de Bourges excelled in the composition of music. Women also composed in the new form of opera, received everywhere with enthusiasm. On the wedding day of Duke William of Bavaria, for instance, Orlando di Lasso arranged the performance of an opera by Mme Madeleine Casulana and of another opera by Caterina, niece of Adrian Willaert.

5.

Advantageous marriages could not always be found for daughters of the nobility. For the highborn girl who could not become a patroness of music and art and be a mistress of beauty at some court worthy of her birth, the convent was the alternative. And in the monastery, women were subject to the Church's age-old repression of their sex. An example of the definite regulations ordered by the ecclesiastical authorities can be seen in an edict given out in Rome on May 4, 1686:

Music is most detrimental to the modesty befitting the female sex, as it distracts from more proper actions and occupations; and on account of the dangers to those connected with it, instructors as well as listeners, no young girl, married woman, or widow, though for educational purposes, or else in convents or music schools under any other pretext, although studying music to the end of performing it in these convents, shall be permitted to take lessons in singing or any kind of instrument from men teachers.[8]

The rich convents were full of the sisters of the reigning ladies. They had had in youth the same education as their royal sisters. They carried to the convents the same aptitude, training, and taste for music. And the general trend away from the exaggerated repressions placed upon women by the Church was extending into monastic life. In Cologne, during the year 1550, an edict was given out by the bishop that the nuns might act the part of the Three Marys in the Easter plays. In Italy, many convents produced *sacre rappresentazioni*. Serafino Razzi wrote music for some young nuns in Florence to sing in their leisure time. Little dramas composed especially for nuns and novices began to appear. Marc Antonio Charpentier, for instance, presented the young women at Port-Royal a Christmas cantata that any group of schoolgirls today would enjoy. A story about the nuns of Bologna illustrates the new freedom in the monasteries. It appears that at the convents of St. Agnes and St. Christina there was great rivalry in the performance of liturgical song. During the year 1703 a prohibition was issued forbidding them to sing at all! At St. Christina this ruling was observed for one week, but at a ceremony of the taking of the veil, the choir was unable to suffer restraint. They broke into such sweet singing that crowds of people were attracted, bringing large sums of alms to the convent. Fortified by public approval, they continued to sing and inspired all the other convents to follow their daring example.

French and Italian nuns, like their laywomen contemporaries, profited from the musical renaissance which was taking place all over Europe. By the sixteenth century, women were attracting the musical public to the monastery chapels. At the Chiesa dello Spirito Sancto in Rome, the nuns sang vespers on Easter Monday with such perfection that the critic Pietro della Valle said he had never in his life heard such beautiful music. In the seventeenth and eighteenth centuries, French and Italian nuns received unstinted praise for their wonderful singing and playing. At the convent of San Vitale, Florence, Catabene de Catabeni and Cassandra Pigno were good *tenors*, Alfonsa Trotti a *basso*, singular and stupendous; Claudia Manfredi and Bartholomea Sorianati were sopranos (*soprani delicatissimi*). Rafaella de Magnifici and another Catabene were players of the cornet—playing also every other sort of instrument. Olimpia Leoni (1621) played a viola and sang contralto with great feeling and a beautiful voice. The famous walk to Longchamps (Paris) originated in the eighteenth century as a pilgrimage of enthusiasts who went to hear the nuns sing the Tenebrae on Good Friday.

It was for singers such as these that Palestrina, Lasso, Vittoria, Monteverdi, Couperin, Lotti, and other famous church composers wrote motets to be performed at special services.

In the convents of Italy there were several extremely good women composers. Suor Beatrice del Sera was felt by music lovers to be remarkably original. At the monastery of Santa Margherita in Milan, Maria Caterina Calegari was famous as a singer and organ player, attracting crowds of music lovers from far and near to hear her play and sing her own compositions. Many others received recognition for their motets and organ compositions.

6.

What the Italian ladies did at their courts was done with greater or less success at other European courts down to the nineteenth century. In the latter part of the sixteenth century the courts of England and France were also centers of musical activity. Queen Elizabeth herself was a musician, and English girls of the aristocracy studied music like the Italian girls. Lady Mildmay, a sixteenth-century English girl, in describing her pastimes to a friend, wrote: "Every day I practice my voice and set songs of five parts to my lute." [9] There was the royal pageantry in England and France involving special musical compositions and performances. On one of Queen Elizabeth's "progresses," she was greeted by a party of girls dressed to imitate the Greek graces and hours. They sang what is described as "a sweete song in six parts." When King Henry II of France traveled to Rouen, he too was entertained by a pageant. The chronicle of the festival describes a show chariot on which ladies representing Vesta, Royal Dignity, Triumphant Virtue, Respect, and Awe rode while they sang a song of praise to the King. The very words and music that they sang are still in existence—a four-part motet for three soprano voices and one alto by H. Lecouteux. (See Plate 59.)

> Praise and glory, thanks for the favours!
> Eviva the King, eviva." [10]

In the poorer and ruder land of Germany the courts were at first slow to take up the new fashion. In 1550, when the English ambassador reported to King Henry VIII his opinion of Anne of Cleves as a prospective queen, he said: "Nor yet she canne not synge nor pleye enye instrument, for they take it heere in Germanye for a rebuke and an occasion of lightnesse that great ladyes should be lernyd or have enye knowledge of musicke." [11]

But in the seventeenth and eighteenth centuries the German courts became centers for the patronage of music, supported by a widespread knowledge of composition, singing, and instrumental playing among the ladies of the nobility.

The Electress of Saxony—Maria Antonia Walpurgis—was extravagantly praised by Dr. Charles Burney. On his travels around Europe, he visited her court and described her talents: "This Princess is celebrated all over Europe for her talents and the progress she has made in the arts. . . . Her Highness is a poetess, a paintress, and so able a musician that she plays, sings, and composes in a manner which dilettanti seldom arrive at. She has, among other things, written in Italian two operas which she has herself set to music. . . . She sang a whole scene from her own opera Talestri in a truly fine style." [12]

In the late eighteenth century music flourished in Vienna under the Empress Maria Theresa. Caldara, for example, composed a four-part madrigal called "The Game of Cards" for the four archduchesses. Hasse wrote a charming litany for the Empress Maria Theresa and her eight daughters to sing in their private chapel. The Empress, who had a fine alto voice, took the principal solo part. The girls joined in the choral sections and the future Emperor Josef played the organ.

No women musicians in Europe or England could vie, however, with those of Italian blood and background. From Italy the spirit of the Renaissance flowed out, carried often by the melodious tones of a woman's voice. Sometime around 1700 a Venetian noblewoman, Antonia Bembo, went to Paris and attracted the attention of the great Louis XIV by her beautiful singing. Since she was performing her own compositions, the King believed her competent to be his court musician. While in the royal household and expected to produce a constant supply of new music, she composed freely. One of her most successful works was a Te Deum for mixed voices and instruments. This Te Deum contains a very fine trio for women's voices; the song extols the beautiful eyes of Princess Adelaide of Savoy. It was written by the order of the King to give thanks for the safe delivery of her baby boy. If it had been associated with the name of some great man composer, it would have been a celebrated piece.

Bembo was one of a very small group of talented women who attained the rank of musical leader at court. Only three are known to have been in the position held by countless men—Louise Couperin, a Frenchwoman who worked professionally for Louis XIII, Tarquinia Molza, and Antonia Bembo. Each of them, when under a stimulus somewhat comparable to that enjoyed by men, created the type of music demanded by their employers and demonstrated the ability of women to think and work in terms of contrapuntal music.

7.

So through the centuries, from the time the troubadours began singing to the lady in the castle, there was a series of momentous changes involving the relation of women to music and hence to the whole pattern of social life. By the fourteenth century the taboo against women playing instruments was removed. By the fifteenth century ballroom dancing, even with the kiss before the partners separated, was considered proper. By the sixteenth century disapprobation of women's natural voices changed to approval, and women became normal participants in the singing of madrigals and part songs. Old, young, and even servants were in demand where polyphonic music in the home required several performers. By the seventeenth century the ladies were acting on the castle stages. Castiglione, who described ideal courtly life, thought that music and singing were "pastimes most fitting when ladies were present." He set the standard for a great lady—"She must occupy herself with literature, music, painting, dancing and entertaining." [13] Music and women were no longer incompatible companions in Christian doctrine. A good Christian lady could improve herself with a little music. In this respect, times had changed.

With the freedom to make music, there was a limited opportunity at some courts for professional women musicians to work as conductors and composers. But such brilliant women tended to be unlucky and a little tragic. Society was not organized to sustain them or to further their genius. Where they emerged as composers they were social accidents. For the most part, the function of women at the courts was simply to provide inspiration to men musicians. And this function they fulfilled wherever a sufficiency of wealth and power was represented in some lady, carefully trained in music for her high position as fosterer of the genius of men.

In influencing and often initiating social changes and inspiring men to produce new music for new occasions, the priestess of beauty had a mission. She was the indispensable social background for the creation of secular music in the sixteenth, seventeenth, and eighteenth centuries. Through her, music came to be regarded as a direct extension of the functions of a lady. The aristocracy set the standard for the rising bourgeoisie, and even after the glory of the courts had faded many rich ladies of the nineteenth century retained the musical customs of the castle at their town houses or country estates. These dilettanti—those who delight in music—and amatores—those who love music—were quietly creating and maintaining that cultivated taste without which no men musicians, however great, can thrive.

This priestess of beauty was by no means the one whose coming had been crudely foreshadowed by the priestesses of the pagan religion. She was not a natural being, in the fullness of a free development, standing on the inalienable dignity of her own relation to life as mother and woman. Despite the earnestness of some of these ladies and the intelligent and hard work they gave to their social task, the priestess of beauty was an artificial creation, representing the subordination of the woman to an ideal of aristocratic family pride and power. But even so, the modern world owes much to her. In her, woman found again a real though limited place in the hierarchy of talent and power. The priestess of beauty symbolized for womanhood what Lodovico di Canossa attributed to music: "Music is the charm of life, its light, its sunny grace; no art responds thus to the needs of our nature, none brings us such various and vivid emotions. It calms and penetrates us and raises us to Heaven with the quick beating of its wings." [14]

It had been discovered that life cannot be fully lived without that charm.

CHAPTER XV

THE PRIMA DONNA

1.

*T*HE cultural pattern in which women as musicians function today was set at the beginning of the seventeenth century. At that time modern society, with new and revolutionary uses for music, began to take form.

The change began with the slow crumbling of Church and castle as the guides of the people's spirit and arbiters of their earthly fate. The Protestant rebels against the Catholic Church established their dominance in the northern European nations, which now assumed leadership. Though the Protestants frequently repressed women and limited the use of music, the religious and ethical monopoly of the Church as a whole was broken. Feudalism decayed or was violently destroyed. With its passing the power of the lady of the castle and the palace slowly declined.

Instead of looking to the Church to explain and control the vast powers of the universe, men gained increasing assurance, and increasing practical rewards, from exploring and controlling these powers through science. Instead of looking to princes and lords for material well-being, they began to find ever increasing means of getting well-being for themselves through trade and commerce and manufacturing.

All these new tendencies were best represented in America. Starting at the beginning of the new era with no real traditions based in medieval church and castle, it was free to make the most spectacular and universal application of trade, money-making, science, and invention. Modern America is now the supreme example of the change that had come over music and woman's relation to music.

Quite apart from the extension of music into new fields, during the seventeenth century there came a fundamental change in the idea of the utility of music—a change that amounted to a revolution in the social aspects of the art. The modern state and the modern educational system began to assume responsibility for leadership in thought and in the formation of ideals. As the new institutions gained in authority, music became an activity within the sphere of each, and musical expression from the talented individual found many new outlets. Instead of being inseparable from ritual, dance, and poetry, used primarily for the purpose of enhancing the emotional value of these expressions, music now began to be used as an end in itself. The stage, rather than the place of ritual or locale of work, became the setting for music. "Concert," which had meant music made concertedly by several people for their own edification or diversion, now came to mean a performance by skilled professionals in which the audience took no part. The focus of interest changed from what music could do to people to what people could do to music.

One thing that did not change, however, was the association of music with the most highly valued activities. Music had always been a magic means of inducing a spiritual state. The religious exercises that were believed to bring this about once occupied the most important place in the social life of the times. When religion lost some of its former dominance and other values developed, the nature of musical enterprise adapted itself to the changing environment. Trade, commerce, business, and money-making became the most highly valued activities. In the minds and lives of a great many people, business organizations and activity superseded the Church. And from the seventeenth century on until the present day, music entered a creative career as the handmaid of commerce. Thus the public performance for a price superseded the old religious practices.

The significance of this new relation of music to money is profound. Music lost the power that had been attributed to it from the beginning—the power to have some practical effect on the forces governing life. Music was no longer regarded as magic, but by many people merely as a means of making money, and by others as an amusement or diversion. But the more people were able to deal scientifically with physical and practical ills, the more they were left with a need for some other magic. So music became a means of spiritual escape from care and worry, even from the details of money-making. Other means had to be found to bend the powers of the universe to the will of the individual. But individuals still had no peace, no fullness of joy or reserve of vitality unless they harmonized themselves to the mighty rhythm of the universe. And the supreme means of doing this for modern people is music.

2.

Out of the quest for money and the need for spiritual escape developed the public concert, and with it a new popular goddess, the prima donna.

The popular concert gives to the people what formerly was the monopoly of court and castle and church. One does not have to ask the church or the lady of the castle for leave to enjoy skilled performances of music. One simply pays a price so small that any thrifty worker can afford it. This is an immense release to the spirit of man, and especially of woman. A woman buys her ticket equally with a man and attends what she pleases. The box office knows no sex.

The popular concert takes the ideal of the lady as priestess of beauty and gives her to the people as prima donna, the lady of their own worship. The lady of the castle and of the Renaissance palace had been a remarkable social institution. In her, aristocratic society had achieved a synthesis of the function of mother and wife and of the presiding spirit of music and social entertainment. In ancient society and in polished societies outside the West to this day, the mother and wife are one person, the hostess, musician, and entertainer quite another—a courtesan, a geisha, a singsong girl, often beloved and admired and highly cultivated, but deprived of the status of her who bears the burden of the race. In the lady of the castle and palace, the honorable wife and mother took over some of the arts, the charms, the social freedom, and the privilege of the courtesan. She could sing and dance in mixed company. She could be the object of the praises and admiration of men and musicians.

When the public concert developed, the people appropriated this lady and made her their own. A woman's charm and talent became legitimate public property. She could display it to any public audience, yet remain in person and in private reputation inviolate. The lady's voice was also appropriated. The Church could and did make rules against women's singing. But the people paid no heed. What they sought was a spiritual escape. There was no musical instrument that gave wings to the average person's spirit on which he or she could more easily soar away than the voice of a woman.

So out of the extension of the functions of the priestess of beauty to include all who could make a small votive offering at the box office, and out of the people's response to the woman's voice, there gradually evolved the prima donna. She thus became the modern goddess of music at whose altars a worshiping public burns incense of praise, on whom are showered all the gifts of the world, and whose managers profit by the devotion of her followers very much as pagan priests may have profited from the worship of old-time goddesses. And since women's voices early proved to be among the supreme attractions of the public concert, a way was opened for women to make large sums by the exercise of their own talents and to wield the power that money gives.

3.

The drift toward public performances featuring women's voices had begun in some of the palaces and castles whose owners made their own buildings and grounds serve, on occasion, the functions of community centers by opening them to the public. This was what happened when the Duke of Mantua allowed his master of music, Claudio Monteverdi (1567–1643), to develop the idea of drama set to music, which had already been tried out in Florence and elsewhere, into a stupendous performance for an invited audience of five thousand people. This drama or opera, the *Ballo dello Ingrata,* opened with an elaborate scene showing the Inferno, with the souls of the damned coming through its flames, two by two, singing of their sins and their eternal torment. The voices of women who took some of the singing parts thrilled the Duke's court.

Slowly the woman singer began to emerge from the safe seclusion of castle or court into some public places without losing caste. One intermediate step was the appearance of women singers of noble birth at the *accademie,* which were men's social clubs. Diana Paleotti, one of the famous seventeenth-century singers, was extravagantly admired by a certain Roman nobleman, Marc Antonio by name, and was followed by him from house to house where the *accademie* met, and where she sang and played. Yet when she appeared at some public entertainments, he exclaimed in surprise that a noblewoman would dare to sing before so many people.

Another intermediate step was the appearance of a composer's wife as a singer in an opera composed by her husband. Several of the writers of the new musical drama were married to skilled singers. When the Teatro San Cassiano, the first public opera house, was opened in Venice in 1637, the first opera to be produced was *Andromeda*. The composer, F. Manelli, sang the role of Neptune himself, and his wife, Maddalena, impersonated Andromeda, but the roles of the goddesses Juno, Venus, and Astrea were taken by castrati.

So great a revolution as the appearance of honorable women upon a public stage could not come to pass without stirring the opposition of the Church. Naturally, the authorities took steps to prevent girls from adopting musical careers. A series of decrees was issued. The first one appeared in 1588 and affected only the Roman theater, but in 1676 Pope Innocent XI extended the prohibition to cover the whole of Christendom.

When women did perform in a public place, an apology seemed to be in order. The prologue to the second part of the opera *The Siege of Rhodes,* one of the first English operas, is spoken by a woman who says: "Hope for our women less, whose bashful fear wondered to see me dare to enter here." When in Russia, at exactly the same period, orchestras were being organized and theaters opened by Peter the Great, even this notable reformer could not break down the tradition of the monastic ideal in which Russian women had been nurtured for centuries. He was obliged to import actresses from Germany for the first Russian operas. Russian women themselves shrank from the public gaze.

But as the seventeenth century progressed and the musical world went mad over opera, women solo singers were in great demand. The impressarios fully realized the sales value of a beautiful female voice. Unlike the Greeks, Europeans could not dispense with the actress, so they made her attractive offers in the forms of educational opportunities and financial rewards for singing in public.

With the rise of the middle classes in the eighteenth century, the career of the woman singer began to be soundly established along with the custom of public concerts and stage performances. Concerts of vocal and instrumental music, operas with ballet, and oratorios were performed in the public theater for the benefit of all who could pay admission. The fact that noblewomen were so accustomed to playing, singing, dancing, and acting in the castles undoubtedly in-

59. During the Renaissance period, women musicians participated in pageants and are so depicted upon a decorated chest. (See page 224.)

60. In a French lithograph from about 1830, a modern women's chorus can be seen in the making. The man, instead of waiting, is now in the center of the scene. Compare the men in Plates 13, 17, 19, 30, 32, 53. (See page 255.)

61. The seventeenth-century artist Florigerio has symbolized the relation of Western European women to music by painting an entertainer as the companion of men. A nun retreats from the group and the natural woman is missing. (See page 282.)

62. In this photograph of Martha Graham's "Primitive Mysteries," the grouping of the women and the position of their hands is similar to that in Plate 9. But while the Sherbro women *live* their rituals, these dancers merely *act* them on the stage. (See page 241.)

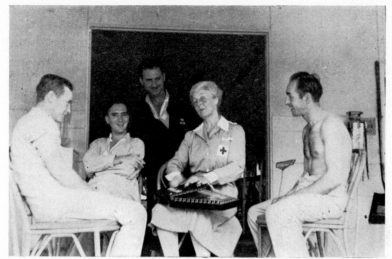

63. A Gray Lady with an auto-harp invokes the healing power of music for the rehabilitation of wounded veterans. (See page 290.)

64. Photographed in action, Vereda Pearson conducts a Neighborhood Home Festival. (See page 293.)

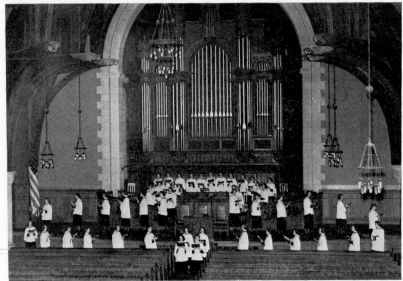

65. Vassar girls in vestments officiate at their chapel services. (See page 293.)

66. In a crayon drawing, the artist has expressed her appreciation of the spiritual sustenance she derives from singing in a women's chorus. (See page 293.)

fluenced public opinion in the matter of accepting women and girls of the middle classes as actresses and singers on the public stage. Even the continued opposition of the Church and the competition of the castrati could not turn the tide against the popular determination to make the public woman singer a trained musician with an honorable social status, whose highly lucrative career should be open to any girl of talent.

The alternative to women's singing was the singing of women's parts by castrati. Throughout the seventeenth and eighteenth centuries, sometimes women, sometimes castrati sang. The toleration of these curious substitutes for women was part of a general lack of verisimilitude in early Italian opera. No one seemed to be artistically offended if Hercules had a high soprano voice or if a maiden nymph was impersonated by Vittoria Tesi, a popular singer with an alto voice as deep as a man's. All interest was centered in vocal technique, in the ability of the singer to trill, shake, make "divisions," and reach incredible heights or depths of tone. Through the eighteenth century, wherever the Italian operas went, the castrati went with them. Upper-class groups and court circles pampered them. Clad in silk, velvet, and lace, with diamonds glittering on their soft, white, plump hands, they continued to warble and posture and to assume incredible airs, even in dealing with kings and potentates. In the portrait Seneseno had painted of himself, he represented himself as a Roman emperor, with ladies kneeling and kissing the hem of his coat of mail. Caffarelli complained to Louis XV that he did not receive the royal privileges accorded ambassadors. "All the ambassadors in the world could not make one Caffarelli," he said.[1]

While these creatures remained the darlings of some upper-class audiences, the genuine popular taste would have none of them. As the people with their increasing prosperity asserted themselves and the greatest opportunity for the singer came to be the concert stage, the castrati disappeared and the prima donnas took their places. Finally Napoleonic law made it a crime to castrate a boy. Apropos of the subject of incentives and stimuli to productive musical imagination, it is an important fact that, throughout their long history, castrati (or eunuchs) are never spoken of as composers and are not associated in any way with creative work.

The prima donna, who had already proved her worth in competition with the castrati, rose to greater heights of fame in the nineteenth century. The romantic movement sounded the death knell of artificiality. It was now the thing to capitalize human feelings. Love, longing, hate, despair, and other emotional states became the subject matter of music. The more a composer's music was capable of manifesting a mood, the greater its appeal. Audiences demanded men with bass voices and women with deep, rich, stirring voices to sing the new romantic songs and operas. The more passionately the women performers sang or played, the more fuel was added to the fire of enthusiasm for their musical service. The very qualities that had formerly made women unacceptable in vocal music now became their best assets.

While few singers could reach the heights of the great operatic prima donnas or concert singers, the way was opened for many skilled musicians to take the lesser parts. In the nineteenth century the limitless funds of the Americans and the ready enthusiasm of our great audiences made concert singing a most lucrative profession for the European women musicians. An American tour could make their fortunes for life.

4.

At her best the prima donna entirely transcended sex appeal and theatrical glamour and became a great representative figure, for women no less than for men. One of the most beautiful descriptions of Jenny Lind was that of Clara Schumann, who saw her with the eyes of a great woman and great artist.

"The Lind" has a genius for song which might come to pass only once in many years. Her appearance is arresting at first glance, and her face, although not exactly beautiful, appears so because of the expression in her wonderful eyes. Her singing comes from her inmost heart; it is no striving for effect, no passion which takes hold of the hearer, but a certain wistfulness, a melancholy, which reaches deeply into the heart, whether one will or no. At the first moment she might appear to some as cold, but this is not so at all; the impression is caused by the purity and simplicity which underlies her singing. There is no forcing, no sobbing, no tremolo in her voice; not one bad habit. Every tone she produces is sheer beauty. Her coloratura is the most consummate I have ever heard. Her voice is not large in itself, but would certainly fill any room, for it is all soul.[2]

Music like Jenny Lind's was made possible because it was wanted. The people had called forth in her powers such as had been dormant in other women for centuries. She could transcend the narrow and silly patterns of femininity still prevalent in the middle of the nineteenth century in a serene assurance of her power over so many hearts and minds everywhere. Wealth and praise were showered on her in her spectacular American tour, but she did not sing only for wealth or adulation. The lavishness with which Americans were ready to pour these at the feet of a prima donna rather overwhelmed her. In the midst of splendor she remembered her simple childhood and said wistfully, "Herrings and potatoes—a clean wooden chair and a wooden spoon to eat milk soup with—that would make me skip as a child." [3] The greatest prima donnas could always say in the words of Edith Wynne Mathison, "Nobody pays me for my art. That I give to the best of my ability. What I am paid for is what I must put up with in trying to give the world my art." [4]

At the present time, the popularity of the virtuosa—be she vocalist or instrumentalist—is undimmed. Newcomers on the stage are the wonderful Negro singers. When Marian Anderson was invited to sing one Easter afternoon on the steps of the Lincoln Memorial, the people of Washington thronged to hear her until the open spaces were filled with a vast surging crowd. This musician belongs to a race that, until only yesterday, had been barred from the professional musical life of European and American culture. Once the taboo was removed, once prejudice against the Negroes subsided sufficiently to give them liberty of action, several great singers rose to well-deserved fame. No better illustrations could be found of the way force of custom and taboo operate against the free use of human energy.

5.

While the prima donna was beginning to win her extraordinary place in modern music, the solo singers of the eighteenth century opened the way for the professional choral singer and her professional training. Before the eighteenth century there were no choruses in the modern sense. One or two performers to a part were regarded as sufficient to reproduce the composer's intention. Among the many new developments in musical customs was the rendition of music by large groups of trained people. Gluck's innovation in opera created a demand for the chorus. By introducing choral sections in addition to the solo parts, he required the participation of many more singers. As choirboys and castrati were far from plentiful enough to make up a large chorus, girls were pressed into service. The romantic movement increased the demand for them. No one would have been satisfied if beautiful young girls with trained voices had not sung the parts of the Polovetzian maidens in *Prince Igor,* or the priestesses in *Boris Godunov,* or the three Rhine naiads in *Das Rheingold.* The new interest in dramatic verity made women indispensable and opened up a wide avenue for musical activity.

The problem was to provide enough trained girls to take the feminine parts. Even as late as 1825, Spontini had to dress up choirboys in the robes of vestal virgins for his opera *Les Vestales.*

The demand for trained singers to take part in operas and oratorios prompted musicians to found special schools for the instruction of music. Hence, one of the new movements of the seventeenth and eighteenth centuries was the institution of schools for girls. Previously, girls had received their education at home from private tutors, or they had attended the monastic schools where they were educated as if they were to become nuns. One of the first schools for the professional woman performer was founded in France by Lully. He persuaded Louis XIV to allow girls to dance in the ballets of the operas he was composing. This was the origin of the Académie Française. Several princes in Germany founded singing schools for girls. In Hamburg a municipal theater was established—a unique institution in the history of German opera. A description of the activities there stated that "the female personnel is made up of daughters of destitute merchants and artesans." In 1711 seven girls are named in the records, their good social position being expressly specified, as if the authorities wished to make the profession respectable. Later, almost every city in Europe, England, and the Americas had several conservatories of music and, probably without exception, expected the attendance of girls, whose tuition fees were needed by the teachers to make their business profitable.

6.

The prima donna also broke ground for instrumental players as artist performers, though instrumentalists lacked an undeniable advantage or disadvantage in tone production. Women had here the competition of men, especially of those who started the fashion of playing on the new and improved pianos with a touch loud and heavy enough to break the strings. Nevertheless, many women have excelled in playing both the old-fashioned harpsichord and the new piano in public performances.

Supreme among all women pianists was Clara Schumann. All that makes the drama, the glory, and the tragedy of a woman artist's life was hers in full measure. Trained by her father as a child wonder and taken on concert tours by him, she was treated with the utmost harshness by him when she married the impecunious musician and composer Robert Schumann. Her father took her savings from her earnings and would let her have nothing to begin married life. Though her husband loved her dearly, admired her art, and constantly spoke of the inspiration she gave him, they both took it as a matter of course that she would make a daily routine that would be convenient to him. In her diary Clara wrote: "My playing is getting all behindhand, as is always the case when Robert is composing. I cannot find one little hour in the day for myself." [5]

Seven children and a husband who spent his later days in an asylum drove her to resume her concert career. A woman of thirty-five, she took up the task of making Beethoven's work, then considered baffling and abstruse, known through her exquisite playing. She was the inspiration and critic of Brahms, who was fourteen years younger than she and who adored her. She devoted herself to making his music known, by her beautiful playing, along with that of Beethoven and her husband. In city after city of Europe the lovely lady, "almost a widow," her slight figure very slender in its tight bodice above her full skirts, sat at the piano. Steadily, tirelessly, with a standard of execution that was the wonder of all the musicians who heard her, she kept up her tours, playing to bring her husband back to health, playing to support her children, playing to make known new and beautiful music the world had not learned to appreciate. These were her incantations.

For those talented girls who could not attain the success of a Clara Schumann, a Mme Carreño, or many others, the piano proved to be a practical means of providing a satisfactory career in professional performance and especially in teaching others to perform. In modern times, no other instrument has surpassed it in popularity and in practicability for the woman musician.

Next to the professional piano players, violinists presented themselves to the public. Maddelina Lombardini, a particularly brilliant musician of the eighteenth century, rivaled Tartini in her playing. Like the ladies of the courts, she often played her own compositions.

In the nineteenth century numerous others performed before admiring audiences. Soloists of either sex performing on wind instruments in public were extremely rare until the most recent times.

7.

But the genius of individual performers could not break down entirely the old taboos against women in music. What was yielded to an individual woman of genius or charm was not yielded to women collectively and as a right. In no field do the curious anomalies that have been inherited in our culture from a dark past show more clearly than in the barriers women encounter as players in orchestras.

Among men, professional instrumental players of lesser skill found many opportunities for a musical career in the opera and symphony orchestras, which were increasing by leaps and bounds throughout the nineteenth century. But here women were, and still are, at a grave disadvantage. Players and conductors in the newly forming orchestras at first consisted entirely of men who used music as a means of making a living and who resented the competition of women. For some unknown reason, harpists proved to be an exception to the general taboo against women appearing in an orchestra. A single woman playing the harp graced almost every concert. Since the First World War, competent instrumental players have been pouring out of the conservatories, seeking employment in the large orchestras, in various types of chamber orchestras, or in jazz bands. But still controversy rages over the question of the participation of professional women instrumental players in orchestra associations supported by the public. The women have their supporters and their antagonists announcing diametrically opposed opinions as to the worth of women musicians.

On the one hand, these instrumental players have many supporters, especially in localities where women themselves are accustomed to independence. At Long Beach, California, for instance, an all-women orchestra is maintained by municipal tax. A short time ago Leopold Stokowski said: "I find that women are equally as talented as men." And in the New York *Times* of September 29, 1940, appeared a statement by Izler Solomon, conductor of the first all-women symphonic orchestra to appear regularly on the air: "It is perfect nonsense to say that women are inferior to men in the world of music. . . . In many instances, they are better than men. . . . Women are more sensitive and are apt to have a finer perceptive reaction to phrasing." Hans Kindler, in 1946, represents the most liberal attitude toward women players: "Their ability and enthusiasm constitute an added stimulant for the male performers . . . they were a veritable godsend to most conductors during the war years. The National Symphony has re-engaged its fifteen women players." [6]

On the other hand, José Iturbi goes so far as to agree with some of the nineteenth-century conductors in believing that women can never be "great musicians." On that account, he refused to accept girl graduates from the Eastman School of Music as players in the Rochester Symphony Orchestra. In a recently published article, Sir Thomas Beecham boldly announced that "Women Ruin Music." He explained his meaning by adding: "If the ladies are ill-favored the men do not want to play next to them, and if they are well-favored, they can't." [7] In this remark he makes himself out a cad, or, as his countrymen say, a "bounder." But he also places himself in the category of the early Church Fathers, who wished to make the life of the spirit, including music, a man's business with no thought of women's emotional needs.

Even today, in most parts of Europe, England, North and South America, however, women have an uphill fight to secure a desk in a professional orchestra. Many irrelevant reasons are advanced for their exclusion. Women, it is said, cannot attend rehearsals on account of their home duties, women cannot travel, women interfere with men's liberty to swear and spit, girls might flirt with the patrons. . . . These difficulties are overcome by managers of theatrical and ballet troupes because girls are essential to the success of their business. Orchestral music can be performed without women. Hence, excuses are made to exclude them.

As a result of excluding women from the regular civic orchestras, women have organized instrumental groups of their own. Musically, these groups are without justification, since in instrumental playing the sex of the player should make no difference, unless, of course, feminine sex charm is advertised as box-office appeal. What the serious woman musician hoped was that skill, when demonstrated, would enable her to be employed in a regular orchestra on terms of merit. But when the women's organizations first appeared, they were met by the critics with a conspiracy of silence. In 1896, for instance, the concerts of the Women's String Orchestra of New York were never reviewed by the press. Later, sarcasm was employed. Patronizing remarks about women's orchestras are still the rule rather than the exception. It is the reporter's favorite joke to compare women players to sirens or angels. The old idea of the Jewish rabbis and the Christian Church Fathers, that a woman musician must be either a seducer of good men or a sexless spirit, dies hard. Most critics, indeed, treat with levity the legitimate attempts of women to earn their living by means of instrumental music: "Eight hundred feminine members of the American Federation of Musicians campaigned for the right to toot the trombone and blow the bassoon—for pay. They charged that the eighteen thousand masculine members of the union so dominate the field of professional music in New York that a woman can obtain jobs only by playing the harp, piano, or organ." [8]

Unless a girl attains the rank of a successful virtuosa, she has far less chance for a profitable and interesting career as an instrumentalist than if she were a man of equal native talent and proficiency.

8.

Despite the cultural backwardness of some men musicians in positions of authority, the prima donna was a constant inspiration to the woman musician. As she soared to her great glory in the nineteenth century, women engaged in a determined but uphill battle to assert leadership in other kinds of endeavor associated with music. Within the last two or three decades this is beginning to show some real results, especially in America. As conductors, as critics and musicologists, as composers, as teachers, and as dancers, women have been able to do more or less original work—not nearly as much as they might do, but an increasing amount with increasing freedom and effectiveness. A few individuals have been able to compete successfully with men on men's own ground. For a representative of leadership in every modern department of the modern musical world, there is Nadia Boulanger. As performer, conductor, composer, and teacher, she attracted men and women from the four corners of the earth to her institute at Fontainebleau, and has become a distinguished leader in the advancement and dissemination of intellectualized music.

Nowhere has women's initiative in enterprises associated with music been more original than in creating new forms of the dance. Since the dance as a religious expression was forbidden by organized religion, ballets in operas developed in the most artificial and barren manner. But by the end of the nineteenth century the public became ravenous for new sensations. At the same time women were beginning to be sufficiently emancipated to act as free lances. From Isadora Duncan on, a steady supply of women artists has been revitalizing the old primitive dance forms that expressed subconscious desires and strivings. Like her primitive ancestress, the dancer of today usually combines the functions of creator, performer, and leader. (See Plate 62.)

In conducting music, however, the same barriers that keep women players out of orchestras were, and still are, effective. Men were already intrenched in musical leadership, and exclusion from classes in conducting added to the handicaps confronting a woman leader. When Antonia Brico, now a successful orchestral conductor, worked her way to Berlin and persuaded Karl Muck to accept her in his class, he was at first reluctant. Even in 1920, a woman leader seemed to be an anomalous creature. When a woman did succeed as a conductor, she had to overcome the general prejudice against women as leaders of public enterprises. The majority of people (including women) questioned a woman's ability to understand or demonstrate the music. Although she might have proved her authority, still they condemned her. Emma Steiner, a brilliant musician in New York City, successfully led the Anton Seidl Orchestra of eighty players. One of her admirers, Heinrich Conrad, said that he would like to promote her to be a conductor of the Metropolitan Opera Association, but that he did not dare to brave public animosity against a woman. Although prejudice against women leaders has abated sufficiently for several to have achieved marked success, still, except occasionally as guests, women are not asked to conduct the most important symphony orchestras.

On the other hand, a forecast of better times brings hope to young women musicians. Many of them are benefiting from a change not only in the attitude of teachers toward them but also in the new liberality of public opinion toward women leaders. Girls who enter the Westminister Choir School at Princeton, New Jersey, suffer from no suspicion of incapacity. This school is affiliated with the low-church Protestant groups that have taken the lead in breaking down barriers against the participation of women in the religious ceremony. The girls are trained not only to be choral singers, but also to be choir directors and organists. Young women graduates are as much in demand as their men companions. For missionary outposts and rural communities, married couples are at a premium. As a result of the general change in attitude toward the natural women, the number of competent women conductors is annually increasing.

9.

It is especially in the art of teaching that women have been able to break new ground by emphasizing social values of music that tend to be neglected by men musicians. The exclusion of women from musical activities where men have strong vested interests has forced women to initiative and enterprise, which, in time, if women prove to have a sounder sense of social responsibility, may prove to be a boomerang to men.

Many farsighted women have worked hard to establish music teaching in public and private schools and to develop methods of their own. As far back as 1850, an Englishwoman, Sarah Ann Glover, invented a sol-fa system for reading music. By virtue of it, hundreds of new choral societies sprang up in England. Opportunity for more individuals to participate in choruses and choirs was tremendously increased. From her day, almost a hundred years ago, to this, there has been a steady stream of women leaders intent upon breaking down the pre-emption of musical authority by the few and upon helping more people to experience music firsthand. A contemporary leader among women musicians is Olga Samaroff, the distinguished pianist. Realizing the lack of an adequate technique in so many adults for hearing music, she planned a course of study to give a person who has never been musically educated the elementary training for listening. The "Layman's Music Course" has been widely circulated to the enrichment of thousands previously incapable of enjoying music.

Though women, in general, have lacked adequate institutional support, this also is granted to gifted individuals on occasion. An outstanding example of this is the permission granted by the Catholic Church to a nun, Mother Georgia Stevens, to train the teachers, both men and women, who were needed to carry out an important reform in the musical usage of the Church. It is now ordained that the members of Roman Catholic congregations shall be taught to give their responses to the priest in Gregorian plain chant, according to a very ancient custom. Hence children in the parish schools are now given systematic instruction in singing.

For this a nun, Mother Georgia Stevens, who sums up in herself the long tradition of music in women's convents, organized and directed classes and trained teachers, many of them women. She wrote a graded series of six music textbooks to teach sight reading and the elements of composition—entitled the *Tone and Rhythm* series— which are a beautiful example of the application of intelligence, imagination, tact, and charm to teaching music. This teaching she designs not for the purpose of making skilled performers, but to restore to music its rightful place as a universal language for the deepest human emotions.

In her work as a teacher up to her death in 1946, and in the books she has left behind her, Mother Stevens has brought into the life of children and young people in the United States something of the leadership and power of the great nuns of the Middle Ages. Any child trained in her methods will henceforth possess music as a natural language and a spiritual resource. As regards participation in congregational singing, Catholic women and girls will eventually be in a position vastly superior to that of their Protestant sisters. Unfortunately, as yet the number of teachers trained in Mother Stevens' methods is insufficient to reach more than a few parishes. Like so many of the new musical customs in which women are having the chance to participate in a natural manner, only a beginning has been made, and only a very few women are profiting from changing attitudes.

10.

Mother Stevens' work was a long step in the right direction. But elsewhere in the great educational system that had been developing throughout western European and American civilization, the cleft between different types of musicians was widened. There were patrons, producers, impressarios, publishers, conductors, performers, and composers. Each group required intensive training and often cultivated quite different capabilities. All together, they served as a hierarchy of men and as purveyors of men's musical ideas to an expectant public. Women were no more in this hierarchy than they had been in the priesthood, except in the capacity of performers of men's music. Here the prima donna shone. But she shone alone. The expression of collective womanhood through music was lacking.

Under some circumstances the brilliant achievement of the prima donna might have provided a more vital stimulus and braver musical leadership for women. But she reached her height in connection with a general social tendency to overrate virtuosity as an end in itself and to underrate creative self-expression through composition. It is true that some prima donnas were composers. When the excellent professional singer Josephine Köstlin-Lang was a young girl of fifteen, Mendelssohn spoke with enthusiasm of her talent: "She has such a gift for composing and singing songs as I have never heard. She gives me the greatest joy musically I have ever experienced." [9] In later life, Josephine sang at her own recitals and also published many songs that were received with admiration. She was only one of many women performers who both composed and sang or played her own music. Clara Schumann composed for the piano and for the voice. The brilliant pianist, Mme Carreño, composed a stirring song that became the national anthem of her country.

But as the demands of virtuosity compelled performers to devote themselves completely to their task of acquiring a more and more brilliant technique, the urge to create was stifled. Men, too, became specialized into either performers, conductors, or composers. Anton Rubenstein is a good example of a musically talented boy who neglected his creative impulse in favor of virtuosity on the piano. Pianists and violinists even gave up composing their own cadenzas in concertos. Not the slightest stigma of spiritual or intellectual deficiency was attached to these artists—men or women. It was simply that custom had changed. Women, therefore, followed the fashion and lost the one springboard they had had for creative work.

The glorification of performing artists out of all proportion to their real service to society leads us to a secondhand and vicarious participation in music. Love, joy, grief, symbolic union with the rhythm of life find musical expression through witnessing performance on the stage rather than through actual participation by people themselves. A "festival" too often means a public performance by professionals rather than public participation by the people who are affected by the spirit of such a festival. We are satisfied to celebrate a victory by listening to a symphony. We have accustomed ourselves to hearing requiems away from the presence of the dead, and to watching dancers on the stage step through the paces of a primitive puberty rite, as in the beautiful conception of Martha Graham.

Such vicarious participation in music tends to deceive youth into thinking that men and women can dispense with the work of making every detail of living right and vital and that they are to look for beauty and art only in museums and on the stage. Thousands of girls and boys who should be learning the rudiments of music, who should be regarded as precious raw material from which genius is refined, are diverted from a straightforward, natural attitude toward music. Merely average ability to sing or play becomes mistaken for marked talent. Girls and boys glorify actors, actresses, movie stars, opera singers, and attempt to emulate them rather than aiming at the ideal of incorporating music into their own daily lives.

Overemphasis on virtuosity is now reaping its just reward. Our young composers—men and women—are at a distinct disadvantage when compared with those of former times. Societies have to be organized to "encourage" creative work. Prizes are offered to "stimulate" expression in terms of music. The public is not interested in new works, but places a far higher value on some popular singer or conductor who is able to exert a temporary magical charm over spiritually starved listeners. By following too intensely the ideal of *showmanship*, we narrow the groove for musical expression rather then opening wide the gates to limitless realms of imagination.

So the prima donna has been the representative of two great tendencies in modern music. On the one hand, her refulgent glory has helped gifted individual women to function as musicians. The light shed by her has been a sort of sunshine insensibly melting the frozen and sterile attitudes of the Church toward the natural woman musician. On the other hand, she has become the representative of a deplorable tendency to substitute highly finished performance of others' music for original musical creation, and to listen to music instead of participating in it. In glorifying the one spectacular woman who reaches heights of virtuosity, the influence of the prima donna and her spiritual descendant, the motion-picture star, has not been wholesome. As a popular goddess of music and charm, she is a dangerous deity whose presence in our midst needs now to be challenged if we are to revitalize the spirit of our young men and women by means of music.

CHAPTER XVI

THE CAMILLAE

1.

WHEN the priests and priestesses of ancient Rome approached the altars, they were attended not only by boy acolytes, but also by girl acolytes. These girls were called camillae.

So the modern priestess of beauty, the prima donna, has her attendants in the many amateurs who have been inspired by music. These are her camillae.

These amateurs have two functions. One is to act as patronesses or sponsors of performing artists. The other is to perform music themselves, in co-operation with or under the leadership of professionals.

For recognition and support, musical talent depends upon intelligent music lovers. As organizers of musical enterprise in all its forms, women continue to play an important role. The ranks of the few aristocratic ladies who patronized musicians in palatial residences have now been increased by thousands of prosperous ticket buyers for public concerts. In almost every city, women are associated for the purpose of assisting local artists and of helping to support the large orchestras and choruses. While there are still those who agree with Cosima Liszt that women were put into the world to serve great *men*, an increasing number are making a point of supporting women artists. Many a women's club now engages women musicians to sing or play at the meetings. And this tendency found a broader expression in 1939, when the General Federation of Women's Clubs, meeting in New York, stated that it would henceforth encourage those orchestras that employed women as well as men players.

Although women are so active and so beneficial an influence in the essential task of advertising and planning music, and although more women than men attend concerts, still the directing boards of the large orchestras and opera companies are made up primarily of men. The reason for this is that since the performance of music must be a profitable business, members of the board must have business, rather than musical, experience. To register her disapproval, the patroness may boycott an individual or an organization, but rarely from the inner circles does she make ultimate decisions about new trends in music. Her control is more negative than positive, more conciliatory than self-assertive. She herself determines this attitude and deliberately chooses to curb her power. In the musical world women actually have more power than they are exercising at the present time, but they allow their relation to music to be governed by their relation to men and to the type of culture in which they live.

Just as our modern art of music depends on amateurs as patrons, so it also depends on amateurs as performers in private and for their own pleasure. On the desire of amateurs to perform music themselves, a vast musical enterprise flourishes—including teachers and music publishers. Without these acolytes many professional musicians could not find means to live. As amateur performers of all kinds, women are now as numerous, as enthusiastic, and as powerful as men.

2.

But there is one field that requires a special discussion, and some historical background, for here amateurs participate to the virtual exclusion of professionals. This is the field of choral music. In this department of our musical civilization, amateurs are essential. Without their voluntary and temporary service on the stage, the great choral groups of modern times would be a financial impossibility. For women who love and crave music but who do not wish to be professionals, this custom has enormous benefit—for it enables them to participate in the greatest music with a professional conductor, accompanied by a professional orchestra and soloists, without interfering with their home life.

The rise of the middle classes to prosperity enabled many more people to pay admission to concerts. In the seventeenth century these new public audiences clamored not only for operas but also for other types of choral music. The men and boys trained in church choirs could not entirely satisfy the demand. Students' choral societies from the men's universities often gave both private and public concerts. Older men, too, who had singing societies and glee clubs for their own diversion, invited guests to hear them sing the popular part songs and madrigals. But such men as these and the trained church choirs were hardly fitted to present great oratorios and other forms of sacred music to the public. Then it was that volunteer choirs of men and women offered their services and immediately became indispensable. As early as 1680, mixed choruses appeared in France. By 1780 they were found in practically every city of Europe, England, and the United States.

Oratorios were first written about 1600, at the same time as the first operas. An oratorio differs from an opera in that it deals with a religious subject. The name "oratorio" was used because the oratory of churches was generally the place of practice and performance. It is said that the first oratorios were action songs, just like the operas. And it seems certain that women participated. But the presence of women in concerts of a sacred character, especially when they were performed in church, was objected to by many church officials and by the pious conservatives. In the first mixed choruses organized for singing oratorios, women sang only the soprano parts. Often, in public performances, they merely reinforced the choirboys' voices. In 1784 at the Handel commemoration in Westminster Abbey, for instance, *eight* ladies were permitted to assist the boys. Forty-eight men sang the alto parts, and indeed, until very recently, in many English churches and concerts men continued to sing alto. In one of the early American choruses, women seemed to be admitted out of a feeling of tolerance for their eagerness to sing. The Stoughton Musical Society, organized in 1774, gave women the treble but not the alto parts. Men sang the alto line and women merely imitated the tenors an octave higher in the treble range. Only gradually did the women take a natural place among the singers. When Mendelssohn and Spohr organized groups, they insisted upon giving women the alto parts to sing. After about 1840, women supplanted choirboys and even the male altos, and thus established beyond recall the modern mixed chorus.

The latest development of the mixed chorus has come about through the colleges for women and co-educational colleges. The establishment of institutions where women could gather for study and training made centers where women could function collectively as amateur chorus singers. They immediately established their high value for music. Men's colleges now send formal invitations to the girls to join with them in producing the great choral works.

Some of these mixed choirs are famous, appearing on the stage in special hierarchal costume. The St. Olaf Choir is clothed in purple velvet and the Westminster Choir in red with white satin surplices. So as far as the performance of vocal music is concerned, the mantle of the nun-priestess musician of former times has fallen on the shoulders of the modern college girl.

This has made a great many changes in choral music. Not only has the personnel of the chorus changed, but the sound of the music has changed. The B Minor Mass, Handel's oratorios, the Missa Solemnis, and other choral works that were written with the sound of falsetti, or boys, in mind are now associated with the sound of women's voices.

Another change has been the change in the character of the music. Modern audiences respond to music that expresses human emotions. For the purpose of enhancing the emotional effect, they prefer the joint performance of men and women. Brahms composed his German Requiem for adult men and adult women to sing together. Without the quality of maturity and experience with life, this appealing work could not be affectively interpreted. And ever since Brahms' time, this lead has been followed by composers of great choral music.

At the same time that women and girls were edging their way into the mixed choruses and were being trained as professional performers of music, some leaders in the musical world agitated for their inclusion in regular church choirs.

By the middle of the nineteenth century, women had been singing in enough choruses to have changed public opinion about the value of their joining regular church choirs. A contributory factor to liberality in the matter was the change that had taken place in the kind of music thought to be suitable for church use. Churchgoers became interested in giving to music that accompanied the religious ceremony the quality of a concert. Organists were expected to be virtuosi; solo singers were employed on a professional basis; women were included in choirs in order to facilitate the performance of elaborate anthems. Presbyterians in America, especially, followed the trend of concertizing all music and sanctioned the solo quartet—two men and two women singers who rehearsed and performed as if at a musicale.

Today, however, a distinction is still drawn between liturgical singing and other religious choruses. Where church music is regarded as a kind of sacred concert—a performance by trained singers for an audience that listens—women are admitted to choirs. But where music is a liturgy and the members of the liturgical choir are thought of as attendants of the priest at the altar, women are excluded. Women may entertain an audience, even in church, and attract people into the service by their voices, but they may not be official representatives of worship. This prohibition applies wherever there is liturgy, in its ancient and traditional sense, in the church service—whether the church be Catholic, Greek Orthodox, Jewish, or Protestant.

Protestant church singing is founded not on liturgical singing but on congregational singing. The formal choir, even in vestments, is composed of trained singers whose function is theoretically to lead the congregation in singing. To such choirs many Protestant churches admit women, and so greatly enhance their music and the interest it has for the public. In Flint, Michigan, working men and women have thus made their city famous by their reverent musicianship. At St. Paul's on the Hill, an Episcopal church in Minneapolis, men and women chant Georgorian plain song antiphonally. Dom Anselm Hughes, the well-known English music scholar, spoke of this choir in 1940 as being the most remarkable he had heard in America. There is clearly no musical reason why women should not sing in church, and the custom preventing them from taking an equal responsibility with men in the religious ceremony is a survival of a taboo on women that is now repudiated by public opinion. The exclusion of women from the liturgical choir constitutes the last barrier to the complete participation of women in the vocal music of our civilization.

3.

The mixed chorus with orchestra is the high point of our musical life. But there are also the separate men's choruses and women's choruses, both of which are sound musical ventures and sound social institutions with a longer history than any other musical group. At the present time, the social need for either has been transcended by the far greater need for choruses of men and women together. But as long as there are men and women, there will be times when men prefer to sing in their own groups and when women, or girls, find satisfaction in singing with each other without men. If a men's chorus is socially justified, then a women's chorus is equally justified.

There is, however, a striking difference between the two groups, and this difference is the cause of public respect for men's choruses and of lack of interest in women's choruses. Modern men's choruses are similar to the men's groups in primitive societies. They are, indeed, a continuation of very ancient secret societies. In primitive tribes today, men perform their own rites and invoke their own spirit at initiation, in preparation for war or hunting, and at many other times. The modern men's chorus is an offshoot of the synagogue or church choir in which men's religion (their relation to God) is expressed. Whether the men in a men's club today have ever sung in a synagogue or church choir or not, whether they believe in the Jewish-Christian God or not, they believe wholeheartedly in the power of men collectively. They sing with vitality, self-confidence, and in the assurance that they are right. In the glee club or college chorus, men celebrate their own moods, be they grave or gay. They sing music composed by one of their own members or by a professional man musician. They have their own leader. The secular chorus is merely one more institution organized by men themselves for the affirmation of their manhood.

As men sing now, so women once sang to their own deities, inspired with a proud, collective sense of their importance as women. And so they still sing among many primitive and peasant groups. But at the moment, the talent of peasant women in many countries has been forced into a channel that is still flowing swiftly and deeply like a mighty underground river, fertilizing the soil above it but only here and there surging up to the surface. In these groups women themselves are often conscious of their repressed power. Even a hundred years ago, strong personalities like the Gaelic Máire Ni Dhiubh burst out regretfully: "Where are the dark women of the glens, who would keen and clap their hands. . . ." [1]

And in our civilization women are so far devitalized by the long suppression of their real inner life and its voice in music that they do not even know why they are still not in the right relation to music. When women gather to sing now they have no background. Owing to the negative attitude of organized religion as a whole toward women and girls, the women's chorus of modern times has never been a religious expression, as the primitive and peasant women's choruses are. Even the Protestants missed the opportunity, which had presented itself so forcibly in the Reformation, to dignify their daughters and to crystallize the trend away from the debasement of women. They planned nothing for their girls in the way of official participation in religious music, and to this day accept the negation of womanhood. This principle, supported also by women themselves, has conditioned the whole development of the women's chorus and even the music composed for it by men.

When our civilization developed, only the nuns in the convents had music, and some wonderful music was composed for nuns by men. Even today this constitutes the best music for women's choruses—that is, the most nearly equal in quality to music for mixed choruses.

So far as early secular singing by women in groups is concerned, there is no record of the music sung by women together in the castles. We know of no music composed for them by men until the sixteenth century. Then some madrigals were written for especially skillful singers. Later in private chapels a few pieces were composed by men for women to sing. Much of the music now regarded as classics for women's choruses was composed for and sung by boys.

The women's chorus, as we know it, began in the music school or in the girls' boarding school—both products of the seventeenth century. At that time, singing teachers in France were gathering their pupils together to give them practice in "ensemble." And Mme de Maintenon was persuading Louis XIV to endow a boarding school for girls of the French aristocracy. In this school at St. Cyr, the Ursuline canonesses in charge of the girls taught them to sing beautifully in their private chapel. So charming were the girls' voices that Racine was inspired to write the operas *Esther* and *Athalie* for the girls to perform. His friend J. B. Moreau composed the music. Both operas were given several times before the king and royal guests with such success that the attention of the church was attracted. Objections were made to the nuns' and their pupils' spending so much time on secular music, and development along these lines stopped short.

In Protestant England, the girls' schools were often centers for the performance of new music. Purcell's lovely opera *Dido and Aeneas* came to life at Mr. Priest's school for girls in Chelsea. One of the pupils, Lady Dorothy Burke, took the leading part, and her companions sang and danced in the choruses. Like Mr. Priest, other schoolmasters were often skilled in music and advertised the teaching of song and dance as a particular advantage of school life. They fre-

quently composed masques and operettas for their pupils. Susanna
Perwich is an example of a young woman musician who had the incentive of leadership to develop her creative musical imagination.
She and her mother directed a school for girls. As music teacher, she
conducted a chorus, a ballet, and an orchestra. She herself invented
the dances and wrote the orchestral compositions for the pupils. In
America the Moravians in Bethlehem, Pennsylvania, were unique,
apparently, in making adequate provision for their girls to be choristers. Division of the congregation into "choirs" according to sex and
age brought each group into prominence as singers and made antiphonal singing a feature of the service. In the famous Moravian
School for Young Ladies, founded by the Countess von Zinzendorf
in 1742, the girls were taught to regard singing as a serious contribution to community life, and from their ranks came a number of
hymn writers.

Russian "institutes," or boarding schools for aristocratic girls, were
founded by various empresses. The first one in St. Petersburg was
called "The Society of Genteel Maidens" and became known later as
the Smolny Institute. Music played a great part in the lives of the
girls who attended these schools. Choirs were organized as a matter
of course. The girls often gave performances for guests or in celebration of some national event, and in that way had opportunity to participate in operatic music. In 1773, for instance, the pupils at the
Smolny Institute performed Pergolesi's *La Serva Pardona,* and in
1775 they commemorated the treaty of peace just signed with the
Turks. Dressed in the attire of vestals, four hundred girls took part
while forty of them guarded a sacred flame upon an altar erected for
the purpose.

During the nineteenth century, high-ranking musicians such as
Glazounoff and Liadoff composed special cantatas for the girls to
sing in welcoming church dignitaries and members of the imperial
family. Most of these schools had private chapels in which the girls
performed religious music with wonderful sincerity and skill. At the
services held every Saturday evening and every Sunday morning, the
choir was customarily led by one of the older girls and assisted by
soloists drawn from the student body. The most wonderful singing
was achieved during Lent and especially at the midnight service on
Easter Eve. At the Vladimir Girls' School, where women teachers
were trained for the parochial schools, the choir was particularly

famous. It was the custom for legends and facts about the choirs, their leaders, and the soloists to be passed down from class to class, building up an unwritten tradition of effort and excellence.

During the seventeenth and eighteenth centuries, the famous Venetian conservatories for orphan girls gave tremendous impetus to the participation of girls in singing and playing instruments. In music-loving Venice, when prosperity enabled influential citizens to spend money for the arts, it was only natural that public institutions should also benefit from the prevailing interest in music. The directors of the four orphan asylums hit upon the happy plan of training the girls to contribute to their own support by means of concerts. Musical directors of high standing—among them such great masters as Hasse, Porpora, Gasparini, and Vivaldi—were engaged to compose vocal and orchestral music for the girls. The result was that soloists, the girl choirs, and girls' orchestras became famous all over Europe. Visitors flocked to the conservatory of the Incurabli to hear the choir, to the Pietà to hear the orchestra, to all four conservatories in order to hear the enchanting solo voices. Especially during Lent, when the theaters were closed, the fashionable world crowded into the churches attached to the institutions to enjoy the concerts given by these girls and their nun teachers.

Strangely enough, the Church, although it required a promise from the girls that they would not go on the stage after leaving the asylums, did not object to these concerts. Even when frankly secular music was performed, the ecclesiastical authorities shut their eyes to the activity. The decline of the conservatories did not come from suppression by the Church. It followed the Napoleonic invasion, with its consequent disruption of social life. In the history of women and music, the Venetian conservatories stand out as a milestone. A choral literature for women's voices arose; prejudice against a women's choir was somewhat overcome; the foundation was laid for later developments in other schools and centers where girls congregated; and precedents for the participation of women in music were established. These have not since been reversed.

In the latter part of the eighteenth century and in the early years of the nineteenth century, J. A. Hiller in Leipzig deliberately undertook to train amateurs for oratorio singing and orchestral playing. Hiller organized classes for different classifications of singers, giving the beginners only simple music and graduating them into groups capable of singing polyphonic motets and oratorios. His idea was to increase the supply of singers for oratorios and especially for church choirs. The Swiss Nägeli, too, had amateurs grouped together according to their proficiency. In 1824 he incorporated the several choruses and published the rules for membership. Respectability was one of the first requirements. The early nineteenth century still regarded group enterprises on the part of women as open to criticism. Nägeli gave a great impetus to the movement by his genuine faith in the ability of girls to sing religious music competently. He announced publicly *that the voices of young girls between the ages of twelve to sixteen compared favorably to those of boys and proved to be more supple and educable.* In a newspaper entitled *Morgenblatt für die gebildeten Stände* for November 8, 1808, an article appeared that praised extravagantly Nägeli's work and also the wonderful singing of his young girl pupils. What the public had long expected to hear sung only by boys trained in Protestant choir schools was now performed much better, so the critic said, by these girls with their higher, clearer, and more flexible voices. Nägeli's own conviction, too, that the most beautiful effects in religious music could be obtained by capitalizing the natural contrast of male and female voice lent authority to his efforts in behalf of the natural girl and woman. As time went on, nearly every music school had a chorus, formed by the girl students as an integral part of its social life. (See Plate 60.)

The Hamburger Frauenchor, for which Brahms composed practically all of his literature for women's voices, is well known to all choral singers. In 1859, when Brahms lived in Hamburg, one of his piano pupils, Friedchen Wagner, used to entertain him at her house. She asked him to arrange folk songs for her and her two sisters to sing. Brahms was pleased with the opportunity to exercise his skill, and suggested that the group be enlarged, promising to bring new music for each meeting. A concert was once given in St. Peter's Church. Upon another occasion the original group joined with the pupils of Grädener's Conservatory and gave a private concert. The Frauenchor has become famous because Brahms became famous, just as Nanette Fröhlich's pupils are mentioned in *Grove's Dictionary* because Schubert composed music for them. Hundreds of other groups functioned in the same way. The leader, associated with a conservatory, was the prime mover, and his (or occasionally her) interest lay chiefly in the musical experience to be derived from conducting and composing.

After about 1870 women began to organize their own music clubs, but these, too, generally depended upon a professional leader drawn from the conservatory or university group. This movement toward independence had no place in Russia, Italy, Spain, or, indeed, in any of the countries dominated by the Greek Orthodox or the Roman Catholic Church. It belonged to the Protestant and to the democratic nations. In Germany, especially, the choral singing of women was woven into the warp and woof of the aristocratic and upper-middle-class woman's life. Meeting in the drawing rooms of the large houses, some women joined several groups and went from one to the other, often singing four or five hours a day. And while in the nineteenth century no one group developed into an institution to promote the choral singing of women, the great number of isolated units in many parts of the Christian world brought about the revival of the women's chorus.

But women's choruses did not perform on the public stage. The appearance of more than one woman at a time implied collective independence and strength—a state for womanhood in which people took little interest. Even in the United States, where women had so much personal liberty, a public concert by a woman's chorus in 1888 received sarcastic comment. A well-known music critic wrote that were the choir composed of angels and led by St. Cecilia, it would still be musically unsatisfactory.

The conventional attitude toward a suppressed and reticent womanhood was reflected in the music produced by men for adult women to sing. Nineteenth-century composers who knew the love and companionship of individual women had not yet been sufficiently leavened by the romantic movement to regard *collective* womanhood as of the same caliber. The music these men composed for women is, as a rule, sentimental, sometimes mawkish, and generally inadequate to bring out the strength inherent in the female voice. The contrast between the bridesmaids' song in Glinka's opera *A Life for the Czar* and the Russian peasant mothers' wedding cycle illustrates with remarkable clarity the gulf between the artificial and the natural. Glinka has made a song for wavering, timid twittering of repressed young misses. One can imagine that he subconsciously desired the listeners to experience a sense of unfulfillment—a sense of longing for the bass voices of men to support the treble. How different is the musical effect produced by the deep, rich, emotionally satisfactory voices of the peasant mothers!

The composers often chose texts depicting women as sirens, witches, Loreleis, fantastic creatures without the creative power of the spirits of antiquity. Legends about the "errant," or wandering, moon lady became converted into sentimental poems about an "erring" girl mourning the loss of her chastity! Or the words of songs are inconsequential, placing women in the class of devitalized dolls, angels, even morons. Still more depersonalized for a women's chorus are the words of a man's love song—like Brahms' *"Minnelied,"* Op. 44, No. 1. In this choral literature, the real flesh-and-blood women, as well as the expression of strong, human attitudes, are conspicuous only by their absence.

In 1905, when Gustav Holst first went as director of music to St. Paul's Girls' School in London, he wrote his daughter: "I find the question of getting music for the girls' schools perfectly hopeless. I get reams of twaddle sent me periodically, and that is all the publishers seem to think is suitable for girls." [2] Even in the twentieth century, England's most intelligent girls were being treated like musical children.

After the First World War there was a great acceleration in the development of women's choruses, owing to the vastly increased attendance of girls in schools and colleges and the institution of women's clubs. As women became more independent in their daily lives, their choruses sprang up like mushrooms after a fertilizing rain. Many more women are joining choruses; more have organized the societies themselves; more choruses have women conductors. The newer the group, the more likely it is to be independent. The military girls, Wacs, Waves, Spars, and their British equivalents, invariably had bands and choruses with their own leaders.

Many of the Catholic church schools have wonderfully trained girl choirs. The most renowned of these is the group at Manhattanville, trained by Mother Stevens. These girls sing from the gallery at the Sunday services of the Church of the Annunciation, attracting visitors from near and far to hear their beautiful voices and polished performances. In at least some of the secular women's colleges, choral singing by the girls now forms an integral part of college life. Vassar girls, trained to keep on pitch for a whole evening's performance, enrich their chapel services with beautiful and appropriate singing. Mt. Holyoke girls have made their college famous by their sympathetic rendering of Christmas carols. The singing of Bryn Mawr girls has been metamorphosed and electrified by the arrival of a young woman conductor, Lorna Cooke Devaron.

Through the organization of clubs, women have been establishing new customs for their participation in music. The chamber-orchestra or chorus constitutes one activity in the larger life of the group. At annual meetings, these amateur musicians give a concert. No effort on their part to attract an audience is required, since the club members and their invited guests expect to be so entertained. In adopting this method, women have shown initiative in creating ways and means *convenient to them* for the gratification of their musical aspirations.

One significant result of such independence has been a change for the better in the quantity and quality of music composed for French, English, and American women's voices. In Germany, on the other hand, the decline in output is marked. In Italy, modern music composed for women's voices is practically nonexistent, since the amateurs' movement of the nineteenth century never materialized there. But where the women's clubs and college choruses evince an attitude of independence on the part of women, several composers and conductors are beginning to appreciate the enormous musical possibilities of women's choruses. They are featuring rich and moving alto parts, making interesting experiments with the low range of women's voices, testing a dynamic balance of soprano and alto, and introducing varied instrumental accompaniments. Most modern composers are setting their music for women's voices to appropriate texts, which treat women's interests and reactions with dignity.

Women's choruses are now a recognized social institution and their public appearance on a stage is no longer a cause for facetious comment. This change has occurred only since 1912. In that year Margarete Dessoff was asked to bring her women's chorus from Frankfort, Germany, to participate in a great German Brahms festival. She conducted it in singing Brahms' choral works for women, on a par with other performing groups. This was a landmark in the history of women's choruses. For the first time in history, a women's chorus made a public appearance on an equality with other musical groups in a serious musical enterprise. Since 1912 the development of women's choruses has been greatly furthered by the women's colleges and the women's part of co-educational colleges. Here women are gathered in strength under conditions that make for study and training and collective authority. Having developed music for and within its own group, the college women's chorus is in a position to appear on the public stage with prestige.

In recent years two great women's choruses conducted by women have set very high standards for performance. One was the Adesdi Choir of fifty women conducted for ten years, from 1925 to 1935, in New York City, by Margarete Dessoff. She made this chorus unique in that it sang only music composed originally for women's voices, and of the highest quality. The standard she set was maintained and even surpassed by the chorus of girls trained by Mother Stevens. At a concert given by her pupils in Philadelphia in 1940 three thousand people came to hear her and praise a girls' religious choir, trained by women and conducted by a woman. Before the war, these two remarkable American women's choruses were matched by others, also directed by women, in England, France, Germany, and South America. A significant fact, entirely unrecorded by critics or historians, is that the outstanding women's choruses of modern times have been under the leadership of women.

On the whole, the women's chorus has made phenomenal gains since its inception in the schools of the seventeenth century, but from the psychological point of view, the choral singing of women is still in a state of repression. People are still saying that women's voices alone are beneath the serious attention of a composer and that a chorus of women is uninspiring to a musical audience. Yet people do not complain that the low voices of men alone are inadequate to satisfy either the composer or the audience. At least ten times as much music has been written for men's voices alone as for women's. At least a hundred times more concerts have been given by men's groups than by women's. Curiously enough, there is still some indefinable barrier that keeps a women's chorus from being a complete success. The reason for this is not, however, far to seek. It is a social, not a musical, reason.

All musicians know well that a men's chorus is an inferior musical instrument to a women's chorus. Women's voices have more brilliance, clarity, and flexibility than men's. The missing sonority can be readily supplied by organ or by other instruments, whereas no instrument can adequately supply the mass of high tones lacking in men's voices. Finally, women's voices lend themselves more easily than men's to a greater variety of musical climaxes. There is no valid *musical* reason for the slur cast on the women's chorus.

But a women's chorus is not like the primitive and peasant groups —the ritual and musical expression of women collectively. The modern women's chorus is not an offshoot of church choirs. Jewish and Christian women have been excluded from religious choirs for many centuries. And nuns never sang to *affirm womanhood*. A few modern groups of women singers have been successfully conducted by women, but even they do not win public recognition as an expression of women's moods, thoughts, and desires. Without a new point of view, indeed, they cannot, since the ideal for Jewish and Christian women is a negation of the principle that women have anything to express.

Like the nuns' choirs, the modern women's chorus has been adapted by men (with the consent of women) to conform to the creed that men only are creative in body and spirit. Jewish and Christian women have been in this relation to men for so long that their ability, and even their desire, to assert themselves by means of group music is dormant. People think that what is missing in a women's chorus is the sound of men's voices. Rather it is the vitality with which men endow the sounds that is lacking. Women's choruses will never be as socially or as musically acceptable as those of men until women and girls feel inwardly—as primitives and peasants do—that their singing is merely one manifestation of their power and natural authority as women.

Because of the present-day emphasis on virtuosity, women find it impossible to regain this sense of power. Singing in a women's chorus should be one of the means by which women can revitalize their own depleted psyches. But to achieve this, such a chorus must fulfill several conditions that are generally neglected. It must be led by a woman, not by a man. The woman leader must have a full rich sense of the spiritual power of music and the latent spiritual power of women, and the ability to communicate this inspiration. Women must first meet to sing with no idea of training for a concert. They must be seeking *first* what music can do for them, not for an audience. A concert should be the by-product of success in achieving spiritual entity, not the end and aim of musical participation. Especially valuable in group singing is the companionship with others in orchestras and chorus—the thrill of hearing one's own part in strength, the discipline of giving way in turn, in order to perfect the sound of the whole. The chorus then becomes a tremendously important musical experience. The participants are stimulated to learn our great heritage of musical art by actually playing and singing it themselves. The necessary foundation is laid for spiritual enrichment and for collective self-expression.

4.

The *principle* of a dynamic participation in music applies equally to choruses of boys and girls in schools and colleges—which are now the best places for education in music. But unfortunately the over-development of the concert, and of the ideal of virtuosity, has cast a shadow over the rich experience. School authorities, influenced by current ideals, run a grave risk of overemphasizing the value of public performance.

In this they apply to music a standard they would not tolerate in connection with literature and language. Students are taught English, or any other language, with the primary object of mastering the use of the language terms and of becoming intimately familiar with the masterpieces of its prose and poetry. The acting of a play or the reading aloud of a novel in public is never made the goal of a season's work, but merely the occasional offshoot of activities that are broader in scope. In music, the giving of a concert is too often the end toward which all the efforts of the chorus or orchestra are directed. If practically all the available hours are spent preparing for the display of one composition, then there are not enough hours left for becoming familiar with other great compositions. No literature class would be satisfied with knowing only *one* of Shakespeare's plays; at least a speaking acquaintance with them all is required of an educated person. How few people know, much less have sung, half a dozen of Bach's two hundred cantatas, or Brahms' choral music other than his Requiem!

School and college years are the golden time for acquiring musical literacy. A similar opportunity rarely occurs again. Too many students leave their schools or colleges without the proper foundation for using music as a normal activity in postgraduate life. The prevailing attitude toward the value of virtuosity definitely deters the average girl and boy from taking a direct, natural approach to music as a language.

Women as camillae, or acolytes at the altar of music, are suffering from the juxtaposition, in our culture, of two sterile influences, one applying to them as women, and the other a general characteristic of our Western civilization. They have been spiritually starved as women by the long tradition of the Church, and by the requirement that, in matters of the spirit, they accept men's formulations and men's music. And they share with men the overdepartmentalization of music that limits music lovers to passive listening to virtuosi or to vain attempts to become virtuosi themselves. As audiences, as students of voice or instrument, as singers in mixed choruses or in women's choruses, the camillae may be serious and hard-working, but the deity they serve is not capable of giving them a tithe of the spiritual sustenance they obviously crave.

CHAPTER XVII

ST. CECILIA

1.

SINCE the sixteenth century, the virgin Cecilia has been the patron saint of music and the misleading symbol of woman's participation in music during the period of its great modern development. Her picture, with eyes upcast to heaven and cherubs showering roses on her as she plays, hung over the piano in thousands of nineteenth-century homes. Here was inspiration to guide the fingers of generations of little girls through the daily chore of piano practice.

Piano playing and, if a girl had a "voice," a little parlor singing were something a lady acquired by diligent and even painful effort, along with a waist laced in to be three inches smaller than nature made it, a foot that would fit a slipper half an inch shorter than itself, and a soft, flattering recognition that man is the woman's natural god. "He for God only. She for God in him." [1]

So St. Cecilia beamed and languished, as "divine woman," inspiration, and patroness of masculine genius. Over the centuries from 1550 till today, music was developed into a great and complex art by a series of great men—and not a woman composer of first-class stature among them. As representing opportunity for a participation by women in the creation of music expressing their own hearts and lives and their unique function as the mothers of the race, St. Cecilia is an utter fraud. The very word "patroness" has something spurious about it. It is made by the lacy addition of "ess" to the word "patron," whose root means father. An honest word for an honest woman saint of music would be founded on a word whose root meant mother, as the word "matron" does.

Why Cecilia was chosen for her anomalous position is one of those perplexities in men's scholarship and writing of history that baffles a sincere woman's mind. St. Cecilia did not compose music. She created no ritual such as the primitive women had created. She helped no woman to approach the divine altar, to understand the rhythm of her own being, and to demonstrate its implication for the life of the spirit. St. Cecilia was a Roman girl of noble family who in the second century was martyred for her faith. Her connection with music consists in the fact that her father arranged to have an organ played at her wedding to a young man named Valerian. But she refused to be married "and sang in her heart to God alone." [2] In no remote sense did she reflect the activities of Christian women in religious music, as the old musician goddesses had reflected the musical activities of the women of earliest times.

When St. Cecilia was established in 1550 as the presiding spirit of music, women had not had, for many centuries, sufficient free participation in music to warrant any woman's being made a saint of music. As a symbol of something to come, St. Cecilia held out a false hope. At best she represented a sentimental sanctification of the Renaissance conception of the priestess of beauty.

Yet, in a sense, St. Cecilia is a true representative of the pattern within which women as musicians have been confined during the whole of the modern period.

In that period the great structure of wonderful music has been reared by men, pleasantly encouraged by women as purveyors of beauty and charm. Compared with the early woman musicians in the crude dignity of their ritualistic approach to the divine life, the priestess of beauty was no priestess at all when she first began to reign in the courts of the Renaissance. She seemed to have a greater degree of honor and liberty than the forcibly silenced and suppressed woman of the ruder Middle Ages, but she had this only within the limits that had been set in the fourth century. The pattern itself had not changed, and it has not changed to this day. It has merely been obscured in some flowers of sentiment. The woman, as priestess of beauty, from the early Renaissance till now, when as queen of beauty she appears in hundreds of public celebrations, serves the male human being only, in his vanity and his power. She officiates at no genuine altar, and such altars as there are she is not allowed to approach save as she kneels at the foot of a male priest.

This is why there are no woman composers of the highest stature. Certainly, women do compose, and some women composers compare favorably with second- and third-rate men. Some compositions of the women composers are better than some of the published material of even the greatest composers. But when one considers what music is, and how it must be composed, it is a wonder that one can say even that.

Music, of all the arts, has its origins in the deepest levels of the subconscious. It is, of all the arts, the most profoundly religious. It is indeed the voice in which the human being speaks to the life that is over and above this human life. Even in modern times, since 1550, the really great music has had its focus in religious feeling. The musical idiom developed primarily for religious worship has merely been transferred to secular music. It would actually be enough explanation of the lack of first-class music by women to say that they could not compose because they were barred from authoritative positions as church musicians. One could say, with reason, that there is no feminine Bach because no woman had a position like his—which was that of church organist with the duty of composing music for the religious service.

2.

But there is something much more serious to say about what the lack of women composers of the first stature reveals. There is a wrong and a poison at the heart of our society, and an essential falsity in the whole modern tradition of secular learning and religious teaching.

Consider what a woman faces, even today, in free and enlightened America, from the day she begins to have any formal training. She goes to school and begins her struggle to think logically in the words she has already learned from her mother's lips. And then there begins the difficulty with the English pronouns, in some sentence like "If anyone looks at this object closely, *he* will see." Why should "anyone" be a he? Why not a she? Is she not to look at this object closely, too? The teacher explains patiently. When we mean a person of either sex, we always say "he"! But the little girl looks at the little boy near her, who is no brighter than she, and she thinks, But why should he stand for girls and boys too? *I* am *she*. No one tells her that the language in which she must speak for the rest of her life is so distorted because the modern vernacular was formed when men still completely dominated learning, and that the first grammars were written by men. There ought to be a pronoun to represent both men and women. But there is not.

As the girl goes on learning, she faces this problem again and again. There is the word "man." It stands for all humankind. The life of "man" is the life of everybody. But why should a man stand for everybody? She goes further and begins to learn Latin. "Virile," "virtue" come from the word *vir*, meaning man. They are grand words. They mean strength and courage. "Feminine" comes from *femina*, meaning woman. But what does feminine mean? Something soft and mildly attractive. If the girl has a good mother—and according to the testimony of men, good mothers appear to be very numerous—the girl knows that this word "feminine," with its soft, silly connotations, by no means represents what mother is—strong, patient, able to keep the family secure and happy. Is there no word for women's *strength*, in a world where women must have so much strength, if not of muscle, certainly of nerve and will and soul?

Meanwhile the girl goes to Sunday school and church. If she is a Catholic the truth may dawn on her only slowly, for in the Catholic Church there are Mary and many women saints, and an atmosphere of family love in the innumerable pictures and images of Mother and Child. The girl may innocently suppose that these figures of angels, singing, kneeling, adoring the new baby, are daughters. They look like girls with their long curled hair and long dresses. But if she has a mind and begins to use it as the time for confirmation approaches, the truth may dawn upon her. God is a man only. He has a son but no daughter. He has priests but no priestesses. Mary is only a handmaid, not an equal partner. Mothers are not fit to serve God at the altar. Women may not even sing in the choir, saying their prayers to music. They can only listen to men singing their prayers.

And why is this? Because a woman is of different sex from a man. And what is this difference? A man starts the baby in what may be only a moment of careless and often irresponsible pleasure. But a woman takes up the burden and carries it alone, through months of unique experience to a great life and death struggle. This is what distinguishes her as a woman. This is her sex. And for no other reason, God, who is male, will not have a mother stand and speak at the altar. The door of the holy of holies, with its symbols of regeneration derived from her own function as life bringer, is closed to her, who brings the child into the world.

3.

In the formation of this dogma, Catholic and Protestant theologians have been equally guilty. Women did not sing in the liturgical choir from the fourth century on, and they do not do so to this day, either in Catholic churches or in Protestant churches *that have real liturgical singers, who are properly speaking the attendants of the priest and priestess.* This is to say that where music is regarded as worship, and so used in the church service, women may not sing in the choir, and the music requiring high voices must be sung by immature boys. The only exception to this was from early times the singing of nuns in their own chapels. But here a special voice was cultivated, clear, high, sexless. Women did not sing in their natural voices.

The Protestant Church based its music not on the liturgy but on Luther's noble principle of congregational singing. For this selected strains of folk music were converted into hymns. These are the basis of Bach's chorales. To ensure a high quality of church music, the Lutherans established schools for boys, like St. Thomas' in Leipzig, where Bach served. No schools trained girls to be official singers, organists, or composers for the church.

In the Calvinist churches in Switzerland and France there may have been trained women's choirs. Goudimel, in 1565, set eight psalms for four high voices. In the preface to his collection he says that he composed the music for both home and church use. But in England the authorities spared no pains to prevent the participation of women and girls in choirs. Henry VIII issued warrants permitting boys with good voices to be impressed for service in the cathedral choirs. In Queen Elizabeth's time boys were taken from their parents without compensation to serve as Children of the Chapel. At the time of the Restoration, 1660, there were no trained choirboys available at all, owing to the fact that the choirs of the Anglican Church had been disbanded during the Commonwealth. The soprano part was played on what was called a cornet. Men, who habitually took the alto parts and still do in many places in England, at that time often sang the soprano in falsetto, rather than allow a woman to use her natural voice in religious song.

In America the early settlers were torn with dissension over the question whether a woman should be allowed to sing to God. One of the questions to be decided by the Massachusetts Bay Colony was: "Whether the people join in singing the Psalms, or the Minister alone?" It was agreed that the congregation should join, and then the age-old question came up for decision—"Whether women sing with men, or men alone?" [3] Even the bravery and fortitude of women bearing the dangers and toil of a pioneer life could not do away with the long prejudice that classed them as inferior in matters ecclesiastical and juridical. The intrepid Anne Hutchinson succeeded in persuading John Cotton, minister of the Boston Congregational Church in 1637, to allow women to sing in his church. Before the other colonial settlements took the liberal point of view, however, Mrs. Hutchinson was expelled from her community for her theological and political dissent. The matter of the church singing was one of the grievances cherished against her by the Puritan authorities.

In most Protestant churches, women's participation in congregational singing became accepted as a matter of course. But for the participants, hymn singing in church has a far greater social than musical value. Inspiring though congregational music is, it has never been developed by any religious group in our culture beyond the elementary stage of unison singing accompanied by all-pervasive organ playing. The trained choir, however, demands a special skill, and the exclusion of women and girls from it had a direct bearing upon their relation to music.

This exclusion has continued in part down to the present day, despite many efforts on the part of liberals to do away with it. When William Tuckey came from England in 1752 to be choirmaster at Trinity Church, New York, he first organized a choir of boys and girls from a near-by charity school, but, as *Grove's Dictionary* expresses it, he soon "succeeded in eliminating the female element" and established choir singing in the proper English manner. Although some Episcopalians favored liberality in the matter, the revival of medievalism by the Oxford Movement in England in the nineteenth century tended to restore the taboos of the Dark Ages, and checked any move to sanction girl choristers. When about 1850 the Reverend Dr. Haweis, a Church of England minister, put surplices on women choristers, he was vehemently attacked by one faction of his parishioners. The Roman Catholic Church made a few compromises, even permitting a Catholic newspaper to publish a favorable comment on Brahms' beautiful religious motets for four women's voices. "No offense could be taken by even the most pious on the *setting* of the liturgical texts," the critics conceded. But instead of following the modern trend, the Catholics reacted against the participation of women in the formal church choir, and explained why in the *Motu Proprio* of Pope Pius X (1903). After stating that women may not be admitted to the priesthood, the edict says: "On the same principle it follows that singers in Church have a real liturgical office, and that therefore *women, being incapable of exercising such office, cannot be admitted to form part of the choir.* Whenever, then, it is desired to employ the acute voices of sopranos and contraltos, these parts must be taken by boys, according to the most ancient usage of the Church."

To this day, women do not sing in every church as a matter of course, nor are they regarded as having an inalienable right to be there. In conservative groups the opposition against women is strong. G. S. Stubbs, organist of St. Agnes' Episcopal Chapel, Trinity Parish, New York City, represents a considerable body of opinion as he writes about women choristers in vestments: "While it is not certain that these choirs will increase to an alarming extent, steps may have to be taken to check their growth." [4] A long correspondence on the subject of mixed choirs was recently carried on between various dignitaries of the Catholic Church. It was finally decreed that men and women could sing with propriety in a religious choir—but not in a strictly liturgical choir—provided they sat in galleries at the back of the church as far as possible from the altar, and provided the sexes were separated by some physical barrier, such as an organ or a railing.[5]

In spite of the new policy of the Catholics toward congregational singing—which includes the participation of women even in a cathedral—the ecclesiastical authorities still object to *choruses* of women within the most sacred precincts. During the year 1938, Mme Lila Pereira, professor of singing at the Conservatory of Santiago in Chile, organized a choir of sixteen women with the intention of singing at certain special services in the cathedral. The choir's repertoire was limited chiefly to religious motets by Palestrina, Victoria, and other great composers of church music. Although Mme Pereira was respected in her city as an individual and as a musician, she had to appeal every three months for permission to take her choir into the cathedral. The women were not allowed to sit in the choir stalls, but had to sing from seats placed in the nave. Eventually, the *vicario* notified Mme Pereira that the pope had forbidden the women to take any part in the religious ceremony. This order effectively prevented the choir from functioning and caused it to disband.

Even the Protestant National Cathedral Chapter, in Washington, D. C., excludes women from its formal choir. A new custom could readily have been established here, since a girls' school and a boys' school are both situated on the cathedral grounds. Both schools are supported by the cathedral chapter. The girls receive musical instruction adequate to qualify them as choristers, but they take no part in the formal musical activities of the cathedral. Conducting their commencement exercises in the crypt is the extent of their participation.

The National Cathedral is sponsored by men and women of all denominations in the United States. It purports to be a national shrine for all people of our country, a center for the dissemination of American democracy and Christian ideals. Yet the authorities allowed Dorothy Maynor to sing from the chancel, while they will not allow mothers and daughters who regularly attend the services to join the choir. Spiritual pastors and masters prefer to exalt the prima donna rather than the women who are the bulwark of our civilization. They cannot yield on the fundamental principle on which all the vested interests of religious hierarchy are based, that the human being who creates half the child and nourishes it from her own body in love and duty is, *by reason of this,* unfit to sing to the Source of all being.

This principle is supported by the cathedrals of all Jewish and Christian sects, whose function it is to set standards for the maintenance of tradition and for correct usage. The Orthodox Catholic Church, the Church of England, the Episcopalian and Lutheran Churches will not tolerate women in cathedral choirs.

People are prone to rationalize about women in church choirs by claiming that a boys' choir is musically "better" than one that includes women and girls; or they say that they prefer the "purity" of boys' voices. But the pure, sexless quality can be produced quite as well by young girls of high-school age. Unless the singers are seen, no musical inferiority, indeed, no difference in boys' and girls' voices can be detected. It is the guilelessness of youth, not the sex of the singers, that recalls the heavenly choir. But even if the boy choir were musically better, that would be no excuse for excluding girls or women. The church is not a place of entertainment, nor is it the primary function of the church to give performances of music. The question is: Who should sing in a representative capacity to the divine force? Is this the privilege only of the male—mature and immature? As for the boys, their young voices are lovely. But behind their present use in cathedral choirs lies a tradition that seems morbid to the modern mind. There is the refined homosexuality of Greece when young boys were substituted for girls as the romantic objects of a mature man's love. There is the long, revolting history of the castrati and their use in ecclesiastical services. The boys' voices should never sound sweet in any decent person's ears till they sing side by side with their sisters. The equally beloved daughters should sing together with the sons to the glory of life's mighty rhythm. The mature voices of mothers, of equal value with fathers, should sustain and support the fourfold human song.

In this attitude of the churches to woman's song much more is involved than the participation of any special group of singers in a special activity. For from the purely musical point of view, even if women and girls were still excluded from the choir of every church, it would today make little difference to them as far as participation in the performance of music is concerned. They are now able to take part in music through many other institutions and in affairs that are musically more important than any sponsored by the churches. But the point is that women and girls who have proved their competence in singing reverently the most sacred motets and masses at a concert, even in a church concert, are not allowed to sing the same music when it accompanies the ritual.

The churches are supposed to represent the organized feeling of the whole community about the relation of human beings to the realities and the mysteries of life. The word "religious" means the relation of individuals to a higher power and the expression of the relation in conduct. These organized religious groups—and the most powerful denominations agree in this matter—are perpetuating the disgraceful fallacy that women are of less value in the scheme of life than men. No primitive taboo upon the free use of human energy was ever more damaging than this dogma. Its result is to deprive women of a reverence for their own way in life and of the confidence that comes only from genuine self-respect. As long as women are denied public recognition of the fact that they are spiritually of *equal value* with men, *equally* able to advance civilization to a higher level, as long as women are not expected to find in worship their most appropriate outlet for musical expression, just so long will they fail to take their rightful place in society and in the art of music. Just so long will our whole communal consciousness be vitiated by this morbid fallacy at its heart.

4.

Though both music and modern learning appear to be secular in origin and tone, the patterns set by Greek classical thinking and by the Church influence professional men to this day. A careless, slighting attitude to women has come down through the ages in clerical and scholarly circles. In the sixteenth century the monk Acidalius announced that women were not human beings, and were therefore incapable of thinking in terms of the spirit. Rousseau reflected current eighteenth-century ideals in his famous saying: "Once it is demonstrated that men and women are not and ought not to be constituted alike in character and temperament, it follows that they ought not to have the same education. Let girls be trained definitely for wifehood and motherhood. *The whole education of women should be relative to men.*" [6] A hundred years later Schopenhauer was saying that women remained big children all their lives. In this opinion he was supported by a group of German scientists who, in the Breslau Conference of 1884, produced what they considered proof of woman's closer resemblance to animals and her resultant deficiency in the higher human faculties.

As recently as 1940, Catholic Church dignitaries, meeting in Kansas City at an educational conference, discussed the familiar affair of Adam and Eve and the apple. Adam was held responsible for the act of disobedience; Eve was pronounced blameless. Because she was a woman, she was incapable of knowing right from wrong. In the thousand and a half of another thousand years, woman has progressed—if one wishes to call it "progress"—from an aggressively evil power to a negative quantity, innocent only because *powerless.*

Many people regard the Catholic Church as too conservative to be representative of the modern spirit toward women. But the same attitude of denial of woman's power can be found in the latest editions of dictionaries. Under the word "woman," for example, the editors of Webster's Unabridged Dictionary quote a passage from Shakespeare—"Women are soft, mild, pitiful, and flexible"—in order to explain the way the word is used. So also in the new language of Esperanto, the word for "mother" has been formed as *patrino,* a derivative of *patro,* father. If generally adopted, this new language term would forever divest "mother" of its connection with independent activity and authority. What theologians formerly did to the goddess symbols, university professors are now trying to do to language symbols.

Even the psychologists, who should be saving woman from the outward mandates of theologians, emphasize the early Christian's negation of womanhood. Only yesterday, in 1944, a group of doctors meeting at Atlantic City concluded that women lack creative imagination. What new name they expected to coin when referring to the many tangible forms of that faculty as demonstrated by many women was not announced. Their conviction that they were right—which significantly enough was not shared by the women doctors present—is evinced by their general use of the words "masculine" and "feminine." All activity is called masculine. Passivity is feminine. A woman is told that any activity she undertakes is a development of the "masculine" part of her nature. In this terminology, the strength —even the existence—of feminine urges and desires is given no recognition.

From the psychologists, too, comes the devastating condemnation of mothers as a beneficent influence over their sons. Not content with a *negation* of woman's power, they give it a *positive,* evil aspect. Because young soldiers and sailors far from home called, in loneliness and fear, for their mothers, doctors pronounced this love a damaging thing. Like the early Church Fathers, they dogmatize reverence for "Mom" as "silly and devoid of reason."

It follows from the peculiar wisdom that the males of our culture have revealed to males that musical art is exclusively masculine. A French critic said of Augusta Holmes, one of the foremost of the women composers of her time: "Why do these women try to make people forget that they are women?" He was only one of many to insist upon the disqualification of women for creative work in music. George Upton claimed that women lacked "objectivity," the power of projecting themselves outwardly and expressing themselves in terms of symbols. Anton Rubinstein, on the other hand, thought that women were lacking in "subjectivity" and initiative, wanting, indeed, courage and conviction. Rubinstein, who like his brother Nicholas managed one of the large Russian conservatories, extended his distrust of women into the field of performance. In this opinion he was supported by Carl Reinecke, who said openly that he believed there was a point where women stopped developing. Even as a performer, he claimed, a woman was prevented by her timidity and indecision from satisfactory demonstration of the composer's intention. Did they not all fail to realize that the timidity and indecision they noticed resulted directly and inevitably from the very denial of the value of women's independent ego?

There is no end to the careless gratuitous insult that these wiseacres heap on the function of giving birth. In 1945 the harp player Salzedo told his girl pupils at his summer school in Maine that only men compose music. "Women," he said, "are born to compose babies." [7] That women are born to compose babies is true enough. The difficulty lies in the silly and illogical deduction that men make from this obvious biological fact. Why, because one lives through—or is physiologically prepared to live through—the most vivid experience life can offer, should one be incapacitated from using the strength and wisdom gained through that experience in other fields? "When old and familiar things are made new in experience—there is art," [8] says John Dewey, and many women have proved and are proving today that this is so. To teach a girl the contrary is, indeed, as death-dealing to her spirit as any doctrine of the early Church Fathers.

5.

Against this the woman struggles, suppressed and reticent. But even so, it might have been possible for her to do something more in music if anything like fair opportunity had been open to her to acquire the training and experience necessary for the production of modern music. In early Greece, women were just beginning to develop real music out of their personal experience, with a steady accretion of knowledge and a refinement of art. But modern music is another creation altogether. It has developed in circumstances that prevented women from sharing the experience that men were accumulating or from obtaining any institutional support for the development of their inspiration. For when the complex forms of modern music were in the making, professional musicians received their training and much of their experience through contacts with the Church. They often combined religious and secular musical posts. Practically all of the great composers of the Renaissance period were primarily composers of church music. Their madrigals and other forms of secular music were merely by-products, written in the same idiom. A favorite device was to clothe a religious text, such as Salve Regina, in a distinctly gay, unecclesiastical setting, and to present the incongruous whole at a social gathering. The organization for Christian music was self-sufficient and, as we have seen, made only special demands upon the natural woman musician.

The obvious result of this new development of polyphonic music was to render the composition of music infinitely more difficult and complicated than in the days when the troubadours sang their melodies to the simple strumming accompaniment of the lute. No one could now attempt serious musical composition without long training and experience. Many rules evolved or were invented—some natural, some arbitrary—that had to be learned, observed, and incorporated into a musical production that would be both correct and pleasing.

Even after the power formerly wielded by the Church began to pass to the university system, every such institution adapted the organization of the Church to further its scholarly, social, or political aims. Women had no corresponding institutions. Even many of their monasteries had been dissolved and their revenues diverted to the universities. Not till late in the nineteenth century did it occur to anyone to found colleges for the higher education of women.

The reason women took to performing men's music rather than creating their own was, of course, not because the intricacies of contrapuntal writing were beyond their powers, but because they were excluded from the Church, and later from the schools, where the knowledge could be obtained and the art practiced.

In one field only has woman's opportunity and recognized function in music been equal to that of men—in the solo performance of the prima donna. But the modern institution of the public concert or stage production for a price has widened the cleft between performer and composer. The teaching of expert performers became the principal justification of the institutions where girls were taught. Virtuosity was the end and aim of the student's interest. Every girl approached music as if she expected to become a concert performer. Since leadership was regarded as being out of their sphere, girls were discouraged from entering classes for conducting. As a general rule, they were excluded from classes in theory and composition—independent thinking being regarded as the prerogative of men. Until late in the century, women could not compete for prizes or receive diplomas at European conservatories.

Although Elizabeth Stirling's orchestral setting for psalm 130 passed every musical requirement for earning the degree of Musical Bachelor at Oxford University (England), in 1856 her application for it was rejected. No authority existed in the university for conferring the honor upon a woman. For the same reason, years later, in 1918, Lili Boulanger was disqualified from receiving the Prix de Rome, which she won at the age of eighteen in an anonymous competition. The donors of the prize had limited the applicants to the class of unmarried men under thirty—this class being the one in their experience most likely to produce a great composer. Far from advising girls to concentrate on music as an intellectual discipline, even serious men musicians treated aspiring pupils with levity. Sibelius once resorted to a trick to rid himself of two girl composition students. When, at his suggestion that they go for a walk outdoors, they had left the room, he turned to the young men and said: "It would be a pity if the young ladies' cheeks were to lose their beautiful country color!" [9] With a characteristic roguish smile, he began to instruct his men students in the theory of music. Such attitudes were effectual in stifling germinating talent. For the composition of major works, a knowledge of counterpoint and orchestration was essential, as well as the faith that intellectual discipline could be borne. Many girls acquired an inferiority complex about their musical imagination, allowing the easy habit of listening and the ideal of virtuosity to dominate their musical lives. Thinking in terms of even the simplest forms of music long ago fell into the discard. Even in eighteenth-century Venice, where the rich ladies in their salons were composing songs and instrumental music and where some of the convents allowed the nuns to spend most of their time at music, the talented girls of the conservatories received but little encouragement to be creative. Pupil and nun-teacher often substituted for the professional director of music, it is true, and pupils were taught to resolve a figured bass at sight. Their authority, however, stopped short of the point where incentives for composition began. The musical directors were always professional men musicians who happened to be in Venice at the time as organists of the large churches. These conductors promised to produce a new suite, motet, cantata, or oratorio at regular intervals. Theirs was the opportunity and incentive for creative work. Women had no such incentive because they had no similar outlet for an achievement.

It was the same story in the newly founded colleges for women, where musical activity was generally limited to a glee club conducted by a man. Young girls neglected to seek training in musical thinking, and young college women apparently made no concerted effort to establish forums for musical experimentation. Their symbol of music was not Artemis with her lyre.

Throughout the nineteenth century the stage, educational system, church, and even home all restricted the musician in some manner. And although singing in a chorus, dancing in a ballet, playing in an orchestra, even teaching and conducting music do not necessarily lead to the development of outstanding musical imagination, yet any restriction upon participation is a barrier to composition. Participation in music is a condition precedent to creative work in music, as it is in any other language. No one would expect to write a book in a strange language, but would first learn the words, construction, and idioms. Any artificial limitation to acquiring familiarity with a language and ease in its use automatically lowers the number of competent craftsmen ready to use it. Women achieved their outstanding measure of success in composing piano pieces and songs—the two types of music with which the greatest number had the most familiar and the most satisfactory experience.

Nor can there be any dispute that leadership in music definitely increases the chances for a musician to find occasions for the exercise of creative imagination. The great body of religious music—hymns, anthems, motets, compositions for organ alone—came from the organist, who was also the choir director, and not from musicians outside the circle. Choral literature for women's voices in the nineteenth century can be traced in almost every instance to the conductors of the choruses—to the men who carried the responsibility of finding music for the group to perform. When women had the responsibility, they too had the practical urge to compose appropriate music, and often did. Luise Reichardt, in the early part of the century, and Mabel Daniels, in the latter part, are examples of conductors who composed music for their own women's choruses to sing. It was while she was the conductor of an orchestra that Emma Steiner seized the opportunity to present a program of her own works. Alma Grayce Miller is a present-day example of a composer whose talents have been stimulated by a definite task. Organist and choir director of St. Agnes' Church, Arlington, Virginia, she has written three Christmas masses and also other music for the use of her choir. As she herself expresses it, whenever she cannot find appropriate music, she composes it. Even the most casual glance at contemporary publishers' catalogues reveals at least ten times as much music composed by women in various positions of responsibility as there was twenty or twenty-five years ago. To the extent, then, that women are excluded from positions of leadership, they are automatically limited in adding a substantial number of women to the ranks from which a possible genius might emerge. Superlative achievement comes only from an already high plateau of experience. And as long as women are regarded as a class apart from men, they will have to build their own plateau.

Persons of discernment never fail to realize that the women composers of the eighteenth, nineteenth, and twentieth centuries possess talent, sometimes to a marked degree. Critics of the women's compositions often concur and, in their judgments, add to information that the composers lacked adequate training and experience in working with contemporary musical idiom. Not being in the class or group from which music was expected, the women of our era had neither the emotional nor the intellectual foundation to enable them to assert freely their own conception of music. What they achieve in creative work is in spite of, not because of, the way of their world. Granting the suppression and the deliberate shaming of woman in connection with her unique mission of motherhood, granting her exclusion from spiritual authority and equality by the institutions of our civilization, granting the persistent discrimination against her by those who held the keys to knowledge and gave the permission to participate in music; granting all this, many people maintain that genius cannot be downed. If a feminine Mozart had been born, they say, she would have been immediately recognized. But these same people ignore the fact that genius in a man is not always recognized, if there is no demand at the time for his particular type of genius. A great general, for instance, does not appear in time of peace; he rises to power only when there is a demand for military efficiency. Even Napoleon could not have manufactured a war if his people had not been in the mood to follow his lead.

Musical talent, too, has often been blocked in men by barriers inherent in the way of life of a particular group. For example, though the Quakers of the seventeenth century at first sang fervent hymns at their meetings, they shortly abandoned the use of music altogether. In neither the religious ceremony nor in community life did they allow music. It is only within the last few years that Quakers in

America have introduced music into some of their schools and colleges. Is it a matter for surprise that, despite their deep spirituality and their high intellectual attainments, neither Quaker men nor Quaker women have been creative musicians?

Again, the America of the eighteenth and nineteenth centuries was clearly not the place for a sophisticated musician. Americans, intent upon developing a new country, had but little time for the arts. They gave their highest rewards and recognition to those who were successful in theological pursuits, or landed or business enterprise. In fact, they definitely discouraged and looked down upon artists and musicians. Consequently, no important musicians of native American stock appeared. At a later period, when the pioneer stage was over, people began to feel the need of music and turned to Europe for their musicians. Only Europeans were expected to be musicians. Even those seriously engaged in the profession of music were forced to adopt foreign names, speech, and manners. As late as fifty years ago, American performers and composers attained only grudging recognition. In the face of these barriers, American men— many of them of German stock—were helpless as musicians. Their native musical talent lay latent. They had to wait until the general background had changed, until the pioneer period was over, until Puritan asceticism had died, until people had time, energy, and money to develop genius along artistic and musical lines.

In Europe composers of the highest stature appeared and disappeared in response to environments that fostered or failed to foster them. Eighteenth- and nineteenth-century western European civilization provided, on the whole, the inspiration and incentives for men to create and to produce music. But despite the general background of a favorable environment, conditions varied locally.

In Germany, environment and racial temperament converged fortuitously to bring out native talent. Hence the Germans were able to carry musical art to its highest expression. Italian and English names, so conspicuous in former centuries, largely disappeared from the lists of great composers. The fact is that barriers against any kind of musical activity by men are always effective in preventing men from performing that activity. Moslem mosques, for example, make no use of music. No Mohammedan Bach has risen to compose great choral and orchestral works.

Wide misunderstanding, indeed, exists as to what constitutes the so-called "musical talent." Different musical capabilities may be inherited—an instinct for rhythm, the melodic impulse, a sense of harmony and of counterpoint. Nonmusical qualities also essential to a great composer—persistence, infinite capacity for taking pains, a sense of artistic proportions—may also be inherited. One might call those gifts of the fates. An individual, however, may possess all these gifts and yet never produce any music of importance. In addition to the possession of native talent, a potential musician must be brought up in an environment that demands music as an integral part of life, must be also one of a class that is expected to create music so that he or she may normally obtain the intensive training essential for serious musical composition.

Many unthinking people whose musical experience is limited to listening assume that a divinely inspired musical genius can pour out a song with the naïveté of a bird. The nightingale, however, has absolutely no talent for musical composition. No note of his unchanging melodic phrase is composed by him, but was unconsciously evolved for him by countless generations of ancestors. While these same people recognize vaguely the mysteries of counterpoint and of orchestration, they assume that to learn to compose a simple song requires little more training than to learn to run an automobile. As a matter of fact, the training in musical composition required for a simple song of importance would more nearly approach that required to build an automobile, or to invent one, if none existed. The compositions by Brahms with which he expressed himself as most satisfied were simple-sounding piano accompaniments to forty-nine folk songs. To the student, these piano parts are marvels of artistic construction and proportion, their simplicity achieved only by the elimination of every superfluous note. Written near the end of Brahms' life, but at the height of his powers, they were the result of long years of artistic musical experience. None but a master could possibly have produced them, yet to the uninitiated they seem as easy as the sleight of hand of a magician's trick.

The more elaborate the composition—and modern compositions become increasingly so—the more complex is its conception and production. Hence longer and more intensive training is required. The difficulties in connection with music are much greater than in literature, where the potential poet or novelist becomes familiar from earliest youth with the use of words. With us, thinking in terms of music and the use of musical symbols by children is unusual. A musical genius, of course, is able to absorb the necessary knowledge and training and so to obtain the techniques infinitely faster than the person of average talent. However, it will be found that all great composers went through a rigorous grind of practice, experiment, and absorption of the musical past before they produced their masterpieces. Mozart, always held up as an example of spontaneous musical generation, was in fact intensively trained by his father as a musician from the cradle. His entire childhood was occupied with thinking, playing, and writing music under encouragement. Had he been born and brought up by unmusical parents on a farm in Kansas in 1880, would his genius ever have flowered?

Even if a girl has been born and brought up in a musical atmosphere, even if she has evinced creative talent, the chances are that she has not been expected by her parents and friends to become a composer, but that she has been directed into performance and taught accordingly. The general public attitude toward woman, and particularly toward woman and her music, effectively discourages confidence in her individual self as a composer and in her women contemporaries collectively as potential creators of music. It also precludes public demand for her to compose—a condition essential for production. Finally, it prevents a naturally endowed girl from procuring easily, and her parents from seeking for her, that early and intensive training necessary for the composition of important music. When combined, these three conditions result in an environment in which the creative musical imagination of only a few women can flower. Until it is changed, the sleeping beauty that is music in the feminine soul will not awaken.

When one sees how effective social barriers are in preventing men from composing music and realizes how many have been the barriers to composition by women, the comparative silence of women musicians during the last three hundred years can easily be understood.

Withal, the real core of the matter is not woman's failure to have created great music. It is what that failure, when analyzed, reveals of the constitution of our society and the deep denial of life on which it rests. Even if women participated equally in every current musical activity, our cultural pattern would still be against their creating music as a spiritual expression of their inner life. This inner life is half the spiritual life of humanity. In so far as it differs from that of men, it differs in the possession by women of a unique experience that touches the heights and depths of emotion and sensation, and calls on a deep and intuitive wisdom, a kind of at-oneness with all the processes of growth and decay, birth and rebirth, in the universe. Primitive woman had begun to put this experience into ritual and music, and had proceeded far enough to give us some hint of the direction woman's genius might have taken.

But just as her attempt to evolve her own religion and music from her own experience began to approach the forms of civilized art, woman received a death blow from man's schematic religions. The bases of her own dynamic relation to life were knocked from under her. The need for her music was not institutionalized. Mary, as a goddess, was a tentative and uncompleted conception. From the Protestants, woman received no symbols.

Nothing now remains of the woman's rites to make her proud and positive. At puberty she begins to go to social dances. And there she dances the dance of life only if a boy asks her. At marriage she is "given away" by her father to her husband. At death she kneels desolate, her old proud power to invoke the rebirth gone, while some man intones. What does he intone? Why should a woman care?

And still St. Cecilia hangs over the piano—insincere, ineffectual. How long now until women learn not to go near these altars from which they were cast down, and take courage to make their own religion and their own music anew, and beat out with faith the measure to which their daughters and their daughters' daughters may dance? (See Plate 61.)

CHAPTER XVIII

ARTEMIS STIRRING

1.

EVERY cultural pattern has its strength as well as its weakness, its place in time, its time for passing. The hour has now come when many different currents of thought and many new conditions are converging to bring about changes in our culture. As far as women are concerned, some of these new influences are tending to nullify the force of the old ideas that regarded women as of inferior value to men in an advancing civilization. If taboos compatible only with a primitive attitude and the equally childish superstitious dogma of the Church Fathers still live, they are threatened, like King Canute, by the swiftly rising tide of an articulate womanhood. It seems today that woman is about to assume a natural relation to life, that Artemis is about to be reborn.

The biological theories of Aristotle, who maintained that men alone possess the creative spark, are now disproved by science. Modern research has demonstrated that to the soul of the newborn child, to that particular bundle of inherited aptitudes and characteristics which will make her or him a distinct individual, mother and father have contributed equally. Science restores to woman her biological dignity and with it her sense of power, as a being creative in her own right.

Science tends also to give validity to women's groping explanation of the mystery of the universe. On the whole, the kind of thinking implicit in the early rites of the life cycle—thinking that was plastic, intuitive, and that sought its expression in the rhythm of birth and rebirth—is consonant with modern science and with our ever widening knowledge of the forces of the universe.

There is today a profound change in the thinking about the symbolic relation of human beings to the invisible, yet perceived, higher powers. The rigid theological propositions of yesterday are losing their appeal. More and more we are returning to the primeval sense that all life is one and indivisible, different manifestations of the same life force. Scientists are daily offering new evidence of the intimate relation of plants, animals, and human beings. Now, too, there is again a tendency to believe that the path toward the spiritual is by way of reverence for all processes of life, in the world around and in both the physical and psychic life of human beings.

Belief in the unity of all life is itself a rebirth for women. The basis of their imagery was destroyed with the introduction of the idea that the spirit can develop only by denying the flesh. In primitive times women were always combining the imaginative with the real, always symbolizing personal experiences, always endowing natural states and normal human urges with spiritual significance. So women may now take up the *principle* behind their old rituals, knowing that the world's thinking will henceforth be with them and not against them.

2.

This changed relation of women to religion is not entirely new. It has been steadily developing for several centuries and coincides, significantly, with a change in men's and women's attitude toward musical activity, an attitude that has also taken some time to become general.

When Christian culture first dominated western Europe, a very small group of men fixed the rules for the use of music. Music was to be controlled by the hierarchy of the Church for the purposes of the Church and for no other purpose. After a thousand years of revolt against these rules, the people finally succeeded in establishing new customs for music. But under the patronage of the nobles, music was confined to the castle or the baronial hall. After 1700 the new hierarchy of professional musicians, which rose to power with the middle classes, carried music into public halls and into secular educational institutions where many more people could hear it and participate in it. The latest development in the social aspects of music is the reaction of amateur musicians against assumption by the professionals of an undue authority over the education and performance of music. Amateurs are again beginning to strive for a knowledge of the language of music for their personal use, for a more direct and intimate contact with it than can be derived from mere listening to the performance of professionals.

Slowly but surely education in music is being incorporated into the school system. It is the type of education that trains ear, eye, and mind for the acquisition of experience in the language of music. Instead of training every child as a possible virtuoso, educators are making sane attempts to train every child to be musically literate. Whereas people formerly supposed that to sing, one must be born with a "good voice," they now begin to realize that all voices are good enough to be trained for the satisfaction of one's self and for intelligent participation in group singing. Scores of girls and boys are demonstrating the feasibility of acquiring enough skill on a musical instrument to join a school or college orchestra. Above all, in the forward-looking schools, musical education is including practice in creative work, with the result that more players and singers are able to make music available socially. This does not mean ability to play or sing "art music" as soloists for an audience, but to be capable of transposing, adapting, and improvising—in other words, to be musically articulate.

It is nothing new, of course, for non-professional musicians to play and sing skillfully for their own satisfaction. The innovation in modern musical custom is to give community encouragement and support to amateur musical activity. This is a return to the Greek idea that "music" belonged to the "Muses," or to the arts and culture in general, and that it should be an integral part of a liberal education. But the foundation upon which the intricate art of our music rests was formerly given to children spasmodically and accidentally only in homes in which the parents happened to be "musical." Now the elements of the language of music are taught to children, and even to adults, in institutions such as schools or summer camps, some being organized especially for the purpose of musical culture.

It is not only educators who are establishing new customs for musical activity. Amateurs already skilled in the performance of music are here and there beginning to give organized effect to their urge for participation in group music.

The adverse conditions of wartime England could not deter thirty of forty men and women from meeting during their summer vacation for the purpose of playing together in an orchestra. Living in tents or lodging in neighbors' houses, they played morning, noon, and night for the sheer delight of it, for the refreshment of their spirits.[1] The experiment of organizing groups larger than a quartet is followed by a New England "musical house party" that is held annually for a ten-day session. Both groups place emphasis upon the fact that the orchestra is organized for the benefit of the players rather than the players existing for the prestige of the orchestra. In England the conductor is an amateur; in America he is a professional, but in the employ of the amateurs and temporarily devoted to their interest.

Meeting in a private house in Merion, Pennsylvania, for the purpose of performing choral music *but with no intention of preparing for a concert,* a hundred and more skilled singers and instrumentalists form the "Accademia dei Dilettanti di Musica." This group is conducted by an amateur—the host—whose only demand upon these expert sight readers is that they love music and that they have had the training to enable them to understand and execute, without previous drilling, such compositions as Bach's cantatas and Brahms' Requiem. The Accademia has been meeting for twenty years, eight or nine times a season. The total number of men and women who have attended these "singing parties" now reaches nearly two thousand. Professionals come as amateurs. No one requires an audience, but each is impelled to come solely by the privilege of participating in great music.[2]

These societies of amateurs are probably as yet unique. Their success has depended upon the strong personalities who originated them and now carry them on. They are pioneer ventures, not yet institutionalized. But a precedent for forming permanent societies to encourage amateurs and choral music can be seen in both England and America. Various organizations serve the purpose of introducing musicians to each other, but of leaving them free to function in any way they wish. As a rule, the benefiting members pay dues, but patrons and patronesses in the community supplement the dues with contributions, thus giving the sanction of society at large to nonprofessional activity in music.

In many ways the musical renaissance of today is a repetition of the rebirth of music in the thirteenth and fourteenth centuries. Then people were overthrowing the restrictive regulations of the Church. Now people are finding the framework for musical activity erected by professional musicians too narrow—again, they are opening new paths for music lovers. When the nobles in their castles instituted new customs in music, they did not interfere with the older customs of the Church but created a demand for more trained musicians. In the same way today, amateurs are not curtailing the need for the virtuosi and other professionals but are adding to the occasions when music can be enjoyed.

The results of these changing musical customs cannot yet be foretold. One trend, however, is already determined—the trend to emphasize the primitive use of music as an affective power for a specific occasion and purpose. In certain uses, music today retains its former application. Music in churches still has this affective purpose—it is supposed to influence the higher powers and also to bring the people into harmony with each other. And who has not felt the power of waltz or rumba rhythm—far more potent an invitation to the dance than the spoken word—or the irresistible command of fife and drum to march behind the flag? Now music is reattaining its primeval value, which in no way interferes with the value of concert giving and virtuosity. Music, which produces an inner harmony, is being introduced into homes, schools, colleges, moving pictures, and theaters, and especially into hospitals for its direct power over emotionally disturbed people.

The need for musical therapy received impetus in the great wars of our times with their aftermath of wounded men and women. The important point made by the experts in this field is that the music used should be of the type that reduces emotional strain. In an age when people are already overtaxed with disruptive forces, they require tones and rhythms that will give them a feeling of security and a sense of harmony with their surroundings. Equally important is the type of person employed as a musical therapist. Virtuosi, or amateurs trained in the spirit of virtuosity, cannot do this work. Many gifted musicians are unsuited to perform music in the sympathetic, adaptable way essential for success in favorably influencing a patient. Different musical qualities from those developed by most musicians are therefore demanded; another set of musical talents is now given community support. How provocative to the imagination it is to learn that scientists have recently discovered the magic in the "sonorous fluid" that primitive men and women have known for countless years! Music has been scientifically proven to be capable of influencing people to think, feel, and act. Music actually can give access to depths in the unconscious where nature and spirit are one. So now a new type of music has the possibility of developing upon the principle behind the great musical art of primitive societies.

3.

Increasing recognition of women's human capabilities, converging with public insistence upon variety in musical enterprise, has radically altered the relation of women to music. Women and girls are at last on the way to approaching music in a free and natural attitude, untrammeled by taboos and superstitions.

It is one thing, however, to make the categorical statement that barriers between women and music no longer exist; it is rather like the boast of a Chinese visitor to this country that his government has forbidden illiteracy. He made the claim as a *fait accompli!* But everyone knows that long years of planning and of hard work on the part of Chinese leaders and teachers combined with the co-operation of the people will be necessary before China can become a nation of literate men and women. So it is now with women and the creative aspects of music. The falling of the barriers is only the beginning of the reform. An attitude of affirmation toward women as potentially creative musicians, accompanied by community backing and intensive training for all who desire it, must lay the foundation, build the plateau from which the creative woman musician can eventually take her natural place in the musical life of her society.

The next step for the friends of women musicians to take is the planning of practices for the future benefit of talented women and the opening up of opportunities for women already trained in leadership and in the composition of music. Obviously, men are firmly intrenched in most of the established musical enterprises of today. For the proving of their capability women will therefore do better to find new fields and untrodden paths. Happily, several opportunities already await further leadership and initiative on the part of women.

The home is the oldest institution we have and the one most closely associated with woman's authority and her creative music. In the home women's songs were sung. Much of our wonderful heritage of folk literature originated in connection with daily work, love, and death. Today these associations have largely ceased to exist. Modern life has robbed this center of many of its former activities. So has the modern utility of music changed. Song is now rarely used as a direct, affective agent. Even the lullaby has been condemned by child specialists. The relation of women to music in the home is now entirely different and comparatively without meaning.

Since the days of the melancholic Robert Burton, fathers have been complaining that the money they spent on their daughters' musical education was largely wasted. Once a girl was married, she neglected her music and appeared content to do without it. This complaint remains true for the twentieth century. Far too often girls "give up" their music. But is it not because custom decrees that it shall lead nowhere except to concertizing? All playing and singing become a concert in miniature, instead of being indispensable to woman's principal business of bringing and fostering life.

But now the idea that music benefits oneself or one's child has captured the imagination of at least some parents. An annually increasing number of young people with a practical musical equipment are becoming parents, and upon the young mother falls the full impact of the demand to make music an integral part of the child's preschool education. Here, in the home, or in the nursery school and kindergarten, is the opportunity for creative work—arranging, adapting, and inventing appropriate rhythms and melodies to be used in giving little children an inner harmony of spirit.

In the larger life of the community, outside of school and home, women have their music clubs. Choral literature for modern women is sadly in need of replenishment and invigoration. What better medium could there be for the woman musician than in the supplying of this demand, bringing fresh musical ideas to her companions, to be sung and played upon convenient occasions, according to women's own interpretation of their spiritual needs?

Some communities have already provided a new outlet for the woman musician in the practice of therapeutic music. Eva Viscelius and Agnes Saville contributed invaluable work toward building morale in the sick and wounded by means of music. Then came Harriet Ayer Seymour, a prime mover in the movement to give music a practical, affective use. During the First World War she had charge of music in army hospitals, and afterward was the chairman of the Hospital Music Committee, where she gave courses for the training of "musical doctors." The last few years of war have greatly increased the demand for women qualified to play and sing "healing" music in hospitals. In the Philadelphia area an experiment was undertaken under the auspices of the Southeastern Pennsylvania Chapter of the American Red Cross to supply instrumentalists and singers.

Selected from the association of Gray Ladies, about twenty women qualified as competent to go about the wards of several hospitals. Working separately or together, each one modifies beautiful, simple melodies into music of therapeutic value adapted to the emotional state of the different patients.[3] (See Plate 63.)

The institutionalization of affective music, already underway in education and in the moving-picture industry, is now taking place in the field of therapy. After the First World War, the National Foundation of Musical Therapy was founded by Mrs. Seymour, and through it scores of devoted musicians have since been working in hospitals and other institutions. At the present time, therefore, both professionals and amateurs are drawn into a common musical cause, the importance of whose social consequences no one can predict. Together they are blazing a path for a new class of official women musicians. The intimate knowledge these pioneers are gaining through experience of the action of music upon the subconscious mind, purifying it of evil influences and revitalizing it, may well be the foundation upon which some gifted woman will create new and wonderful music.

Among our rural people an opportunity for creative work awaits a woman of talent and initiative. By turning her eyes to the Grange and to the now popular festivals celebrating the principal agricultural crop of a country area—such as the Apple Blossom Festival in Virginia and the Potato Blossom Festival in Aroostook County, Maine—a country music teacher may make her position the steppingstone to original composition.

The Grange is one of the most remarkable institutions of American folk life. In it the culture of our country districts centers. Because of the secrecy of its rituals, few outsiders are aware of its importance. Founded in America in 1867 by a group of Masons, the Grange draws on old agricultural rituals that have come down from antiquity through the Masonic orders. Here can be found the old idea of birth and rebirth, reformulated by our American farm population for itself with a Christian coloring but with the use of the old symbols. Nothing is more American than the Grange; yet nothing in our modern life has deeper roots in the earth and in that early religion of nature of which woman was once the priestess and musician.

The opportunity offered by the Grange to the woman composer arises chiefly from the fact that, in this organization, women have a status equal to that of men. While they are still in grammar school, girls and boys are taught the lore of the Grange and learn its traditional motions with songs from the *Grange Song Book.* Girls and boys walk in couples in the processions, and grow up with a full recognition of the honored place of each in the great scheme of life. Women and men also attend the ceremonies in complete equality—"matron" and "patron" of husbandry. The "chaplain" is often a woman. The post of "lecturer" is also often filled by a woman. From the point of view of music, the "lecturer" is the more important of the two, for upon her falls the responsibility of providing entertainment, which must be of educational value and uplifting to the group. So eager are the people of the Grange for anything that enriches their simple ceremonies that a talented woman would undoubtedly find reward for creating appropriate music, perhaps a new and mighty song of rebirth springing from the heart of our fertile land and from the religious spirit of our American farmers.

Community ritual and music has been developed in an entirely new way by Dr. Rachel Davis Dubois, formerly professor of intercultural education at New York University. In co-operation with Dvora Lapson, a musician and mime-dancer, she has made experiments in the cure of socially sick groups and now offers training in the techniques involved at the New School for Social Research in New York.

Rachel Dubois' services as an expert in analyzing social industrial discords are called for where there is trouble in crowded industrial or urban areas, race riots or other disorders beyond the control of regular social agencies. Sometimes she works under the public school system. Sometimes she is called in by a group of churches— usually Protestant, Jewish, and Catholic churches in combination. Sometimes she is sponsored by the Quakers, being herself a Quaker. Sometimes she works in connection with a social agency.

Her mainstay, and the original element in her experienced and competent handling of social disorder, is a new kind of social gathering that she calls a "neighborhood-home festival." With the help of her co-operators in the district, about thirty assorted individuals representing all the types and cultures that cannot or will not mix socially are persuaded to gather at some convenient center. The chosen place is always dressed up for the occasion with the flowers or fruits or evergreens of the season, and with informal seating arrangements. At such a gathering held just before Christmas at the Friends' Meetinghouse in New York City, the vestibule was transformed by evergreen trees and candlelight, the cushions dragged out of the pews inside and placed in a circle on the floor. Flowers, fruits, candlelight, and firelight are the beginning of the magic.

After the people have come and have been charmed into relaxing and waiting to see what will happen next, Dr. Dubois starts a conversation with an observation on something connected with the weather or the seasons. She has discovered a sure social solvent— reminiscence of early childhood connected with seasonal activities. On an autumn day Dr. Dubois gets the group to talking about preparation for Thanksgiving or for Jewish or national harvest festivals, always pushing the reminiscence back to earliest childhood, centered in home and mother. Then Rachel Dubois introduces the critical questions: "Did your mother sing while she was doing this? What did she sing?" And out of the group she begins to draw the old songs they heard or learned in childhood, songs going back to many lands, in many parts of the world. The smooth varnish of Americanism is rubbed off. These people begin to meet on aboriginal levels of folk memory and folk song.

It is amazing to see that any thirty Americans, gathered at random, in our racially mixed city areas, will have among them three or four people who can sing the whole of some unique song. It is a great moment in such a gathering when some unadjusted old woman of foreign birth lifts up her voice and sings. She often breaks down in joyful tears when neighbors upon whom she had looked with distrust draw around her, admiring and obviously moved.

Within an hour after she starts to talk to an apparently dull and uninterested group, Dr. Dubois and her trained musician assistant have the people circling with clasped hands, walking in processionals with lighted candles, singing folk songs and hymns of all faiths, even reverently repeating prayers together. Nine hundred of these "festivals" were given in New York City one season mainly in the least "privileged" part of the city. A visitor to many of them says that each one was entirely different from the others and that every one had some moments of startling and poignant beauty. An artist observer said, "If one could get the secret of this, one would have a new art that would cure almost everything that ails us." [4]

In Rachel Dubois can be seen an educated woman of modern times not only creating a new art, in which music is integrated, but doing so in order to provide rites practical and effective enough to solve a social problem brought about by modern conditions. This is precisely the way her remote ancestors made rituals thousands of years ago when women were creative musicians. Dr. Dubois' remarkable initiative in developing this technique by reviving old rites and music, buried in the memories of people indiscriminately chosen, and by improvising an affective integration of motions and melodies capable of smoothing out the souls of skeptical participants, is significant to the modern woman musician. Not only does it demonstrate that woman's inherent ability to use music creatively is as potent as it ever was; it also suggests that, while women still find it difficult to compete with men in the conventional practice of music, there is now opening to them the opportunity to create healing, beneficent music of immense social value. (See Plate 64.)

But in spite of the giant strides taken by women toward a fuller participation in the musical life of our times, an outworn attitude still holds them back from the full realization of their new opportunities. Women, unfortunately, have long regarded their women's activities as *unimportant* and as *unworthy* of artistic effort. Musicians have a predilection to strive for recognition in men's arenas by writing symphonies and operas—forms invented and used by men for centuries in their own organizations. But if women would sing first for themselves, sincerely and enthusiastically, ignoring critics with preconceived notions about either women or music, their song would eventually burst out of the bounds of home, sickroom, or club and would flow into that stream of rhythm, melody, harmony which is forming the music of tomorrow. (See Plates 65 and 66.)

4.

The woman musician of today is at the crossroads Her relation to music depends upon her relation to the society in which she lives and to the religious expression of that society. This relation transcends any specific barriers that may have been erected in the past between given groups of women and their participation in music. And since all civilization is now in the throes of rebirth, woman's place in the musical life of the new world is dependent upon what new religious ideas will be formulated, what new customs will be made.

Woman's apparent sterility in musical creation, in comparison with man's of our times, is not at all due to any inherent deficiency in her ability to think symbolically. Given the proper environments, where her culture demands music and where her contemporaries confidently expect her to produce it, where she receives from early childhood the training necessary to make her a creative musician, woman has already been at least the equal of her man in composing the type of music required by that culture. And this flowering of woman's natural musical talent has been by no means confined to aborigines of early cultural levels. The Tuareg poetess-musicians, Sappho and her colleagues, the Arabians, Hildegarde and other nuns, many ladies of the Renaissance, as well as the Russian and Lithuanian peasants are witnesses proclaiming woman's power to express herself in the language of music.

Scientists agree that the innate capacity of the human brain for creative, artistic, and intellectual accomplishment has not materially changed during the past sixty thousand years. Neither can the *relative* capacity for men and women for such activity have changed. When we find, therefore, that at many times and in many places, women have equaled their men in music making, we may be sure that the comparative silence of modern women in musical expression is not the result of inherent incapacity or of spiritual inferiority to men.

Nor is woman's comparative silence in music due to the fact that our music has become overintellectualized. Scores of modern women have demonstrated intellectual capacity of the highest order. The intelligence quotient of the average girl is fully equal to that of her brother. Both are equally educable, as has been recently discovered, in the abstractions of mathematics. No chimpanzee could be taught to multiply three by four or to resolve a dominant seventh chord. The existence of many women of high intellectual capacity, of superior artistic imagination, and of ability to express themselves in the modern idiom of music conclusively disproves the possibility that the female sex is disbarred from the sacred circle of creative musicians.

As we have seen, woman's silence in musical expression is, on the contrary, due to historical causes that have brought about a nonpermissive environment for the woman musician. The music of our culture was originally bound indissolubly to organized religion and limited to church use. Women were disbarred from official participation in the religious ceremony and so became automatically cut off from opportunity to create music. Nuns, who had a specified place in the hierarchy, composed only liturgical and extraliturgical music, and within the limits of their opportunities. When men and women freed themselves from the heavy restrictions placed upon the free use of music by the churchmen and began to use music apart from ritual and liturgy, women were *theoretically* able to function again as musicians. But the leaders in music were still those connected with, or employed by, religious officials, and according to the established custom of over a thousand years, were all men. Effective musical education and training was still in the church. Since the supply of men musicians was sufficient, women were not in demand but were expected rather to patronize and to perform men's music. Furthermore, even though ecclesiastical authority waned, authority in church, state, educational system, and home remained largely in the hands of men. And it was an authority reinforced by the religion that women were spiritually and intellectually inferior to men.

The Fathers of the early Church said: "Every woman should be ashamed of the thought that she is a woman."

This is the pernicious doctrine that has determined the relation of women to the body politic and to religious expression, and that has stifled woman's collective imagination. Its poison has survived even in the most up to date of men's teaching. The terms "masculine" and "feminine," when used in association with "activity" and "passivity," tend to give women the same sense of powerlessness and so carry over into modern education the idea that feminine attributes cannot be active and beneficent; that, in order to develop creative imagination, a woman must ignore her sex and build upon attributes and qualities now associated with men. This is as negative and as emotionally conflicting a creed as that taught by the early Christian Church.

How different is the faith in a spirit-bearing womanhood expressed by a great woman of the nineteenth century, Rahel Varnhagen: "I am at one with myself and consider myself a good, beautiful gift." [5]

Here is the clarion call to women—the holy dogma for the affirmation of collective womanhood. In it is implicit all that women need to give them that spiritual independence and self-assertion essential for any kind of creative work. Most of all for the rearing of good and beautiful children.

By regarding herself as a good, beautiful gift, any woman can be sure that she is endowed with every attribute of brain power and spirituality now possible for human beings. She need have no more misgivings about the inherent power of women to evince imagination.

In the words "I am at one with myself" lies the assurance that childbearing, even the female equipment for bringing life, provides one of the most driving incentives to develop imagination that the world has ever seen. Believing this, a mother knows that evidence of creative imagination, or a desire to develop it, does not make her less of a woman and an ineffective imitation of man. She knows that she can accept her natural role without emotional conflict and with the assurance that womanhood is a creative role in the scheme of life.

New ideas are always slow in gaining momentum. Throughout history, they can be traced back far beyond the time they became a force, running parallel to older conceptions of what is right until they either disappear or become the core of another religion. The idea that women are a creative and beneficent power is actually one of the oldest in the world and appears today in the great majority of primitive societies. It reached its most beautiful expression in the oldest known civilizations of antiquity. Wherever the creative power of women is a factor in the making of religious and social institutions, women have authority in such institutions, in the magic arts of healing body and spirit, and in music. From their rites, their music, and from their own leaders (both real and symbolic), women draw the inspiration to revitalize, at fixed intervals, their own powers.

Running parallel to the religion that regards woman as creative and beneficent is the diametrically opposed belief that she is evil, or, in some cases, merely powerless. Even in a few of the most primitive tribes, there are evidences of a movement to degrade the value of the female and to challenge her humanity. This movement reached its climax around the years 400 to 800 A.D., and has had a dominating influence upon the schematic religions founded by men from about 800 B.C. to 600 A.D. Such religions include Brahmanism, Buddhism (although to a lesser extent), Confucianism, Orthodox Judaism, ecclesiastical Christianity, Mohammedanism, and Nazism. It has been the religion of modern civilization. Wherever and whenever the value of womanhood is degraded, women neglect to emphasize the life-bringing value of their natural ways and allow men to pre-empt the creative arts of healing body and spirit, and of music. Although today, in our society, these arts have become separate departments and specialized, they are still endowed with a quality of mystery and magic. Religion, medicine, and music are still the three fields from which men would like to exclude women and in which they most resent women's influence.

It is only very lately that women have taken organized steps to replace themselves in a creative, beneficent relation to life and to reassert their own values. But hardly yet do many face boldly and honestly the crux of the woman problem: religious ideas, symbols, ceremonies, and economic customs that place women in the position of receiving bounties, even the gift of life, from men can never bring women into the right relation to life and free the subconscious for creative thinking.

For women to attain the state of collective spiritual independence, to be reborn as adult human beings, their inner lives must be given the spiritual sustenance so long withheld, and given it more intensively on account of their long starvation.

Instead of those symbols and religious ceremonies that allow a woman only a vicarious relation to the life force, others, giving her a realization of her own potentiality for activity, must be substituted. In ritual, the great truth should be reiterated that woman is a beneficent manifestation of the rhythm of all life. As girl, mate, mother, worker at life's tasks, and finally as one ripe with experience, she should be told and told again that each stage of her life span has its own peculiar wisdom that is needed in the community; that, without her, the torch of life would flicker and die.

So are women now needed to assert their leadership over women, and over men who would work with them, in those departments of life in which women have experiences denied by natural laws to men. Men have great areas in life where their leadership can be properly exercised. But in all matters pertaining to women's female function and to her inner emotional life, the assumption by men of exclusive authority does the feminine psyche grave harm and stifles its free expression. Today it is scientists, doctors, and psychiatrists who possess the modern magic. The exclusion, or the discouragement, of women in these fields is as damaging to women as the exclusion of women from the priesthood was in early Christian times. Healing, religion, and music are the three fields in which woman is pre-eminently fitted by nature and by experience to express herself and to serve her fellows. Unless women are trained in modern methods and equipped with the learning of the ages to be doctors and psychiatrists, able to advise girls in adolescence, in the period of sex relations, in childbirth, and at the threshold to middle age, women will never have the foundation for formulating the new faith, for developing the new rituals and customs that will give spiritual integrity—the foundation of creative expression in music.

Once leadership by women trained in scientific thinking has been established and recognized, women can then make a concerted effort to release their imagination from the age-long repression. They must find their own symbols to remind themselves of their own peculiar power for good. They must find rituals and music to reinforce their own spirits in the crises of womanhood. And they must have representation in the larger life of the community for the authority of the natural woman; then can the Daughters of the Moon proceed boldly and confidently to the task of objectifying their experiences in whatever way they find opportunity and incentive.

Even now, the crescent moon is rising in the sky. One day it will grow again to its full splendor. And Artemis is reaching for her lyre, courageously striking the opening chords of woman's ageless song:

Here, Queen Goddess, light-bringer, divine Moon,
Who move in a path of night, wandering in the darkness.
Torch-bearer of the mysteries, Moon-maiden, rich in stars,
You who gave and diminish, who are both female and male,
All-seeing, enlightener, fruit-bearer, Mother of Time,
Splendor of amber, soulful, illuminator, you who are Birth.
Lover of all-night wakefulness, fountain of beautiful stars!
Whose joy is the tranquil silence of the blissful spirit of night,
The lustrous one, giver of charms, votive statue of night,
You who bring fruit to perfection, visions and sacred rites!
Queen of stars, in flowing veils, who move on a curving path,
All-wise maiden, blessed one, keeper of the treasury of stars,
May you come in beautiful gladness, shining in all your brilliance;
And saving the youthful suppliants who turn to you, Maiden Moon! [6]

NOTES

The very large number of books and articles necessary as a background for the story of women, religion, and music is naturally too great for inclusion here. Only those from which direct references have been taken are listed in this volume. In several instances, I have omitted original sources and have given instead the name of a book in which the source material is used. Such books themselves throw light on the relation of women to music and broaden the base of my approach to this provocative subject.

CHAP. I

1. J. G. Frazer, *The Magic Art* (New York: The Macmillan Co., 1935), I, 125.

2. C. Troyer, *Traditional Songs of the Zuñis,* Wa-Wan Series of American Compositions (Newton Center, Mass.: Wa-Wan Press, 1904), Vol. III, second series.

3. K. Bücher, *Arbeit und Rhythmus* (Leipzig: B. G. Teubner, 1909), p. 401.

4. Personal letters from J. G. Giorgiades, Athens, Greece.

5. Katherine Swan, *The Participation of Russian Women in Music* (MS. at Smith College and at University of Pennsylvania), p. 40.

6. *Records Nos. 12B and 13B Jemima Gibson (Cayuga)* (Six Nations Reserve, Canada, Jan. 23, 1941). Fenton Collection I in Library of Congress from an unpublished MS. of Dr. W. N. Fenton, Bureau of American Ethnology.

7. J. R. Swanton, *Social Organization and Social Usages of the Indians of the Creek Confederacy* (Bureau of American Ethnology, 1924), XLII, 324.

8. Fenton, *op. cit.*

9. F. H. Cushing, *Outlines of Zuñi Creation Myths* (Bureau of American Ethnology, 13th Annual Report, 1891-92), p. 446.

10. Swan, *op. cit.,* p. 10.

11. Alice Fletcher and F. LaFlesche, *The Omaha Tribe* (Bureau of American Ethnology, 1905-06), XXVII, 426.

12. D. A. Talbot, *Women's Mysteries of a Primitive People: The Ibibios of Southern Nigeria* (London: Cassell & Co., Ltd., 1915), p. 205.

13. M. Walters, *Le Peuple Letton* (Riga, 1926), p. 112.

14. F. R. Boas, *The Social Organization and the Secret Societies of the Kwakuitl Indians* (Report of the U. S. National Museum, 1895), p. 584.

ADDITIONAL REFERENCES

Böckel, O. *Psychologie der Volksdichtung*. Leipzig, 1913.

Brinton, D. G. *Nagualism: A Study in Native American Folklore and History*. Philadelphia, 1894.

Frazer, J. G. *The Golden Bough*. New York: The Macmillan Co., 1935.

Katzenelenbogan. *The Daina: An Anthology of Lithuanian and Latvian Folksongs*. Chicago: Lithuanian News Publishing Co., 1935.

Lumholtz. *Through Central Borneo*. New York: Charles Scribner's Sons, 1920. Pp. 310, 350.

Routledge, W. S. & K. *With a Prehistoric People*. London: Edward Arnold & Co., 1910. Pl. CXVI.

CHAP. II

1. T. Michelson, *Autobiography of a Fox Indian Woman* (Bureau of American Ethnology, 1918-19), XL, 319.

2. Personal communication from Marion Szekely Freschl.

3. J. C. Lawson, *Modern Greek Folk Lore and Ancient Greek Religion* (Cambridge: Cambridge University Press, 1910), p. 547.

4. L. von Schröder, *Die Hochzeitsbräuche der Esten* (Berlin: 1888), p. 186.

5. G. H. Dalman, *Palästinischer Diwan als Beitrag zur Volkskunde Palästinas Gesammelt und mit Ubersetzung und Melodien* (Leipzig: 1901), p. 312.

6. E. Martinengo-Cesaresco, *Essays in the Study of Folksongs* (London: 1886), p. 385.

7. B. I. F. Laubscher, *Sex, Custom, and Psychopathology* (London: G. Routledge & Sons, Ltd., 1937), p. 147 & Pl. XI.

8. H. Trilles, *Les pygmées de la fôret equatoriale* (Paris: Bloud et Gay, 1932), p. 412. English translation of the poem by Katherine Garrison Chapin.

9. Swan, *op. cit.*, p. 28.

10. J. T. Bent, *The Cyclades* (London: 1885), p. 183.

11. A. Hauffen, *Die deutsche Sprachinsel Gottschee* (Graz, 1905), Example 105.

12. M. T. de Lens, "Sur le chant des moueddin et sur les chants chez femmes a Meknès," *Revue de Musicologie*, Nov. 1924, pp. 152-63.

13. M. C. Fauriel, *Songs of Greece*, tr. by C. B. Sheridan (London: 1825), p. 230.

14. D. Corkery, *The Hidden Ireland* (Dublin: M. H. Gill & Son, 1925), p. 39.

15. J. G. von Hahn, *Albanesische Studien* (Vienna: 1853), II, 135.

16. *Ibid.*, p. 136.

17. Poem translated by Frances Herskovits, *New Republic*, Sept. 4, 1935.

18. P. H. Buck, *Vikings of the Sunrise* (New York: Frederick A. Stokes Co., 1938), p. 205.

19. Marjorie Kennedy-Fraser, *Songs of the Hebrides* (London: Boosey & Co., 1917), I, 115.

20. M. J. Herskovits, *Dahomey: An Ancient West African Kingdom* (New York: J. J. Augustin, 1938), II, 320.

ADDITIONAL REFERENCES

Buschan, G. *Illustrierte Völkerkunde*. Stuttgart: Strecker und Schröder, 1926.

Coomaraswamy, R. K. *Catalogue of the Indian Collection at the Boston Museum of Fine Arts*. Boston: Harvard Press, 1926. Part VI, Pl. IV, pp. 14, 657.

Hall, Mr. & Mrs. S. C. *Ireland, Its Scenery Characteristics*. London: 1841.

Herzog, G. *Jabo Proverbs from Liberia*. London: Oxford University Press, 1936.

McConnel, Ursula. "Mourning Ritual on the Gulf of Carpenteria," *Oceania*, 1936-37. Vol. 7.

Ortoli, J. B. F. "*Les voceri de l'ile de Corse*," *Collection de chansons et de contes populaires*, 1887, Vol. 10.

Rathery, E. J. B. "*Les chants populaires de l'italie*," *Revue des Deux Mondes*, 1862, Vol. 38.

Warmelo, N. J. von. *Contributions toward Venda History, Religion and Tribal Ritual*. Union of South Africa, Dept. of Native Affairs, Ethnological Publicators, Vol. III.

CHAP. III

1. Kennedy-Fraser, *op. cit.*, II, 110.

2. J. Combarieu, *La Musique et la magie: étude sur les origines populaires de l'art musical: son influence et sa fonction dans les sociétés* (Paris: Picard, 1909), p. 123.

3. C. Velten, *Gebräuche der Suaheli* (Göttingen, 1903), p. 17. Poem translated by Henry S. Drinker.

4. Wm. Thalbitzer and H. Thuren, *On the Eskimo Music in Greenland* (Copenhagen: 1914-23), p. 155.

5. F. La Flesche, *The Osage Tribe* (Bureau of American Ethnology, 1927-28), XL, 687.

6. Swan, *op. cit.*, p. 18.

7. Talbot, *op. cit.*, p. 77.

8. G. W. Stellers, *Beschreibung von dem Lande Kamschatka* (Leipzig, 1774), p. 332.

9. M. Friedlaender, *Brahms' Lieder*, tr. by C. L. Leese (London: Oxford University Press, 1928), p. 248.

ADDITIONAL REFERENCES

Earthy, Dora. *Valenge Women*. London: Oxford University Press, 1933.

Hála, Ján. *Pod Tatrami*. Mikuláši: Vydal "Tranoscius" v Liptovskom Sv., 1942.

Kheiri, M. A. *Indische Miniaturen der Islamischen zeit*. Berlin: Ernest Wasmuth. Pl. 42.

Sachs, C. *Die Musikinstrumente Indiens und Indonesians*. Berlin: G. Reimer, 1915.

CHAP. IV

1. H. A. Junod, *The Life of a South African Tribe* (London & Neuchatel: David Nutt, 1912).

ADDITIONAL REFERENCES

Evans, I. H. N. "Notes on the Religious Beliefs, Superstitions, Ceremonies, and Tabus of the Dusuns of the Tuaran and Tempassuk Districts of British North Borneo," *Journal of the Royal Anthropological Institute*, Vol. XLII, 1912.

Jochelson, W. *The Koryaks of Siberia*. New York: Publication of the Jesup North Pacific Expedition, 1908. Vol. 6, Pl. III and IV.

"*Lieder u. Sangesweisen u. Geschichten der Wanyamwezi,*" *Berlin Universitat Ausland Hochschule Mitteilungen*. Berlin and Stuttgart, 1901.

Nioradze, G. *Der Schamanismus bei dem siberischen Völkern*. Stuttgart: Strecker und Schröder, 1925.

Underhill, Ruth. "The Autobiography of a Papago Woman," *Memoirs of the American Anthropological Association*, No. 46, 1936 (supplement to *American Anthrop.*, Vol. 38, No. 3, Pt. 2).

CHAP. V

1. S. N. Kramer, *Sumerian Mythology: A Study of Spiritual and Literary Achievement in the 3rd Millennium, B.C.* (Philadelphia: American Philosophical Society, 1944), Chap. II, section 3.

ADDITIONAL REFERENCES

Frobenius, L. *Mdsimu Dsangara*. Berlin: Atlantis-Verlag, 1931. Pl. 36 and 51.

Gusinde, M. *Die Feuerland Indianer* (Ona tribe). Vienna: Anthropos-Bibliothek Expeditions, Series 1-2, 1931-32.

Hentze, C. *Mythes et symboles lunaires: Chine ancienne, civilisations anciennes de l'Asie, peuples limitrophes du Pacifique.* Edition "de Sikkel," 1932.

Obermaier, H. *Fossil Man in Spain.* New Haven: Yale University Press, 1925. Pl. IX.

Stow, G. M., and Bleek, Dorothea. *Rock Paintings in South Africa.* London: Methuen & Co., Ltd., 1930. Pl. 71.

Tongue, M. Helen. *Bushman Paintings.* Oxford: Clarendon Press, 1909. Pl. XXVIII.

CHAP. VI

1. G. M. Haardt and L. Audouin-Dubreuil, *Across the Sahara by Motor Car* (London: T. Fisher Unwin, Ltd., 1924), p. 229.

2. Denham and Clapperton, *Narrative of Travels and Discoveries in North and Central Africa* (London: 1826), p. xiii.

3. Haardt and Dubreuil, *op. cit.*, pp. 212, 231.

4. R. Briffault, *The Mothers: A Study of the Origins of Sentiments and Institutions* (New York: The Macmillan Co., 1927), I, 385.

5. *Ibid.,* I, 385.

6. Janet R. Buttles, *The Queens of Egypt* (London: A. Constable & Co., 1908), p. 168.

7. A. Erman, *The Literature of the Ancient Egyptians,* tr. by A. M. Blackman (London: Methuen & Co., Ltd., 1927), p. 279.

8. *Ibid.,* p. 12.

9. A. Erman, *Zaubersprüche für Mutter und Kind: aus dem paprus 3027 des Berliner Museums* (Berlin: 1901).

10. A. Erman, *Life in Ancient Egypt,* tr. by H. M. Tirard (London: The Macmillan Co., 1894), pp. 320, 387, 389.

11. S. Langdon, *Tammuz and Ishtar* (Oxford: Clarendon Press, 1914), p. 11.

12. *Lyra Graeca* (London: Loeb Classical Library, 1922-27), I, 265.

ADDITIONAL REFERENCES

Bull, L., and Scott, Nora. *The Tomb of Rekh-mi-rē.* New York: The Metropolitan Museum of Art, 1943. Vol. II, Pl. LXVI.

Davies, Nina de G., and Gardiner, A. H. *The Tomb of Amenemhet.* Egypt Exploration Fund, 1915. Pl. XIX.

Evans, A. *The Palace of Minos.* The Macmillan Co., 1931-35. Vol. I, Fig. 167; Vol. II, p. 2, Sup. Pl. XXV; Vol. III, Pl. XVIII, Figs. 38, 39.

Fyzee-Rahamin, A. B. *The Music of India.* London: Luzac & Co., 1925.

Galpin, F. W. *The Music of the Sumerians and Their Immediate Successors, the Babylonians and Assyrians.* Cambridge: Cambridge University Press, 1937.

Gombosi, O. *Music in the Old Aegean World*. American Musicological Society, March, 1940.

Sachs, C. *"Musik der Antike," Handbuch der Musikwissenschaft*. Wildpark-Potsdam: 1931. Pl. 7.

CHAP. VII

1. Briffault, *op. cit.*, I, 358.

2. Briffault, *op. cit.*, I, 346.

3. Clarisse Bader, *Women in Ancient India* (London: K. Paul, Trench, Trubner & Co., 1925), p. 9.

4. H. H. Wilson, *Rig Veda*, Vol. V, Hymn 28.

5. Briffault, *op. cit.*, I, 346.

6. Jane E. Harrison, *Themis: A Study of the Social Origins of Greek Religion* (London: Cambridge University Press, 2nd ed., 1927), p. 205.

7. G. Murray, *The Bacchae of Euripides* (New York: Longmans, Green & Co., 1919), p. 14.

8. *Ibid.*, p. 12.

9. *Loc. cit.*

10. *Ibid.*, p. 10.

11. *Ibid.*, p. 42.

12. Nilla Cook, unpublished translation of an Orphic hymn.

13. H. T. Wharton, *Sappho* (New York: Brentano, 1920), p. 102.

14. *Ibid.*, p. 111.

15. *Ibid.*, p. 110.

16. D. M. Robinson, *Sappho and Her Influence* (Boston: Marshall, Jones Co., 1924), p. 89.

17. Athenaeus, *The Deipnosophistae*, tr. by C. B. Gulick (London: Wm. Heinemann Ltd., Loeb Classical Library, 1927-41), VI, 331.

18. Clarisse Bader, *La Femme Grecque* (Paris: 1872), p. 45.

19. F. Poulsen, *Delphi*, tr. by G. C. Richards (London: Gyldendal, 1920), p. 264.

20. *Lyra Graeca*, I, 73.

21. *Lyra Graeca*, III, 13.

22. J. A. Platt, "Sappho," *Encyclopaedia Brittanica*, 1926.

23. C. R. Haines, *Sappho: The Poems and Fragments* (New York: E. P. Dutton & Co., 1926), p. 77 and Pl. XII.

24. J. F. Rowbotham, *A History of Music* (London: K. Paul, Trench, Trubner & Co., 1885), II, 91.

25. A. E. P. B. Weigall, *Sappho of Lesbos: Her Life and Times* (New York: Frederick A. Stokes Co., 1932), p. 220.

26. Haines, *op. cit.*, p. 138.

ADDITIONAL REFERENCES

Encyclopédie Photographique de l'art. Paris: Musée de Louvre, Editions TEL. II, 172.

Furtwängler, A. *La Collection Sabouroff.* Berlin: 1883. Vol. I, Pl. LI.

——. *Griechische Vasenmalerei.* Munich: 1932. Vol. III, Pls. 125 and 171.

Kinsky, G. *Geschichte der Musik in Bildern.* Leipzig: Breitkopf und Härtel, 1929.

Poestion, J. C. *Griechische Dichterinnen.* Wien: 1876.

——. *Griechische Philosophinnen.* Bremen: 1882.

Thomson, G. *Aeschylus and Athens: A Study in the Social Origins of Drama.* London: Lawrence & Wishart Ltd., 1941.

Weniger, L. *Über das Collegium der Thyiaden, Delphi: über das Collegium der sechszehn Frauen und der Dionysos in Elis.* Weimar: 1883.

CHAP. VIII

1. R. T. H. Griffith, *The Hymns of the Reg-Veda* (Benares: 1897, 2nd ed.), II, 596.

2. Hanna Rydh, "Symbolism in Mortuary Ceramics," *Bulletin of the Museums of Far Eastern Antiquities* (Stockholm: 1929-30).

3. J. Langdon-Davies, *A Short History of Women* (New York: Literary Guild of America, 1927), p. 148.

4. *Ibid.,* p. 59.

5. Jane E. Harrison, *Mythology and Monuments of Ancient Athens* (London: The Macmillan Co., 1890), p. lxxxv.

6. *Ibid.*

7. Weigall, *op. cit.,* p. 82.

8. This phrase is used by Hélène Deutsch in *Psychology of Women.*

ADDITIONAL REFERENCES

Endzelins, J., and Klaustini, R. *Latvjutautas Dainas.* Riga: Izdevusi "Literatura," 1928. Vol. XI, Frontispiece.

Gerhard, E. *Auserlesene Griechische Vasenbilder.* Berlin: 1840. Vol. III, Pl. XXIX.

Lenormant, C. *Elites des monuments ceramographiques.* Paris: 1844. Vol. II, Pl. 7.

Perrot, G., and Chipiez, C. *Histoire de l'art dans l'antiquité.* Paris: Librairie Hachette & Co., 1911. Vol. III, Pl. VII; Vol. VIII, Fig. 24.

CHAP. IX

1. M. Granet, *Chinese Civilization* (New York: Alfred Knopf, 1930), p. 146.

2. M. Granet, *Festivals and Songs of Ancient China* (New York: E. P. Dutton & Co., 1932), p. 41.

3. A. C. Burnell, *The Ordinances of Manu* (London: Trubner & Co., 1884), pp. 130, 131.

4. *Ibid.*, p. 247.

5. Judges 5:3.

6. Judges 5:12, 27.

7. Exodus 15:20.

8. Exodus 15:21.

9. Judith 15:12, 13; 16:1, 2.

10. Ecclesiastes 2:8.

11. Ezekiel 26:13.

12. A. Z. Idelsohn, *Jewish Music: in its historical development* (New York: Henry Holt & Co., 1929), p. 97.

13. Euripides, *The Bacchae,* phrase translated by Henry S. Drinker.

14. G. Murray, *The Bacchae of Euripides* (New York: Longmans, Green & Co., 1919), p. 62.

15. *Ibid.*, p. 53.

16. Aeschylus, *The Eumenides.*

17. S. N. Kramer, "A Sumerian 'Paradise Myth,'" *Crozer Quarterly,* July 1945, XXII, 3.

Chap. X

1. Matthew 22:37; Mark 12:30.

2. John 15:5.

3. W. O. Clough, *Introduction and Notes to Gesta Pilati: The Reports, Letters and Acts of Pontius Pilate* (Indianapolis: 1885), p. 155.

4. E. A. T. W. Budge, *History of the Blessed Virgin Mary* (London: Luzac & Co., 1899), p. 99.

5. F. Legge, *Forerunners and Rivals of Christianity: Being Studies in Religious History from 330 B.C. to 330 A.D.* (London: Cambridge University Press, 1915), p. 300.

6. G. R. S. Mead, *Fragments of a Faith Forgotten* (London and Benares: Theosophical Society, 1906), p. 419.

7. T. Gérold, *Les pères de l'église et la musique* (Paris: Librairie Felix Alcan, 1931), p. 196.

8. G. R. S. Mead, "Ceremonial Game Playing and Dancing in Mediaeval Churches," *The Quest,* Vol. IV, Oct. 1912.

9. W. Bright, *Age of the Fathers* (London: Longmans, Green & Co., 1903), II, 275.

10. J. S. Black and K. Lake, "Mary," *Encyclopaedia Brittanica,* 1926.

11. L. Fendt, *Gnostische Mysterien: Ein Beitrag zur Geschichte des Christlichen Gottesdientes* (Munich: 1922), p. 51.

12. J. Donaldson, *Woman, Her Position and Influence in Greece, Rome and Early Christianity* (London: Longmans, Green & Co., 1907), p. 166.

13. R. Lanciani, *Pagan and Christian Rome* (Boston: Houghton Mifflin Co., 1893), p. 357.

14. J. Quasten, *Musik und Gesang in den Kulten der heidnischen Antike und Christlichen Frühzeit* (Munster in Westfalia, 1930), p. 181 and Pl. 9.

15. Gérold, *op. cit.*, p. 156.

16. Langdon-Davies, *op. cit.*, p. 182.

17. *Pseudo-Matthew*, Chap. VI, Apochryphal Gospels, Ante-Nicene Christian Library, XVI.

18. Donaldson, *op. cit.*, p. 160.

19. Chrysostomus, *Exposito in psalmum XLI* in Migne. Patr. gr. LV, 157.

20. J. Julian, *Dictionary of Hymnology* (London: John Murray, 1925), p. 206.

21. Gérold, *op. cit.*, p. 109.

22. *Ibid.*, p. 34.

23. Clement of Alexandria, *Protrepticus.*

24. M. L. MacClure and C. L. Feltoe, *The Pilgrimage of Etheria* (London Society for Promoting Christian Knowledge, 1919), p. 45.

25. K. Meyer, *Der Chorische Gesang der Frauen* (Leipzig: Breitkoff und Härtel, 1917), p. 1, note 3.

26. Ephraemus Syrus, *Select metrical hymns and homilies,* ed. and tr. by H. Burgess (London: 1853), Hymn XVII.

ADDITIONAL REFERENCES

Abbott, N. "Pre-Islamic Arab Queens," *American Journal of Languages,* July, 1941.

Baumeister, K. A. *Denkmäler des klassichen Altertums zur Erleuterung des Lebens der Griechen und Römer in Religion, Kunst, und Sitte.* Munich: 1885. Vol. I, Fig. 218.

Eckenstein, Lina (revised by Celia Roscoe). *The Women of Early Christianity.* London: The Faith Press, Ltd., 1935.

Ramsay, W. M. *The Church in the Roman Empire before A.D. 170.* New York: G. P. Putnam's Sons, 1893.

Rush, A. C. *Death and Burial in Christian Antiquity.* Washington: Catholic University of America Press, 1941.

Sachs, C. *The History of Musical Instruments.* New York: W. W. Norton & Co., Inc., 1940. Pl. VIII.

Vucasovic, V. V. "Funeral Customs and Rites among the Southern Slavs in Ancient and Modern Times," *The International Folk-Lore Congress of the World's Columbian Exposition.* Chicago: Sergel Co., 1898. Vol. I.

CHAP. XI

1. Luke 23:28, 31.
2. Tertullian, *Decultu feminarium* in Migne, Series Prima, Vol. II, col. 1305.
3. Clement of Alexandria, *Paedagogus*, LL, 2.
4. Luke 1:38.
5. Bright, *op. cit.*, I, 523.
6. G. Reese, *Music in the Middle Ages* (New York: W. W. Norton & Co., 1940), p. 65.
7. S. Glennie, "Traditions of the Archaic White Races," *Transactions of the Royal Historical Society, 1889*. Quoted from von Bunsen, *Egypt's Place in Universal History*, IV, 396.
8. W. Christ and M. Paranikas, *Anthologic-Graeca Carminum Christianorum* (Leipzig, 1871).
9. A. W. Chatfield, *Songs and Hymns of the Greek Christian Poets* (London: 1876).
10. W. Wright, *Apochryphal Acts of the Apostles* (London: Williams & Norgate, 1871), II, 155.
11. Meyer, *op. cit.*, p. 13.
12. L. M. O. Duchesne, *Early History of the Christian Church: From Its Foundation to the End of the Third Century* (New York: Longmans, Green & Co., 1909), p. 110.
13. Meyer, *op. cit.*, p. 10.
14. *Ibid.*, p. 10, note 2.
15. Bright, *op. cit.*, II, 33.
16. Quasten, *op. cit.*, p. 169.

CHAP. XII

1. Lina Eckenstein, *Women under Monasticism: Chapters on Saint Lore and Convent Life between A.D. 500 and A.D. 1500* (Cambridge: Cambridge University Press, 1896), p. 60.
2. *Ibid.*, p. 65.
3. Gregory of Nyssa, *The Life of St. Macrina*, tr. by W. K. L. Clarke (London: Society for Promoting Christian Knowledge, 1916), I, 34.
4. *Ibid.*, pp. 50-2.
5. *Ibid.*, p. 68.
6. *Ibid.*, p. 59.
7. Eckenstein, *op. cit.*, p. 390.
8. D. I. Lanslot, *Handbook of Canon Law* (Rome: Ratisbon, 1911), p. 277.
9. Eckenstein, *op. cit.*, p. 317.
10. *Ibid.*, p. 326.

11. Rush, *op. cit.*, pp. 182, 204.

12. Eckenstein, *op. cit.*, p. 253 and Appendix.

13. L. von Strauss und Torney, *Deutsches Frauenleben in der Zeit der Sachsenkaiser und Hohenstaufen* (Jena: Eugen Diedrichs, 1927), p. 80.

ADDITIONAL REFERENCES

Bobillier, Marie. *La Musique dans les convents de femmes depuis le moyen age jusqu'à nos jours.* Paris: Schola Cantorum, 1898.

Gmelch, J. *Die Kompositionen der heiligen Hildegard.* Düsseldorf: 1913.

Nisard, C. *"Des Poesies de Radegunde attribuées jusqu'ici à Fortunat,"* *Revue Historique,* 1888.

Ursprung, O. *"Katholische Kirchenmusik,"* *Handbuch der Musikwissenschaft.* Fig. 19.

CHAP. XIII

1. Eckenstein, *op. cit.*, p. 260.

2. Von Strauss und Torney, *op. cit.*, p. 68.

3. J. Combarieu, *op. cit.*, p. 52.

4. E. K. Chambers, *The Mediaeval Stage* (Oxford: Clarendon Press, 1903), III, 235.

5. Alice Kemp-Welch, *Of Six Mediaeval Women: to which is added a note on mediaeval gardens* (London: The Macmillan Co., 1913), p. 32.

6. Dorothy Gardiner, *English Girlhood at School: A Study of Women's Education through Twelve Centuries* (London: Humphrey Milford, 1929), p. 59.

7. *Ibid.*, p. 59.

8. Collection of Jean Beck.

9. J. H. Smith, *Troubadours at Home: Their Lives and Personalities, Their Songs and Their World* (New York: G. P. Putnam's Sons, 1899), pp. 102, 105.

ADDITIONAL REFERENCES

Farnell, Ida. *Lives of the Troubadours.* London: Nutt, 1896.

Ploss, H. H., and Bartels, M. and P. *Woman: An Historical, Gynaecological and Anthropological Compendium.* St. Louis: C. V. Mosby Co., 1936. Vol. II, Fig. 545.

Rokseth, Yvonne. *"Les femmes musiciens, du XII aux XIV siècle,"* *Romania,* Oct. 1935.

CHAP. XIV

1. O. Böckel, *Deutsche Volkslieder aus Oberhessen* (Marburg: 1885), p. 13.

2. E. Lovett, "The Vessel Cup," *Folklore*, March 1902, XIII, 1.

3. M. A. R. de Maulde la Clavière, *Women of the Renaissance: A Study of Feminism* (New York: G. P. Putnam's Sons, 1900), p. 450.

4. *Ibid.*, p. 274.

5. A. Solerti, *Ferrara e la Corte Estense* (Citta di Castello, 1899), p. 134.

6. O. Kinkeldy, *Orgel und Klavier in der Musik des 16 Jahrhundert: ein Beitrag zur Geschichte der instrumental Musik mit Notenbeilagen* (Leipzig: Breitkopf und Härtel, 1910).

7. Solerti, *op. cit.*, p. 134.

8. C. Ricci, *Vita Barocca* (Milano Cogliati, 1904), p. 59.

9. Gardiner, *op. cit.*, p. 182.

10. Meyer, *op. cit.*, p. 64.

11. L. C. Elson, *History of American Music* (New York: The Macmillan Co., 1925), p. 8.

12. C. Burney, *The Present State of Music in Germany, the Netherlands, and United Provinces* (London: 1773), p. 125.

13. De Maulde la Clavière, *op. cit.*, p. 261.

14. Nesta de Robeck, *Music of the Italian Renaissance* (London: The Medici Society, 1928), p. 91.

ADDITIONAL REFERENCES

Rokseth, Yvonne. "Antonia Bembo, Composer to Louis XIV," *Musical Quarterly*, April 1937.

Rubsamen, W. H. *Literary Sources of Secular Music in Italy*. University of California Publications in Music. Vol. I, No. 1, 1943.

Schubring, P. *Cassoni: Truhen und Truhenbilder der Italienischen Fruhrenaissance*. Leipzig: 1915.

Treverrow, Ruth C. *The Beginnings of Virtuosity in the Italian Madrigal of the 16th Century*. Smith College: May 1945.

CHAP. XV

1. W. H. Hadow, "The Viennese Period," *Oxford History of Music* (London: Oxford University Press, 1929), V, 25.

2. J. N. Burk, *Clara Schumann: A Romantic Biography* (New York: Random House, 1940), p. 243.

3. *Ibid.*, p. 244.

4. Personal communication to Marjorie Barstow Greenbie.

5. B. Litzmann, *Clara Schumann: An Artist's Life*, tr. by Grace E. Hadow (Leipzig: 1913), I, 313.

6. *New York Times*, Oct. 20, 1946.

7. *New York Times*, Oct. 20, 1946.

8. *Philadelphia Evening Bulletin*, May 19, 1938.

9. Friedlaender, *op. cit.*, p. 167.

CHAP. XVI

1. Corkery, *op. cit.,* p. 170.
2. Imogen Holst, *Gustav Holst* (London: Oxford University Press, 1938), p. 217.

ADDITIONAL REFERENCES

Bennett, W. "The Celebrated Women Chorus Singers of Lancashire," *The Choir,* Feb. 1936, p. 27.

Krille, Anna Marie. *Beiträge zur Geschichte der Musikerziehung und Musik ubung der deutschen Frau (von 1750 bis 1820).* Berlin: 1938.

Locke, A. W. *Selected List of Choruses for Women's Voices.* Smith College Monographs, No. 2, 1927. New Edition, 1946, containing 514 compositions for women's chorus, 10 of which are by women.

Les Spectacles à travers les âges. Paris: Editions du Cygne, 1932. P. 122.

CHAP. XVII

1. John Milton, *Paradise Lost,* ed. A. W. Verity (Cambridge: Cambridge University Press, 1921), Bk. IV, line 299.
2. S. Baring-Gould, *The Lives of the Saints* (Edinburgh: John Grant, 1897).
3. Elson, *op. cit.,* p. 8.
4. G. E. Stubbs, "America, the Music of the Episcopal Church." Gardner and Nicholson, *A Manual of English Church Music* (London: Society for Promoting Christian Knowledge, 1923).
5. L. Bonvin, "Women in Church Choirs," *The Caecilia,* Sept. 1934, Vol. 60, No. 8, p. 339.
6. W. Boyd, *History of Western Education* (London: A. & C. Black Ltd., 1921, 3rd ed. 1932).
7. *Time,* July 16, 1945.
8. J. Dewey, *Art as Experience* (New York: Minton, Balch & Co., 1934), p. 267.
9. K. Ekman, *Jean Sibelius* (New York: Alfred Knopf, 1938), p. 136.

CHAP. XVIII

1. Bernard Robinson, Bothamstead, Berkshire, in 1927 started Music Camp.
2. Mr. and Mrs. Henry S. Drinker, Merion, Pennsylvania, in 1928 organized the Accademia dei Dilettanti di Musica.
3. Mary Padgett, "Gray Ladies Praised for Hospital Music." *Philadelphia Inquirer,* Jan. 16, 1944; *The Inquirer's Everybody's Weekly,* Feb. 20, 1944, with illus. taken at Valley Forge Army Hospital.

4. Rachel Dubois, *Get Together Americans* (New York: Harper & Bros., 1943).
   "Try a Neighborhood Festival," ed. by Marjorie Greenbie, *Parents' Magazine,* Sept. 1943.
5. Mary Hargrave, *Some German Women and Their Salons* (London: T. W. Laurie, 1912), p. 107.
6. Nilla Cook, unpublished translation of an Orphic hymn.

ADDITIONAL REFERENCES

Barnes, E. N. C. *American Women in Creative Music.* Washington, D.C.: Music Education Publication, 1936.

Ebel, O. *Women Composers: A Biographical Handbook of Woman's Work in Music.* Brooklyn: F. H. Chandler, 1902.

Elson, A., and Truette, E. E. *Woman's Work in Music: Being an account of her influence on the art, in ancient as well as modern times; a summary of her musical compositions, in the different countries of the civilized world; and an estimate of their rank in comparison with those of men.* Boston: L. C. Page & Co., 1931.

Hughes, R. *Contemporary American Composers.* Boston: L. C. Page & Co., 1900. Chap. V.

Sutro, Florence C. *Women in Music and Law.* New York: Author's Publishing Company, 1895.

SOME BOOKS AND ARTICLES DENYING THE CREATIVE POWER OF THE WOMAN MUSICIAN

Barbacci, R. *"La Inferioridad mental de la mujer y su reflejo en la actividad musical."* Lima: *Revista Musical Peruana,* Ano 1, no. 9, Sept. 1939, pp. 1-5.

Brower, Edith. "Is the Music Idea Masculine?" *Atlantic Monthly,* March, 1894.

Drewes, H. *Maria Antonia Walpurgis als Komponistin.* Leipzig: 1934.

Ladd, G. *Why Women Cannot Compose Music.* New Haven: Yale Publication Association, 1917.

Towers, J. "Woman in Music," *Musician,* April, May, and June 1897.

Upton, G. R. *Woman in Music.* Chicago: A. C. McClurg & Co., 1909.

INDEX

313